CHILD LABOUR

Problem and Policy Implication

CHILD LABOUR

Problem and Policy Implication

Dr Lata Kaushal

MD PUBLICATIONS PVT LTD

NEW DELHI

www.mdppl.com

Published by :

MD Publications Pvt Ltd
"MD House", 11, Darya Ganj,
New Delhi-110 002
Phone : +91-11-41563325 (Customer Service)
+91-11-41562846 (Editorial)
E-mail (orders) : order@mdppl.com
Website : www.mdppl.com

ISBN : 978-81-7533-212-6

Published and Printed by Mr. Pranav Gupta on behalf of **MD Publications Pvt Ltd** at Printext, New Delhi.

PREFACE

Child labour continues to be a global issue, and infringes on the rights of tens of thousands of children. In most developing countries the phenomenon is quite evident, but in developed countries, although perhaps more obscured, the problem is far from solved. Child labour has occurred in all countries of the world at one time, and because abolition was successful in some areas, it begs to question if we cannot learn a lesson from history.

Child labour, or child labor, refers to the employment of children at regular and sustained labour. This practice is considered exploitative by many international organizations and is illegal in many countries. Child labour was utilized to varying extents through most of history, but entered public dispute with the beginning of universal schooling, with changes in working conditions during industrialization, and with the emergence of the concepts of workers' and children's rights.

Poverty and lack of education are the two primary reasons for the ever-growing social malice of child labour. Parents in the poverty zone of society give birth to money-making machines, and not children. They carry infants to earn more on the streets from begging. Then as they grow they make them beggars, and eventually sell them to employers.

Child labour is common in some parts of the world, and can be factory work, mining, prostitution, quarrying, agriculture, helping in the parents' business, having one's own small business (for example selling food), or doing odd jobs. Some children work as guides for tourists, sometimes combined with bringing in business for shops and restaurants (where they may also work as waiters). Other children are forced to do tedious and repetitive jobs such as: assembling boxes, polishing shoes, stocking a store's products, or cleaning.

Child labour is not an easy issue to resolve; while it seems noble to immediately withdraw investments and cooperation with firms and factories that employ child labour it may do more harm than good. Many of these children are from very poor families and work to pay for their family and/or their education. Depriving them of this income has led to some children seeking different, lower paid work, and even prostitution in some cases. Other ways with schemes to help children would likely be needed so that this labour can be phased out. The same has been suggested by the International Labor Organization (ILO), at a meeting in Mexico City in 1999, who also pointed out that child labour affects over 250 million children, 30 percent of which are in Latin America. A gradual phase out is said to be a more preferable solution.

Global Report under the follow-up to the ILO Declaration on Fundamental Principles and Rights at Work, International Labour Conference, Geneva, 95th Session, 2006, Report I (B), describes how the abolition of child labour has become a global cause for the new millennium, explores changing manifestations of child labour throughout the world and how girls and boys are affected differently; presents new data, interlinked causes as well as overall actions taken worldwide at all levels.

I am very grateful to Mr. Pranav Gupta, Director of MD Publications Pvt Ltd, New Delhi for his cooperation and support for this book.

Dr Lata Kaushal

CONTENTS

1

Child Labour
An Introduction

Child Labour

Societies have long sought to eliminate child labour. Yet two hundred years after the first Factories Act and despite a level of prosperity that our forefathers would have deemed unimaginable, there are an estimated 186 million child labourers worldwide –5.7 million in forced labour, 1.8 million in prostitution and 0.3 million soldiers. In design-ing policy to mitigate this persistent problem, it is vital to have a theoretical and empirical understanding of child labour and its consequences. Well-meaning but poorly con-ceived interventions could cause more harm than good. Perhaps the past provides some lessons.

In a new study, use the reminiscences of 617 working class men who lived through the Industrial Revolution to provide insight. Drawn from economically and demographically representative families, the memoirs contain rich detail on early employment. Children were motivated to work by various mechanisms, some operating through family ties and some through incentives like improved status and small subventions from their own earnings. Violence was sometimes used to drive children and was more likely where the incentives of piece rates, competition for jobs and the threat of dismissal were irrelevant.

Children's Occupations

Children's jobs were specific but integral to production processes. In textiles, mechanisation created new jobs for children and these were then duplicated en masse. In mining, it was the expansion of output with little change in production methods that increased child labour. Similarly, agriculture continued to provide huge employment for children even as it slowly contracted. Elsewhere, subdivided production processes, either of old goods like boots and shoes or new ones like biscuits, created new niches for children. The continuing importance of agriculture in children's employment fits with evidence from the censuses but has been obscured by the classical fixation on mills and mines.

The ability of children to hold their ground in agriculture suggests that the physical demands of jobs rarely operated to exclude young workers. Eighteenth and nineteenth century farm work was hugely demanding in terms of strength and size but tasks were broken down and divided up in ways that made it possible for children to contribute. Mining was another sector where heavy physical demands did not screen out child workers. Children did not do the same work as adult males; hewing coal from the rock face was physically beyond them. But the work that they did do was psychologically stressful and physically demanding. The increasing importance of clerical jobs for children could be dismissed as an artifacts of the sample: autobiographers likely being particularly bookish. But it also reflects the invention of new jobs designed for children, such as monitors in the novel Board Schools and boy clerks in the multiplying offices of commercial Britain.

Services comprised another sector where the subdivision of labour created new opportunities for employing children, not separated out from mainstream activities but as ancillaries working in conjunction with adults. Finally some new jobs (railways, utilities) appear in the children's labour force of the mid-nineteenth century while as yet absent from an earlier generation of adults' jobs.

The Nature of Jobs

In almost all cases, children's pace of work was determined exogenously: by adults working on piece rates, by machinery, by throughput or by the need to accomplish a task by a specific time. In agriculture for example, even if children were not capable of adult tasks they worked with adults and were locked into a pace of work dictated by the latter. The autobiographers recorded their fathers' occup-ations along with their own first jobs, allowing movement between occupations to be tracked. Comparison with a model of perfect mobility confirms the importance of occu-pational inheritance and its intensification within high and low prestige groups, results found in most mobility tables.

But one further common characteristic of mobility tables, the correspondence between the amount of movement between two categories (relative to the standard) and their nearness in prestige, which is taken to be a manifestation of the underlying order of the occupational groups along the prestige continuum, is less evident. Instead, the analysis suggests greater movement between groups which enjoyed vocational, training, or technical linkages, and provides individual-level support for the recent findings from large-scale data sets on the importance in the British case of a dynamic tertiary sector, and insight into the microeconomic processes involved in Britain's precocious structural change.

Children's Earnings

Evidence on earnings suggests clear progressions by age and physical competence. Even young children could earn 10-20% of men's and even more of women's wages. Teenage boys could earn more than their mothers; their rates of pay were higher, they had wider opportunities, and unburdened by domestic cares, they could work longer hours. Where families had a choice it made sense for sons to seek employment while mothers remained at home. Eighteenth-century families were heavily dependent on husbands and fathers for economic support, but if men died or disappeared, their contributions ceased. If they sought work away from home, or served in the army or navy, supply lines back to dependents became strained.

More mundanely, family needs often exceeded men's wages. Children were available "added workers". Mothers, who were responsible for the feeding and clothing of younger siblings, found it hard to resist the potential earnings of older children. However reluctantly, they often found children their first jobs and battled to keep them employed thereafter by ensuring their punctuality and discipline. Child labour thus emerges as the outcome of the fragility of the male breadwinner family structure in a context where men's support was irregular or insufficient, and a compact between children and their mothers, whereby working children surrendered their pay to their mothers who in return spent it carefully and in the interests of the family as a whole. In this way, older children helped to support their younger siblings, which was vital in an era of high fertility and large families.

The responsibility that children felt for their mothers and siblings prompted their entry into work and disciplined them on the job. But duty was leavened with other compensations for working children, who enjoyed improved status and carefully judged *baksheesh* from their own wages. They spent these coppers on nutritional treats and only when their earnings had increased and hunger abated, on market commodities. New clothes rarely spurred children's efforts. Jam, biscuits, sweets, even bread, are not as glamorous as new fabrics or tropical groceries and not as readily tied into mainstream narratives of an Industrial Revolution highlighting the cotton industry or expanding empire, but they may be important nonetheless.

Regulation and Abuse

Children were prevented from starting work or caught working under-age and expelled with sufficient frequency to suggest that scepticism about the effectiveness of regulation may be misplaced. Feelings about such expulsions were mixed;

children in needy families were dismayed to no longer be able to contribute but grateful for the relief afforded. In some cases, autobiographers reflected that protective labour legislation saved them from impending physical collapse. Violence was used to drive children. But it was not as important a motivator as the responsibility children felt for family wellbeing, particularly for the diets of siblings and mothers. Nor were factories the most violent workplaces, for they had alternative ways of ensuring discipline: supervision, piece rates, competition for jobs, and the threat of dismissal.

Violence was more likely where these incentives were irrelevant, as in the case of unpaid and orphaned children consigned by the state as pauper apprentices to specific employers or enterprises, and where the earnings of adults depended on child helpers and coercion was hidden by the isolation of the workplace. Where parents or co-workers could afford some check by their disapproving presence as well as active intervention, abuse was contained. Child labour reconstructed through these memoirs is not the same as the version portrayed in classic accounts of industrialisation. But the child labour of working-class memoir slots neatly into revised interpretations of the British Industrial Revolution, where economic change has been pushed back in time and identified with the dynamism of the tertiary sector and productive agriculture.

Modern Implications

Even more important perhaps are the implications for understanding child labour today. Two can be mentioned here. First, it is not inevitable that growth will drive child labour to the economic margins before rooting it out completely. As in the past, if associated with an unequal distribution of income and child-intensive production processes, economic growth can increase child labour rather than eliminate it. And once in place, child labour can be difficult to uproot as child workers forgo schooling and apprenticeship and so grow up to be unproductive adults, who, in turn, cannot earn enough to support their children through education or training.

It only takes one generation of child workers to trap an economy in such a low-productivity equilibrium. Second, despite the spectre of avaricious parents, the children most at risk of early, hazardous, and even slave labour are those without adult kin. Where families have been broken up and denuded of prime-age adults by wars and epidemic disease, the prospects for preserving childhood look bleak.

POLICY

Much of the early debate on child labour was concerned with whether the existence of child labour deserved a policy response. In the heydays of the *laissez faire* it had seemed to many observers that if child labour was a product of the market then it must be efficient to have child labour. And if one were committed to the efficiency of the market, then it was best—so went the argument—to leave things as they were. The state had no reason to be involved in the market. The chinks in this argument were obvious enough. Education involves externalities and so a decision taken by an individual or a household may not be in the best interest of society. This argument was cogently summarized by Grootaert and Kanbur (1995) in a paper that has been influential in sparking off debate.

Then there was the problem of a child's agency. The decision as to whether a child will work, study, or play, is usually taken by the child's parents or guardians; and the standard consumers- sovereignty argument does not apply to cases where one person decides for another. Even when one recognizes these caveats, the laissez-faire prescription of non- intervention and waiting for the benefits of growth to trickle down and remove child labour, has been defended by some as a kind of best *available* strategy. This is the position taken by Nardinelli (1990), who reads the experience of industrial revolution and its aftermath in Britain as evidence of how legal interventions are futile in the face of market forces that gives rise to child labour. A similar line, based on an econometric analysis of American historical data, is taken by Moehling (1999).

We shall however argue, based on our understanding of the modern theory and data, that government intervention for controlling child labour is both desirable and possible. However, one has to craft policy recognizing the powerful market forces that give rise to child labour in the first place and therefore will no doubt respond to any intervention; and also being aware of the many pitfalls and risks of backlash that occur in this area of complex interaction between household economics and market structures. In conducting this discussion, it is useful to state an important ground rule that we shall follow.

Any policy in the area of child labour (including the policy decision not to do anything) must be justified primarily in the interests of the children. In other words, we shall not be interested in arguments such as: "policy x concerning child labour will leave children worse off but is justified in the interest of helping boost the country's exports and through that its GNP". In brief, we take here a child-centric view of policy. The policy interventions that we will discuss can be divided into two kinds: 'collaborative' measures and 'coercive' measures.

Collaborative Measures are, broadly speaking, interventions which alter the economic environment of the decision makers, which make them now more willing to let children stay away from labour and spend more time on other activities and, especially, schooling. Thus a policy which improves the functioning of adult labour markets that adult incomes rise and unemployment falls, is always desirable from the point of view of curtailing child labour. Given that parents, typically, want to keep children away from work and in school, if they find that they have enough income of their own so as to render child labour to be unnecessary, they will themselves tend to withdraw children from work and may be put them in school.

Does this mean that just giving unconditional income subsidies to poor households will curtail child labour? Though we feel the answer will generally be yes, one has to be careful here. From what we have already seen, it is possible that such subsidies will be used to buy land or other businesses and this, in turn, could increase child labour by creating an easy productive environment for employing children. Closely related to this is the policy of improving credit and insurance markets, so that adults who fall into bad times can borrow money on decent terms and do not need to take their children out of schools and send them to work to help the household ride over the rough patch. The link between credit markets and child labour has been noted in the literature. But, by far the most direct collaborative measures are the ones which reward children who go to school instead of working.

Around the world many such interventions have been tried and there is now a small body of empirical literature studying these programs. *Bolsa Escola* in Brazil, *Progresa* in Mexico, *Red de Protection Social* (RPS) in Nicaragua, food for education program in Bangladesh, mid-day meal schemes in India, the school construction programs in Indonesia and the "back to school" measures aimed to prevent a rise in child labour and sustain school enrolments in Indonesia after the financial crisis are all examples of policy intervention which builds in incentives for parents to send their children to (or for autonomous children to go to) school. Most of these programs find that schooling does in reality respond to such incentives. Thus Dreze and Kingdon find that female school participation is 15% higher when the local school provides a mid-day meal. They find that girls schooling responds more to such incentives than boys schooling. This is an important finding since we need to make special effort to keep girls away from work, which, though often invisible, could add up to more than what boys do.

Mexico's Progresa now extends to approximately 40% of all rural families as beneficiaries and can provide large incentives to schooling (including required medical tests and nutritional programs). In poor areas, the grant that the mother receives if her daughter is enrolled in the 9th grade is 255 pesos per month, which is 44% of an average male day-laborer's wage or about 2/3rd of what a child of this age would earn if she worked full time. Schultz (2001) finds that the program's net effect on enrollment is positive and statistically significant. Skoufias and Parker (2003) estimate that the labour force participation of children aged 12 to 15 years is reduced by 15-25% relative to the probability of participating prior to the program, and that children are much more likely to attend school and to spend more time on school activities. The estimated increase in the education attainment of children dominates the enrolment gains from increased provision of schools.

Nicaragua's *Red de Protección Social* (RPS) is a conditional cash program modeled after *PROGRESA*. An evaluation of recipient households in a pilot program against a randomly selected group of comparable households shows that RPS had a significant and substantial effect on schooling matriculation and enrollment during its first year of operation. Moreover, it led to a substantial reduction in child labour within the target population. In contrast to the Mexico case, these gains occur even at the earliest ages, suggesting that the *PROGRESA* type interventions may hold promise for the poorest countries with the worst educational outcomes in the region. Bourguignon, Ferreira and Leite also find that such incentives increase schooling in Brazil's Bolsa Escola program (though it is less successful in mitigating poverty). But does this increase in schooling cause child labour to decrease?

Almost always the answer is yes and almost always the answer is that this happens by less than the increase in schooling. In some of the poorest regions, even with subsidies, schooling becomes possible for children only if they can also do a little work to finance their schooling and, presumably, also their consumption. The above are 'collaborative' measures. They do not require coercion and may not even require any legislative backup. Coercive measures have been very hotly debated in international fora and policies such as having a 'social clause' which would enable the WTO to take punitive action against a country that has child labour have been proposed by many. What position does one take on such coercive measures? Unfortunately, on these there is not enough empirical work. But these are such important matters that we cannot look away from them on that ground. One has to use the best available theory and intuition to take a stand on these, no matter how tentative. We argue that coercive measures also have their role but need to be used much more carefully than collaborative policies.

First of all, hazardous labour ought to be legally banned. It is true that this may cause other forms of hardship to some very poor families in the short run, but to allow for such labour to directly hurt children, who or whose parents often cannot properly assess the long-run damage that such labour can do to them, makes little sense. Even for nonhazardous labour there may be scope for using legislative bans and this is typically and closely associated with the theory of multiple equilibriums. We have seen above that in static and dynamic models we may often have multiple equilibriums with children typically doing better in the equilibrium in which children do not work or do very little work. Should there be such multiple equilibrium in an economy, with the economy settled in a situation with high child labour, a legislative ban can deflect the economy to the 'superior' equilibrium and may be justified on that ground.

Such action, however, needs to be preceded by careful empirical evaluation of the situation, since, if there are no multiple equilibriums, then such a law can exacerbate the suffering of the children. For one, it can deprive children from work which was essential for their survival. If the law is effective only in some sectors, it can drive child labour underground, to sectors that may be more harmful for the children. And finally, note that such laws are typically implemented by imposing a fine on the employer, who employs children in violation of the law. That is exactly how India's Child Labour Deterrence Act, 1986, works. It empowers the state to impose a fine on firms that violate the law by employing children in activities that are disallowed. Such laws can, ironically, have the effect of raising the amount of child labour.

The reason is easy to see. By making the employment of children more costly to firms, such a law ensures that child wage will now be lower (for otherwise it is not worthwhile for firms to employ children). Now in case children were working to meet some minimum tolerable income target (for instance, to escape abject poverty), then the lower wages would mean that children have to work longer hours, and often harder, to reach that target. Hence, the slapping of a small fine can have the opposite effect of what is intended. Partial measures are, in general, a bad idea and this is relevant when we think of global action to deter child labour. This is part of the larger debate on international labour standards.

The two major problems that have concerned economists are, first, that once an instrument of global action is created to thwart the flow of goods from nations that violate minimal labour standards, this will be used for protectionism by the industrialized nations, and second, that international action to stop child labour inputs into traded goods will simply drive children into the non-traded sector and this may be worse for them. In a study of India's garment export industry, Stahl and Stalmarker (2002) found little evidence of bonded labour and the 'worst forms' of child labour. This does not preclude these practices occurring elsewhere, but suggests that the export sector is not one where they occur.

There is evidence for both these. It was discussed in Basu (2001) how the Sander's Amendment in the US, which is a desirable amendment to the Tariff Act, meant to prevent forced child labour, has been used to block imports into the US and settle other scores. There is also evidence that some initial attempts to stop child labour in export industries, such as carpets in Nepal, has driven children into prostitution (UNICEF, 1995). And conversely, there is evidence that market integration may lead to less child labour. Edmonds and Pavcnik (2002) found that opening up the Vietnam economy resulted in rice price to rise and this caused child labour to decline. Hence, while there is scope for coordinated action among developing countries to raise labour standards (so as to discourage international capital from fleeing from one country to another), we must be wary of policies that use punitive action, like trade sanctions, to enforce labour standards.

It is not surprising that there is no one simple policy measure to eradicate child labour. Its persistence through two centuries is testimony that there is no easy solution. Yet today we understand much better the causes of child labour, and have the opportunity to craft policy that can sharply reduce and ultimately eradicate it. Child labour, or child labour, refers to the employment of children at regular and sustained labour. This practice is considered exploitative by many international organizations and is illegal in many countries. Child labour was utilized to varying extents through most of history, but entered public dispute with the beginning of universal schooling, with changes in working conditions during industrialization, and with the emergence of the concepts of workers' and children's rights. Child labour is still common in some places where the school leaving age is lower.

Child labour is common in some parts of the world, and can be factory work, mining, prostitution, quarrying, agriculture, helping in the parents' business, having one's own small business (for example selling food), or doing odd jobs. Some children work as guides for tourists, sometimes combined with bringing in business for shops and restaurants (where they may also work as waiters). Other children are forced to do tedious and repetitive jobs such as: assembling boxes, polishing shoes, stocking a store's products, or cleaning. However, rather than in factories and sweatshops, most child labour occurs in the informal sector, "selling many things on the streets, at work in agriculture or hidden away in houses—far from the reach of official labour inspectors and from media scrutiny." And all the work that they did was done in all types of weather; and was also done for minimal pay. According to UNICEF, there is an estimated 158 million children aged 5 to 14 in child labour worldwide, excluding child domestic labour.

CHILDREN RIGHTS

The United Nations and the International Labour Organization consider child labour exploitative, with the UN stipulating, in article 32 of the Convention on the Rights of the Child that:

> *...States Parties recognize the right of the child to be protected from economic exploitation and from performing any work that is likely to be hazardous or to interfere with the child's education, or to be harmful to the child's health or physical, mental, spiritual, moral or social development.*

The first general laws against child labour, the Factory Acts, were passed in Britain in the first half of the 19th century. Children younger than nine were not allowed to work and the work day of youth under the age of 18 was limited to twelve hours. In many developed countries, it is considered inappropriate or exploitative if a child below a certain age works, excluding household chores or school-work. An employer is often not allowed to hire a child below a certain age. This minimum age depends on the country; child labour laws in the United States set the minimum age to work in an establishment without parents' consent and restrictions at age 16.

During the Industrial Revolution, children as young as four were employed in production factories with dangerous, and often fatal, working conditions. Based on this understanding of the use of children as labourers, it is now considered by wealthy countries to be a human rights violation, and is outlawed, while some poorer countries may allow or tolerate it. In the 1990s every country in the world except for Somalia and the United States became a signatory to the Convention on the Rights of the Child, or CRC. However according to the United Nations Foundation Somalia signed the convention in 2002, the delay of the signing was believed to been due to Somalia not having a government to sign the convention. The CRC provides the strongest, most consistent international legal language prohibiting illegal child labour; however it does not make child labour illegal.

Poor families often rely on the labours of their children for survival, and sometimes it is their only source of income. This type of work is often hidden away because it is not always in the industrial sector. Child labour is employed in subsistence agriculture and in the urban informal sector; child domestic work is also important. In order to benefit children, child labour prohibition has to address the dual challenge of providing them with both short-term income and long-term prospects. Some mai ja bhosdinaloda youth rights groups, however, feel that prohibiting work below a certain age violates human rights, reducing children's options and leaving them subject to the whims of those with money. In 1999 the Global March Against Child Labour the movement began with a worldwide march when thousands of people marched together to jointly put forth the message against child labour.

The march, which started on January 17, 1998, touched every corner of the globe, built immense awareness and led to high level of participation from the masses. This march finally culminated at the ILO Conference in Geneva. The voice of the marchers was heard and reflected in the draft of the ILO Convention against the worst forms of child labour. The following year, the Convention was unanimously adopted at the ILO Conference in Geneva. Today, with 169 countries having ratified the convention so fat, it has become the fastest ratified convention in the history of ILO. A large role in this was played by the Global March through our member partners. In an influential paper on "The Economics of Child Labour" in the *American Economic Review* (1998), Kaushik Basu and Pham Hoang Van argue that the primary cause of child labour is parental poverty.

That being so, they caution against the use of a legislative ban against child labour, and argue that should be used only when there is reason to believe that a ban on child labour will cause adult wages to rise and so compensate adequately the households of the poor children. Child labour is still widely used today in many countries, including India and Bangladesh. CACL estimated that there are between 70 and 80 million child labourers in India. Even though the respective national laws state that no child under the age of 14 may work, the law is often ignored. Children as young as 11 go to work for up to 20 hours a day in sweatshops making items for US companies, such as Hanes, Wal-mart, and Target. The get paid as little as 1 cent per item proauced.

CHILD LABOUR IN VICTORIAN BRITAIN

The Victorian era became notorious for employing young children in factories and mines and as chimney sweeps. Child labour played an important role in the Industrial Revolution from its outset, often brought about by economic hardship; Charles Dickens for example worked at the age of 12 in the Blacking Factory, with his family in debtor's prison. The children of the poor were expected to help towards the family budget, often working long hours in dangerous jobs and low wages. Agile boys were employed by the chimney sweeps; small children were employed to scramble under machinery to retrieve cotton bobbins; and children were also employed to work in coal mines to crawl through tunnels too narrow and low for adults. Children also worked as errand boys, crossing sweepers, shoe blacks, or selling matches, flowers and other cheap goods. Some children undertook work as apprentices to respectable trades, such as building or as domestic servants (there were over 120,000 domestic servants in London in the mid 18th Century). Working hours were long: builders worked 64 hours a week in summer and 52 in winter, while domestic servants worked 80 hour weeks.

A high number of children also worked as prostitutes. Children as young as three were put to work. In coal mines children began work at the age of five and generally died before the age of 25. Many children (and adults) worked 16 hour days. As early as 1802 and 1819 Factory Acts were passed to regulate the working hours of workhouse children in factories and cotton mills to 12 hours per day. These acts were largely ineffective and after radical agitation, by for example the "Short Time Committees" in 1831, a royal commission recommended in 1833 that children aged 11-18 should work a maximum of 12 hours per day, children aged 9-11 a maximum of eight hours, and children under the age of nine were no longer permitted to work. This act however only applied to the textile industry, and further agitation led to another act in 1847 limiting both adults and children to 10 hour working days.

CAMPAIGNS AGAINST CHILD LABOUR

Child labour was approached from the beginning of the Industrial Revolution. For example, Karl Marx called for "Abolition of children's factory labour in its present form" in his Communist Manifesto. Concern has also been raised about the buying public's moral complicity in purchasing products assembled or otherwise manufactured in developing countries with child labour. Others have raised concerns that boycotting products manufactured through child labour may force these children to turn to more dangerous or strenuous professions, such as prostitution or agriculture. For example, a UNICEF study found that 5,000 to 7,000 Nepalese children turned to prostitution after the United States banned that country's carpet exports in the 1990s. Also, after the Child Labour Deterrence Act was introduced in the US, an estimated 50,000 children were dismissed from their garment industry jobs in Bangladesh, leaving many to resort to jobs such as "stone-crushing, street hustling, and prostitution," all of them, according to a UNICEF study, "more hazardous and exploitative than garment production". The study says that boycotts are "blunt instruments with long-term consequences that can actually harm rather than help the children involved."

Recent Child Labour Incidents

After the news of child labourers working in embroidery industry was uncovered in the Sunday Observer on 28 October 2007, BBA activists swung into action. The GAP Inc. in a statement accepted that the child labourers were working in production of GAP Kids blouses and has already made a statement to pull the products from the shelf. In spite of the documentation of the child labourers working in the high-street fashion and admission by all concerned parties, only the SDM could not recognise these children as working under conditions of slavery and bondage. Distraught and desperate that these collusions by the custodians of justice, founder of BBA Kailash Satyarthi, Chairperson of Global March Against Child Labour appealed to the Honourable Chief Justice of Delhi High Court through a letter at 11.00 pm.

This order by the Honourable Chief Justice comes when the government is taking an extremely retrogressive stance on the issue of child labour in sweatshops in India and threatening 'retaliatory measures' against child rights organisations. In a parallel development, Global March Against Child Labour and BBA are in dialogue with the GAP Inc. and other stakeholders to work out a positive strategy to prevent the entry of child labour in to sweatshops and device a mechanism of monitoring and remedial action. GAP Inc. Senior Vice President, Dan Henkle in a statement said: "We have been making steady progress, and the children are now under the care of the local government. As our policy requires, the vendor with which our order was originally placed will be required to provide the children with access to schooling and job training, pay them an ongoing wage and guarantee them jobs as soon as they reach the legal working age. We will now work with the local government and with Global March to ensure that our vendor fulfils these obligations."

BBC recently reported on Primark using child labour in the manufacture of clothing. In particular a £4.00 hand embroidered shirt was the starting point of a documentary produced by BBC's Panorama (TV series) program. The program asks consumers to ask themselves, "Why am I only paying £4 for a hand embroidered top? This item looks handmade. Who made it for such little cost?" in addition to exposing the violent side of the child labour industry in countries where child exploitation is prevalent. As a result of the program, Primark took action and sacked the relevant companies, and reviewed their supplier procedures.

The Firestone Tire and Rubber Company operate a rubber plantation in Liberia which is the focus of a global campaign called Stop Firestone. Workers on the plantation are expected to fulfill a high production quota or their wages will be halved, so many workers brought children to work. The International Labour Rights Fund filed a lawsuit against Firestone in November 2005 on behalf of current child laborers and their parents who had also been child laborers on the plantation. On June 26, 2007, the judge in this lawsuit in Indianapolis, Indiana denied Firestone's motion to dismiss the case and allowed the lawsuit to proceed on child labour claims.

On November 21, 2005, An Indian NGO activist Junned Khan, with the help of Police, Labour Department and NGO Pratham mounted the country's biggest ever raid for child labour rescue in the Eastern part of Delhi, the capital of India. The process resulted in rescue of 480 children from over 100 illegal embroidery factories operating in the crowded slum area of Seelampur. For next few weeks, government, media and NGOs were in frenzy over the exuberant numbers of young boys, as young as 5-6 year olds, released from bondage. This rescue operation opened the eyes of the world to the menace of child labour operating right under the nose of the largest democracy in the world.

On October 28, Marka Hansen, president of Gap North America responded, "We strictly prohibit the use of child labour. This is a non-negotiable for us - and we are deeply concerned and upset by this allegation. As we've demonstrated in the past, Gap has a history of addressing challenges like this head-on, and our approach to this situation will be no exception. In 2006, Gap Inc. ceased business with 23 factories due to code violations. We have 90 people located around the world whose job is to ensure compliance with our Code of Vendor Conduct. As soon as we were alerted to this situation, we stopped the work order and prevented the product from being sold in stores. While violations of our strict prohibition on child labour in factories that produce product for the company are extremely rare, we have called an urgent meeting with our suppliers in the region to reinforce our policies."

In early August 2008, Iowa Labour Commissioner David Neil announced that his department had found that Agriprocessors, a kosher meatpacking company in Postville which had recently been raided by Immigration and Customs Enforcement, had employed 57 minors, some as young as 14, in violation of state law prohibiting anyone under 18 from working in a meatpacking plant. Neil announced that he was turning the case over to the state Attorney General for prosecution, claiming that his department's inquiry had discovered "egregious violations of virtually every aspect of Iowa's child labour laws.". Agripro-cessors claimed that it was at a loss to understand the allegations. Child labour is used in the production of cocoa powder, used to make chocolate.

DEFENSE OF CHILD LABOUR

According to Friedman's theory, before the Industrial Revolution virtually all children worked in agriculture. During the Industrial Revolution many of these children moved from farm work to factory work. Over time, as real wages rose, parents became able to afford to send their children to school instead of work and as a result child labour declined, both before and after legislation.

Austrian school economist Murray Rothbard also defended child labour, stating that British and American children of the pre- and post-Industrial Revolution went "voluntarily and gladly" to work in factories. However, the British historian and socialist E.P. Thompson in The Making of the English Working Class draw a qualitative distinction between child domestic work and participation in the wider (waged) labour market. Further, the usefulness of the experience of the industrial revolution in making predictions about current trends has been disputed. Economic historian Hugh Cunningham, author of Children and Childhood in Western Society Since 1500, notes that:

"Fifty years ago it might have been assumed that, just as child labour had declined in the developed world in the late nineteenth and early twentieth centuries, so it would also, in a trickle-down fashion, in the rest of the world. Its failure to do that, and its re-emergence in the developed world, raises questions about its role in any economy, whether national or global."

Big Bill Haywood, a leading labour organizer and leader of the Western Federation of Miners and a founding member and leader of the Industrial Workers of the World famously claimed "the worst thief is he who steals the playtime of children!"

According to Thomas DeGregori, an economics professor at the University of Houston, in an article published by the Cato Institute, a libertarian think-tank operating in Washington D.C., "it is clear that technological and economic change are vital ingredients in getting children out of the workplace and into schools. Then they can grow to become productive adults and live longer, healthier lives. However, in poor countries like Bangladesh, working children are essential for survival in many families, as they were in our own heritage until the late 19th century. So, while the struggle to end child labour is necessary, getting there often requires taking different routes -and, sadly, there are many political obstacles.

Few issues in developing countries draw as much popular attention as does child labour. The purpose of this chapter is to provide a detailed overview of the state of the recent empirical literature on why and how children work as well as the consequences of that work. A less detailed overview of recent developments in the child labour literature can be found in Edmonds and Pavcnik (2005a), and an older review with a more theoretical focus is Basu (1999). Child labour has received considerable attention in economics throughout the discipline's history. Early writings tended to focus on child labour solely through the lens of labour demand. Adam Smith emphasized the value of children in labour shortage societies as motives for fertility. Friedrich Engels wrote extensively on the conditions of working children in the early industrial revolution, and to Marx, child labour was created by the industrial revolution. In his view, machines replaced the need for muscle power, allowing children to do the work formerly performed by men.

Though his views on labour supply are not transparent, in *Das Kapital* he seems to assume that parents and capitalists inevitably exploit all opportunities to employ children. Interestingly, one exception to this assumption that working parents will take all opportunities to have children work is in Malthus. He argues that the prevalence of child labour in the late 18th century is evidence that families were unable to meet their most basic needs. Modern writings on child labour are largely based on the human capital theory as developed by T.W. Schultz, Gary Becker, and others. In thinking through the determinants of investments in education, Schultz (1960) emphasized the importance of foregone earnings in human capital accumulation. Investors (parents, children) weigh the return on additional education investments against the costs such investments entail which includes the foregone economic contribution of children. Becker (1965) extended this argument to emphasize that non-wage uses of time are apt to be an equally important influence on the opportunity cost of child time in school.

Rosenzweig and Evenson (1977) appear to be the first published study to apply this framework explicitly to analyze child labour in a developing country context. In recent years, there has been an astonishing proliferation of empirical work on child labour. An Econlit search of keywords "child labour" reveals a total of 6 peer reviewed journal articles between 1980 and 1990, 65 between 1990 and 2000, and 143 in the first five years of the present decade. This rise in interest appears driven by three factors. First, child labour has drawn considerable policy and public attention over the last decade.

This public interest seems to be motivated by a concern about child labour as a human rights issue and its implication for long-run growth and development through its interaction with education.

The rise in interest in recent years may owe to rising trade and globalization more broadly. They have both raised awareness about the pervasiveness of child labour and elevated concerns among rich country residents about their role in its perpetuation. Second, concurrent with this rise in public interest is a booming theoretical literature on why children work. Prominent theoretical publications such as Basu and Van and Baland and Robinson have spurred a large battery of empirical research. Third, large-scale, nationally representative household surveys from developing countries have become increasingly available over the last fifteen years. This has both lowered the costs of working on child time allocation and increased the complexity of the types of questions that can be addressed empirically. Any study of child labour must begin with a definition of what the researcher means by child labour.

The next surveys different definitions used in the existing literature and discusses some examples from a variety of countries about how children work. The types of activities popularly viewed as child labour are not usually the focus of empirical studies labeled "child labour." Often, academic studies of child labour are better viewed as child time allocation studies, and it seems clear that research must consider as wide a scope of activities as data permits in order to understand the dynamics of child time allocation. Data sources and data problems such as children that are hard to observe with randomized surveys are also discussed. Historically, activists sought to move children out of work so that children could enjoy their childhood, and the Progressive Era's "sacralization" of childhood persists in contemporary, anti-child labour resolutions such as the 1989 UN Convention on the Rights of the Child.

Part of the reason for viewing working child work as a

moral issue is that parents may make decisions for children about whether and how children work without fully internalizing the costs of such activities. Research on child labour tends to avoid moral arguments about how children should spend their time by focusing on quantifying the costs of working. Human capital theory generally post-dates the anti-child labour movements in developed economies, but most of the academic interest in child labour today is because of its consequences for human capital accumulation. Many studies examine whether specific types of work or groupings of activities appear to affect education, physical and mental health, or the nutritional status of working children. This begs the question of why focus on child labour as anything other than something to explain schooling or health changes. This literature is of academic interest in its own right for all the same reasons that adult labour supply is of interest to research.

Moreover, studying the determinants of common forms of work also can be informative about the case for attention to common activities. That is, how the common forms of work are affected by changes in the family's broader economic and social environment can reveal how family decision-makers view the most common forms of work in low income countries. Policies aimed to influence how and where children work can be useful for understanding the causes and consequences of working. A simple analytical model helps fix ideas in this chapter and can illustrate most of the basic points that have been emphasized in existing research on child labour.

This model is presented in the remainder of this introduction. This model is meant to be heuristic. Cigno and Rosati (2005) present a more general time allocation model that can incorporate most of the important recent theoretical contributions in the child labour literature. Leisure and play is likely complementary to schooling in the production of child welfare, but such statements about cross-partial derivatives are not necessary for the present discussion. Importantly, time spent in education is not necessarily limited to time in the classroom. Also, beyond the opportunity costs of education inherent in the time constraint, schooling entails direct costs, and the direct costs are assumed to be increasing in the time spent in education. Thus, direct schooling costs entail in foregone consumption today.

Work outside of the household is freely available in the formal labour market and brings an exogenous wage. First, the residual claimant on child time outside of work is not schooling, and there is a return to leisure that parents may value and could be important for the child's future welfare. Second, if one is interested in child labour because of its impact on schooling, there is no theoretical reason to focus on work outside of the home alone. Consider a child that does not attend school. What are the possible explanations for this? The family's marginal utility from the foregone consumption caused by schooling costs plus the is at least as large as the family's marginal utility that comes through marginal utility of time improving child welfare from additional education.

The marginal utility of time will depend on how the family values the contribution of play to child welfare, the marginal utility of the standard of living, and how time spent in the wage market and in household production affects the standard of living. There is no reason to presume that the wage contribution is more likely to dominate schooling than is the household production contribution. In fact, most children work at home rather than in the wage labour market. This implies that, for most children, the return to time in household production is at least as large as the value the family places on the child's wage contribution. The idea that studies of child time allocation should consider as broad a definition of child work as the data permits is a main theme. Of course, there are many reasons to be interested in why children work beyond its implications for schooling.

This framework also implies several key reasons why children work. First, poverty is a key influence on child labour supply. It influences the family's valuation of child time in household production and the formal labour market, and it may affect the production function for future child welfare. Second, the relative return to child time in schooling may be an important factor. The relative return depends in part on the returns to education as well as the returns to play, the return to child time in home production, the return to formal labour income, and the direct costs of schooling. Schooling improvements, labour demand factors including trade, technological change, and labour regulations all potentially affect child labour through these mechanisms. Similarly, living arrangements, fertility, and market imperfections in credit, land, or goods markets may all influence child labour through their impact on the relative return to child time? Third, parental preferences play a key role in child time allocation decisions. In this set-up, preferences do not drive differences in the allocation of child time between the formal labour market and household production, but they affect the family's valuation of child time in work activities relative to non-work activities.

The marginal utility from the child's contribution to the production of the standard of living (through wage income and the lack of educational expenditure) is at least as large as the marginal utility from the return to education. To the extent that preferences are important, then questions of intrahousehold allocation such as how household decisions are made and who makes these decisions become important in understanding child labour supply. With so many influences on child labour, what types of policies will be useful in reducing it? There is very limited evidence to suggest that anything other than long-term poverty reduction and development is likely to substantially alter the child labour picture although some findings from conditional cash transfer programs are encouraging. However, it is important to note that the general lack of evidence reflects a lack of scientific research more than a failure of programs.

Moreover, very little is known about why children participate in some of the worst forms of child labour, where human rights issues are most relevant, and very little formal analysis has been done on the policies being pursued to help these most vulnerable children. Any discussion of child labour must begin with a precise description of what the term means. The phrase "child labour" conjures images of children chained into factories, sold as slaves, or forced into prostitution. Fortunately, while many children work in the developing world, few experience such atrocities. The International Labour Organization (ILO) is the international body charged with counting child labour, and it estimates that in 2004 there are 218 million child laborers in the world (ILO 2006). Most of these working children labeled "child laborers" are helping their family at home, on the family farm, or in the family business. Economics research on "child labour" tends to focus on these more commonplace activities, both because of their greater prevalence and the relative ease in collecting data on the typical types of activities children perform.

There is controversy about whether the types of activities that children typically participate in are harmful or beneficial to children and others. The present section aims to describe the different definitions of child labour and child work that are prevalent in the literature and overview how children typically work in low income countries. It should be clear from the discussion in the introduction that if one is ultimately interested in influencing the allocation of child time to a particular activity such as some form of work or schooling then researchers need to consider as broad a set of activities as possible. Children do not typically participate in the formal wage labour market. When children do not participate in the formal wage labour market, the shadow value of child in the analytical time (model) is determined by the child's involvement in chores, the family business, schooling, etc. Hence, focusing on a limited set of activities can bias a researcher's understanding of the dynamics of child time allocation. Of course a broad focus on child time allocation overall inevitably means a paper on "child labour" will consider types of work that are very different than the popular use of the term.

TERMINOLOGY MARKET AND DOMESTIC WORK

In both research and policy discussions, there is extraordinary heterogeneity in how child labour is defined and in what words are used to describe the different categories of work in which children participate. The purpose of this subsection is to review how words are typically defined in the literature. There is no consensus. There is currently work underway to define statistical standards and develop a fixed terminology that is the basis for much of this section, but that work is still in its infancy. Both producers and consumers of research need to be careful to define exactly what is being studied in a particular research paper. According to the SNA, "the production of economic goods and services includes all production and processing of primary products whether for the market, for barter, or for own consumption, the production of all other goods and services for the market and, in the case of households which produce such goods and services for the market, the corresponding production for own consumption".

The production of economic goods and services will include wage employment, self- employment, and participation in agriculture, milling, handicrafts, construction as well as water and wood collection. Aggregate statistics of child employment typically cover the economically active population. Economically active is defined as being involved in economic activity and it includes wage workers, employers, own-account workers, members of producer cooperatives, unpaid family workers, apprentices, members of the armed forces, and the unemployed. Economic work or market work is used similarly to economically active individuals, except the unemployed are excluded. Participants in market work are sometimes separated by whether their work is for the consumption of others (market oriented work) or their own family (non-market oriented work).

One can imagine how this distinction is important in national accounts, but there is no clear reason why this distinction is important in studying child time allocation.

Wage work is a subcategory of market oriented work, and many authors focus on studying wage employment alone. One unique challenge in classifying children engaged in market work outside of their own household is that children are not always paid directly in wages. They either receive pay in-kind (goods and services) or their labour is contracted for a fixed fee. Typically, these children are grouped with those paid in cash under "wage work", but some studies separate them, labeling them unpaid out of household market or economic work. Child involvement in non-SNA activities is studied infrequently in child labour studies.

A February 2005 review of empirical papers on child labour indexed in EconLit and published in peer reviewed economics journals since 1995 found that all but two considered wage work, half additionally considered other forms of market work such as work in the family farm or business, and 10 percent considered work that would fall outside the SNA definition of economic activity. The phrase non-economic work is sometimes used to denote partici pation in the provision of goods and services to family members or other members of the community that fall outside of the scope of the official definition of economic goods and services. This includes for example community service work that helps build or maintain local schools. It also includes domestic chores such as caring for family members, cooking, cleaning, or shopping. The phrase "housework" is sometimes in place of domestic chores or it is used to refer to domestic chores excluding shopping.

Finally, "domestic work" is used in reference to non-economic work exclusive of community service and volunteer work. The use of the word "economic" in the SNA is confusing. Since the early 1960s, economists have emphasized how important these "non-economic" activities are to the household's standard of living. Moreover, non-economic can be interpreted to imply that the associated activities are inelastic with respect to economic factors, an assumption that is not born out by the data. Many writers avoid using the phrases "economic" and "noneconomic" work. Instead, they classify work into market work and domestic work. The remaining classification of work, community service and volunteer work is rarely studied and poorly understood. There are two obvious problem with using this market and domestic work lexicon. First, market work and market oriented economic work are apt to be confused.

Second, domestic work performed for compensation outside of the child's own household is considered a type of market work and is often referred to as domestic service or domestic work. The safest solution is for researchers to be explicit in how they are defining the activities under study. Two commonly used terms to be avoided are child work and household work. Child work is typically used synonymously with market work. However, asserting that a child who works in substantive hours in the provision of services to their home is not working is difficult to justify. One could make the case for defining child work as covering both domestic and market work, but simply using the phrase "work" to refer to these activities together is apt to generate the least confusion given child work's common use as market work. Household work is often used as a synonym for domestic work. However, this is confusing, because market work most often occurs within the household.

Child labour researchers often avoids labeling any one activity as child labour. Official definitions of child labour vary. Some countries officially define child labour as wage work (e.g. Pakistan) or market work that is harmful to the future well-being of children (e.g. Vietnam). This later standard is based on the precedent of the International Labour Organization's (ILO) C138. C138 on the Minimum Age for Admission to Employment was passed in 1973 and has been signed by 135 countries to date. Signatories agree to pursue a national policy to abolish "child labour" and to increase the minimum age of employment to "a level consistent with the fullest physical and mental development of young persons" (C138, Article 1). Neither "child labour" nor "employment" is defined in the convention, but the age appropriateness of various activities depends on consideration of their effects on the health and development of the young. In general, the minimum age of employment is the minimum age of completion of compulsory schooling or at least 15 years old, although 14 can be consistent with the convention in very poor countries. Light work that is deemed consistent with schooling attendance and unlikely to be harmful to health and development is consistent with the convention in children as young as 12.

For statistical purposes, defining whether an activity is harmful to a child's health or development is a challenge, because whether an activity is harmful depends on what the child would be doing in the absence of work. The ILO's Statistical Information and Monitoring Program on Child Labour (SIMPOC) is the international body charged with tracking child labour around the world. Their definition of what exactly is "child labour" varies over time, in part because of controversy over what can be considered harmful. At the time of writing, a child laborer is defined by SIMPOC as an economically active child under 12 that works 1 or more hours per week, an economically active child 14 and under that works at least 14 hours per week or 1 or more hours per week in activities that are "hazardous by nature or circumstance," and a child 17 and under that works in an "unconditional worst form of child labour" (trafficked children, children in bondage or forced labour, armed conflict, prostitution, pornography, illicit activities, ILO 2002).

The ILO (2006a) estimates that there were 218 million child laborers in the world in 2004 under this definition. Some researchers that choose to define an activity status as child labour adopt this SIMPOC definition, but others are also present in the literature. By far, the most common thing to do is to define children in wage work as child laborers. Others define child labour as market work. A few researchers also define child labour by adding in domestic work. Typically, an arbitrary cutoff in hours is employed in classifying some domestic workers as child laborers and others as not just as the SIMPOC definition arbitrarily classifies as 13 year old working 14 hours per week as a child laborer while the 13 year old working 13 hours per week is not. Given that "child labour" carries a particular connotation in the popular imagination, the safest course is likely for researchers to avoid labeling any one class of activities child labour. "Light work" is sometimes used to refer to market work that is not deemed child labour.

That is, light work is market work which is for some reason viewed as unlikely to be harmful to health, development, and does not affect school attendance, participation in vocational training, or the child's ability to benefit from any instruction received. Of course, it is not obvious how would know whether work could be harmful in any of these senses without establishing the counterfactual of what children would be doing absent this light work. Worst and hazardous forms of child labour while the general phrase "child labour" is poorly defined; some specific activities are labeled as a "hazardous form of child labour" or a "worst form of child labour". The minimum age convention, C138, places special emphasis on activities that "jeopardize the health, safety, or morals of young persons" (Article 3 - section 1) and defines 18 as the minimum age of employment for activities that can be described as such.

In 1999, C182 on the Worst Forms of Child Labour asks signatory countries to clarify what types of activities fall under this label and to develop specific plans for their eradication. C182 has proven less controversial than C138 on the minimum age of employment. To date, C182 has 151 signatories. While it is up to the individual country to identify "worst forms" in their own country, Article 3 of C182 contains several guidelines for what types of activities are to be considered for persons under the age of 18. These include all forms of slavery and "practices similar to slavery." This later clause is noted to include the sale and trafficking of children, debt bondage, serfdom, and forced or compulsory labour including for the purposes of armed conflict.

These children as well as children in prostitution, pornography, the production or processing of drugs are in "unconditional worst forms" of child labour. The ILO (2002) estimates 8.4 million children under 18 in unconditional worst forms of child labour. Article 3 (d) is the most ambiguous part of convention 182. It allows worst forms to include "work which, by its nature or the circumstances in which it is carried out, is likely to harm the health, safety, or morals of children." Article 4 of the convention is explicit that it is up to individual countries to define what types of work are considered "worst forms" of child labour under this clause. Activities labeled "worst forms" under Article 3(d) of C182 are often labeled as "Hazardous forms of child labour."

The companion recommendation document for C182, R190 Worst Forms of Child Labour Recommendation, suggests that these hazardous forms of child labour include: "(a) work which exposes children to physical, psychological, or sexual abuse; (b) work underground, under water, at dangerous heights, or in confined spaces; (c) work with dangerous machinery, equipment and tools, or which involves the handling or transport of heavy loads; (d) work in an unhealthy environment which may, for example, expose children to hazardous substances, agents or processes, or to temperature, noise levels, or vibrations damaging to their health; (e) work under particularly difficult conditions such as work for long hours or during the night or work where the child is unreasonably confined to the premises or the employer." (R190, Section II.3.a-e).

It is worth noting that, unlike the more general child labour definitions discussed above, these hazardous forms of child labour are defined based on the characteristics of the work rather than relying on understanding what the child might do in the absence of work. Hence, the labeling of specific activity as a worst or hazardous form does not carry the same assumptions about the impact of that work as does the phrase child labour, and a specific country's policy definition of hazardous work or worst forms of child labour can guide researchers in the use of those terms. 170.5 million Children under 18 are in hazardous forms of child labour (ILO 2002).

Available Data

Sources of data on child labour are increasing almost daily, and with them, our understanding of child labour should continue to increase accordingly. Unfortunately, it does not appear that much work is being done to validate the types of surveys and data collection methods that are being used extensively. Hence, there is considerable scope for work on how to measure the activities in which children participate. Many early studies of child labour relied on cross-country data. Cross-country estimates of economic active populations come from the ILO's LABORSTA database although the most recent release (fifth edition) omits the 10-14 age groups. These LABORSTA estimates of economically activity populations are generally believed to understate the extent of work, because data on work inside the household (even market work) are often not collected.

Moreover, although the LABORSTA data are available over time, very few low-income countries have multiple data sources on child labour over time. Much of the intertemporal variation in child labour in the LABORSTA data must thus be driven by the imputations and adjustments done for LABORSTA rather than independent observations on child labour. As a result, the LABORSTA data is not reliably useful for analyzing changes in child labour over time. When the ILO's Statistical Information and Monitoring Program on Child Labour (SIMPOC) compute global estimates of the incidence of child labour, it does not rely on the LABORSTA data.

Instead, it works wherever possible off available household surveys that facilitate a more complete picture of how children work and are free from LABORSTA's imputations. Understanding Children's Work (UCW) is a joint effort of the World Bank, UNICEF, and the ILO to coordinate studies relevant to child labour, and they maintain a thorough listing of labour force, child labour, and multi-purpose household surveys with information useful for studying how and why children work. This chapter draws extensively from

UNICEF's Multiple Indicator Cluster Surveys (MICS) from 2000 and 2001. They include a child labour module which asks children 5-14 whether they work outside of their household in the last week and the last year as well as how many hours they worked outside the household in the last week. The surveys also collect hours in the last week for work in domestic chores and in the household business (separately).

No information is available on industry of employment, type of employer, nor compensation. An appealing feature of the MICS data is that survey instruments are nearly identical in each country. That said, questions are likely to be interpreted in different ways based on local context. Limitations of household surveys and missing children several issues arise in using household survey data to examine child labour supply. First, there is the general question about who to ask about the child's labour supply. A great deal of attention has been directed by agencies such as SIMPOC and UCW towards what types of activities should be monitored, but it is difficult to find detailed analysis of how this information should be collected. It seems likely that measurement error in hours worked is a first order problem with this data while participation is perhaps less difficult to gauge. Second, measurement of compensation is particularly complicated.

For example, 38 percent of children 5-14 in Niger answer that they work in unpaid work outside of their family. The average across all countries is 6 percent. It could be that this labour arrangement is much more frequent in Niger, or it may be that respondents are interpreting the question in a different way than are respondents in other countries. Moreover, it is not obvious that even in wage work any one respondent will be fully aware of the child's compensation. For example, a parent may be paid an amount that the child is not aware of for the child's services, but an employer may also compensate the child to reduce moral hazard problems. Third, estimates of the incidence of any type of work will be sensitive to the recall period used. It is not unusual for children to work intermittently, and it is not obvious what the "right" recall period is for any analysis.

For example, in agricultural communities, one often observes high participation rates in market work during harvest seasons but little other than domestic work at other times of year. Systematic evidence on the dynamics of child labour is extremely rare. Levison et al (2003) is an exception. Brazil's urban, monthly employment survey follows approximately 35,000 household for fourth months (the survey is set up as a rotating panel). Levison et al use this data to document the intermittent nature of market work participation in urban Brazil from 1982-1999. In their sample, they observe that the percent of children employed in any given month is roughly half the number of children employed in at least one of the four months. Moreover, depending on the city, between 20 and 40 percent of children 10-14 experienced 2 or more employment transitions in a four month period. Hence, child labour measures are sensitive to both the types of work considered and the recall periods used to assess employment status. This intermittency of employment raises particular problems for child labour measures based on the intensity of the child's work.

Fourth, some of the most vulnerable children may be impossible to capture with surveys. Either they do not reside in households or their situation is sufficiently rare that the probability that they are sampled in a randomized survey is effectively zero. Moreover, there is often little reason to assume that selection into these activities (relative to other more easily measured forms of work) is random. To get at these rare or hard to find groups of children, researchers often employ contaminated sampling procedures, but it is hard to draw inferences with this data when children outside of the activity are unobserved. This is an active avenue of research. There are two approaches that can be taken to gauge the problem of missing children.

Both have severe limitations. First, enumerators can collect complete fertility histories and then account for all of the children. In general, this approach may be biased by errors of omission if children in particular circumstances are also omitted from fertility histories. Alternatively, this fertility history based approach may overstate the extent of missing children, because children that set up independent households or that are fostered in to other households should appear in those household rosters and would not be excluded from any analysis using representative data. Unfortunately, the data do not identify the timing or age of each birth. It is impossible to decipher the extent to which differences in adult mobility rates are driving differences in the number of absent children or how many of the absent children would be captured in other households in a study of children 10-14 (for example). In many countries, a negligible number of children are missing from the mother's household: less than a percent in Vietnam, Uzbekistan, Tajikstan, Azerbaijan, and Albania.

However, nearly 20 percent of living births are absent in Sierra Leone and Swaziland. 15 percent are absent in Gambia and Guinea Bissau. Altogether, 10 percent or more of births are absent in 9 of 22 countries. It is impossible to tell whether these missing children would be relevant for an analysis of child labour supply or schooling. It is also impossible to identify how many of these children would appear in other households in a nationally representative randomized survey. However, there seems to be ample potential for a substantive problem in some settings. The problem of missing children is most acute in panel data, because children that exit a panel household who would be captured in a representative survey are unlikely to reappear in other panel households. However, panel data permits a second approach to evaluate the scale of missing children. Many household panels collect information on individuals, including missing individuals over time.

This data can be tabulated to gauge the scale of missing children for work. Extrapolating from this tabulation to representative data overstates the problem of missing children as many children that exit panel households would be captured in a survey of non-panel households, but it is an accurate reflection of the incidence of missing children in panel households. A comparison of missing children in the two panels is illustrative, because the questionnaires regarding attrition are very similar, both datasets are World Bank assisted Living Standards Measurement Surveys (LSMS), and at the start of each panel, the two countries have similar living standards as measured by GDP per capita. In the Vietnam data, 93 percent of boys and girls are recaptured.

Of the missing children, 7 percent of boys and 8 percent of girls are potentially missing from the Vietnam data because of work or schooling (this includes children whose absence is not explained). This corresponds to less than a percent of the boys and girls that would be expected to appear in the second round of the panel in the Vietnamese data. While out-migration for work or school is then unlikely to be a significant source of bias in the Vietnamese data (at least for recaptured households), it appears to be a much more substantive issue in the Nepali data. 78 percent of boys and 75 percent of girls are recaptured in panel households in the Nepali panel. Of the missing, 44 percent of boys and 13 percent of girls are potentially missing for work or school. These missing children constitute 10 percent of the boys and 3 percent of the girls expected to be in the household for the second round of the panel. Hence, while the data from Vietnam suggest that missing children is unlikely to be a substantive problem in that data, there is considerably more scope for problems in the Nepali data.

Specific country contexts must be considered in discussing biases owing to missing children. Most household surveys of children capture a large number of children that neither work nor attend school. For example, the 2000 Indian National Sample Survey classifies 13 percent of rural children 10-14 in India as neither working nor attending school. These children are typically labeled "idle," and the exact interpretation of their status is controversial. Biggeri et al (2003) discuss the interpretation of idle status in household surveys from six different countries. They argue that measurement error in activities (especially mismeasurement of domestic work), unemployment, and unobserved health issues are responsible for a significant part of the "idleness" status. Measurement issues may be particularly important in cross-country comparisons as understandings of "work" may vary from country to country. Idleness is not necessarily simply measurement error in work.

That is, true idleness occurs when the marginal utility associated with additional leisure is at least as large as that of the contribution of the child's work to household welfare. Is this ever plausible unless the parents put substantive weight on child leisure? There is no empirical evidence to inform this question, but it could occur when there are not wage employment options open to children (M=0), and the shape of the home production function F(-) is such that the marginal product of child labour can become non-positive. For example, there may be a limited amount of helpful tasks young children can do in a family business. Once completed, children may be more destructive to output (perhaps distractive to adult labour) than helpful. Whether the prevalence of idle children reflects the economic reality of the country or problems in how child time allocation data is collected is not yet answered. Interestingly, Edmonds, Pavcnik, and Topalova (2007) find that the poverty elasticity of idleness in Indian data is greater than is the poverty elasticity of market or domestic work. Hence, even if idleness reflects measurement error, it might not be classical measurement error.

Background on the Activities of Working Children

Types of Activities

The data present a unique opportunity to examine child labour across countries in as comparable a manner as possible (little can be done for cultural differences in the interpretation of the questions). Note that while there is considerable variation in schooling, schooling rates are surprisingly high. This reflects the structure of the questionnaire. It asks whether a child has attended school in the last year while the labour questions refer to the last week. First, work outside of the household is the least prevalent work category in every country except

Azerbaijan, Kenya, and Venezuela. In these three countries participation rates in market work inside and outside of the household are similar. Altogether, 8 percent of children in the MICS data work outside of their household, and only 2 percent work in paid work outside of the household.

It is unclear what the 6 percent of children who work outside their house without pay are doing in the MICS data, but in other datasets, they are often observed working in labour exchanges on neighboring farms, working in schools in exchange for materials or a reduction in fees, helping a relative with their work, etc. Domestic work is the most prevalent type of work. Across countries, 65 percent of children 5-14 report working in domestic work, compared to 23 percent in market work. Second, the countries with the lowest school attendance rates have the highest incidence of "idle" children that neither work nor attend schooling. Work is not the residual claimant on child time outside of school. Moreover, work is not especially prevalent in these countries with high rates of idleness. They do not have the highest rates of work outside of the household or work in market work.

This is consistent with the idea that no single indicator of activity will give a particularly complete idea of child time allocation, and research needs to take a comprehensive view of child time in order to understand how it is influenced. Third, countries with the highest prevalence of work outside the household also have the highest prevalence of work inside the household. Sierra Leone has the highest rate of work outside the household, and the second highest rate of work inside the household. Niger is second with 43 percent of children working outside the household, while it has the fifth highest rate of market work inside the household. We discuss the weak nature of the evidence linking child's market work status and employment opportunities outside of the household, and the high correlation between work inside and outside the household are consistent with the idea that children are not working solely because wage labour market factors draw children away from their homes. Fourth, participation in market work is highest in countries where domestic work is most prevalent.

This positive correlation in participation rates for market and domestic work also appears in hours worked. However, the positive correlations between hours in various categories of work mask a more nuanced view - that participation in various activities is positively correlated when children work a small number of hours in each activity (as is typical) but not with extreme hours. Each contour on the map is a given density. Thus each point on a given contour is equally likely. Density is increasing in color intensity. First, at the peak of the density, children work more hours per week in domestic work than market work. Ignoring domestic work would frequently understate total hours worked by a child by a factor slightly greater than 2. Second, children working a large number of hours in market work are more likely than not to spend additional time in domestic work.

This is evidence by the humps in the market work direction. No such humps are evident with hours in domestic work. Third, as hours per week in domestic work increase, it becomes less likely to observe the child doing significant time in market work. This is evident in the increasing slope of contours as one heads up the domestic hours worked distribution. The joint distribution of hours worked illu-strates the problem with "child labour" definitions that focus on market work alone, especially definitions based on the intensity of hours worked. For example, suppose a researcher decided to be concerned about children that worked more than 20 or more hours per week. If only work outside the household was considered, this would be 8 percent of the MICS 10-14 sample. If market work inside the household is also included, 23 percent of children work more than 20 or more hours per week. When domestic work is also considered, 38 percent work 20 or more hours per week and 17 percent work 40 or more hours per week. Hence, ignoring domestic work may seriously understate estimates of total hours worked and thereby the incidence of child labour if hours worked is used to define the concept.

Among children engaged in market work, most of that work is inside the child's household. The industrial and occupational composition of employment in market work is not available in the MICS data. Comparable cross-country estimates of the industrial and occupational composition of child involvement in market work do not appear to exist. One possible source of this information is that most SIMPOC child labour surveys use similar questionnaires, and they tend to collect information on occupation and industry. In almost every listed country, a majority of children economically active children are involved with agriculture, forestry, or fishing industries.

The exceptions are the 5- 17 populations of Costa Rica, Panama, and the Ukraine where these industries are still the largest employers of children. In most countries, the combination of hotel and restaurants and wholesale and retail trade are the next most important industrial sectors for economically active children. When they can be disaggregated, wholesale and retail trade tends to have a larger share of economically active children than does the hotel and restaurant sector. Of the MICS countries, only Kenya and the Philippines also have child labour surveys. It is interesting to note, that MICS estimates of participation rates in market work differ from estimates of the economically active population in the SIMPOC surveys for these two countries. The difference in the Philippine data is small. 16 percent of children are involved in market work in the MICS data, 11 percent in the SIMPOC survey. However, the differences in the Kenyan data are large. 3 percent of Kenyan children 5-14 are involved in market work in the MICS surveys, but the SIMPOC surveys report an economic activity rate for this population of 15 percent. It is not clear why these estimates differ.

Interestingly, private households are large employers of economically active children in Kenya, Tanzania, and Zambia. Many of these children are child domestic workers and the phenomena of child domestic workers in Africa and elsewhere is infrequently studied in detail within economics. The comparability of industry classifications in the SIMPOC surveys across countries is not as complete as one would like. Nor are the classifications particularly detailed. The 2002/03 Bangladesh Child Labour Survey is unusual in the incredible detail it provides on the industrial classification of economically active children. In examining the detailed industrial composition of employment in Bangladesh, it is important to remember that there is no reason to believe that Bangladesh is representative of other low-income countries. There are an estimate 7.5 million economically active children 5-17 in Bangladesh. This corresponds to 18 percent of children 5-17.

The detailed classifications are useful to see what children are doing within the aggregate sectors. Children involved in agriculture and related industries are involved in the growing of cereals, vegetables, poultry farming, and inland fishing. Cereal cultivation is the largest single sector with 39 percent of all economically active children directly involved. In the retail trade industries, groceries and general stores are the largest employer of children. In manufacturing, wooden furniture and fixtures stand out. For construction, site preparation is relatively more important. The disaggregated occupational composition of economically active children can provide further insight into what children do. 46 percent of children 5-17 are farm crop workers. The next largest occupations are salesmen and shop assistants (7 percent), poultry farmers (5 percent), sales supervisors (4 percent), fisherman (3 percent), and non-motorized road vehicle drivers (3 percent).

Gender differences in activities can be considerable in some countries. Compared to girls, boys generally have higher participation rates in market work and lower participation rates in domestic work. For example, in the MICS countries, girls are 18 percent more likely to be involved in domestic work and nearly 30 percent less likely to participate in paid market work. Estimates of gender differences tend to be extremely sensitive to what types of activities are considered in a study. Studies such as Assaad et al (2003) for Egypt, Levison and Moe (1998) for Peru, Levison, Moe, and Knaul

(2001) for Mexico have documented the misleading picture that omitting domestic work can create for analysis of the determinants of child work. In both market and domestic work, boys and girls often participate in different tasks. This is evident in the large gender differences in the industrial composition of economically active children in Bangladesh.

Boys are involved in a wider variety of industries. Boys are more likely to be engaged in the growing of cereal crops. Girls are more involved in growing vegetables and poultry farming. 14 percent of economically active girls are in poultry and 16 percent in vegetables while less than 2 percent of economically active boys are in each industry. Children involved in textile and sewing handicrafts and private household services are almost entirely female whereas boys are more involved in fishing, wooden furniture manufacture, construction site preparation, retail trade of grocery and general stores, and transport. We should not extrapolate from Bangladesh to assume such distinct gender differences in other countries, but its example shows that these gender differences can be large. Large gender differences in types of tasks can complicate researcher decisions about how to treat gender. Do differences in activities reflect a fundamental difference in how girl time allocation decisions will be made with respect to the household's economic environment? If so, this would suggest that boys and girls should be considered separately in research.

Qualitative evidence from specific country contexts can help inform where girls should be considered separately from boys, but bifurcating data by gender seems a reasonable default position. Substantive gender differences in tasks and determinants of work can be especially challenging for studies that rely on within household comparisons (household fixed effects) of children. Assume average birth spacing is two years, the probability an observed child is a girl is 0.5, and that gender draws are independent within parents. This implies that a household fixed effects study of working children 10-14 will rely on gender differences in activities and tasks for half its variation.

Urban–rural Differences

The research challenges associated with gender also arise with urban-rural data. Children tend to work more and for longer hours in rural than urban areas. 31 percent of rural children 5-14 are engaged in market work in rural areas compared to 19 percent in urban areas. Domestic work also has a higher prevalence in rural areas although the difference is smaller (68 percent compared to 61 percent). 26 percent of children work 20 or more hours per week in rural areas compared to 14 percent in urban, and 9 percent work 40 or more hours in rural areas compared to 4 percent in urban. If children only worked more intensely in rural areas, then researchers could pool urban and rural children in their analysis, but children also tend to work in different types of activities. For example, in the MICS countries, the prevalence of unpaid market work is nearly double in rural areas, and paid employment accounts for 50 percent larger share of all market work in urban areas.

A careful look at the urban-rural differences in the detailed Bangladesh data is illustrative for why researcher's default assumption should be to treat urban and rural child labour decisions distinctly. In general, employment is more concentrated in rural areas in Bangladesh. For boys, urban-rural differences in employment are similar to what one would expect with rural areas more weighted to agriculture. A majority of economically active boys in rural areas are farm crop workers with most being involved in cereals. Salesman and shop assistants, fisherman, and non-motorized vehicle drivers are the next most prevalent occupations among rural boys. In urban areas, boys are most active in sales. 27 percent of economically active boys in urban areas are working as sales supervisors, salesmen, shop assistants, and street vendors.

Much of this appears to be in retail grocery and general stores as well as tea stalls. However, farm crop workers in cereals, fisherman, and non-motorized vehicle operators are also prevalent in urban areas. Urban-rural differences in occupation and industry of the economically active population in Bangladesh are more pronounced for girls. A majority of girls in rural areas are involved in cereals, vegetables, or poultry farming. While poultry is the second largest industry of employment for urban girls, together these agricultural industries are less than a quarter of urban employment for girls. Spinners, weavers, knitters, etc. are unusual in rural areas, but 13 percent of economically active urban girls are in these occupations. Employment of girls in the manufacture of *bidies* or in private households is also much more prevalent in urban areas. A difficulty in bifurcating data into urban and rural segments is that it presumes the two area types are segmented. In some contexts, there is no clear line either defining or separating urban and rural.

In fact, there is an interesting literature that documents how household specialization changes with proximity to major urban areas and that this in turn affects schooling and both market and domestic work. Thus, it is difficult to draw generalities with regards to how and whether urban and rural areas should be treated differently by empirical researchers. Moreover, the example of Bangladesh illustrates that the extent to which urban and rural activities are comparable may differ by gender as well. Age patterns C138 established the idea that whether an activity is viewed negatively for a child depends on the child's age, and this has been codified into SIMPOC's definition of child labour. The idea behind this is that what may be appropriate for a 14 year old might not for a seven year old. This is logical, but implicit in this discussion is that 7 year olds tend do the same sorts of activities as a 14 year old. This does not appear to be the case in the limited available evidence.

The four pictured categories are market work outside of one's own household, market work, any work (the difference between any and market work is children who only work in domestic work), and any work without also attending school. Participation rates in each of these categories looks smooth in age for boys until age 10 when there is a sizeable increase in participation rates in market and domestic work and again for age 12. Girls appear to experience discrete jumps at age 8,

10, and 12. The increase at age 8 for girls appears to be most dramatic in domestic work whereas most of the increase at age 10 and 12 for girls is in market work. Overall "any work" patterns for girls look smooth at ages 10 and 12, suggesting that the increase in market work and 10 and 12 for girls complements the domestic work that began increased substantively starting around age 8. Moreover, within market work, there are changes by age in the types of industries in which children are employed. When available, the industrial composition of employment is also broken down by age.

There are some interesting differences across age. For example, in Tanzania, the fraction of economically active children employed in private households is decreasing in age whereas the fraction in agriculture and related industries is increasing in age. However, the opposite is true for Kenya. Declining shares in agriculture and related industries with age is also present in Ethiopia, Ghana, Namibia, and Nicaragua. But the age patterns are ambiguous in Zambia and the Philippines. Hence, while there is no clear age pattern across countries in the industrial composition of employment, there appear to be patterns within countries that highlight how important age can be in the analysis of child labour. The evidence implies that researchers should be as flexible as possible in how they treat age in their analysis. A full set of gender interacted age effects seems reasonable for regression work, especially for market work.

A related issue concerns what ages researchers should consider. International organizations interested in child labour typically focus on children 6-14 for most activities but the under 18 are often considered in worst forms. However, C182 is careful to allow each country to set appropriated ages for different types of work, and individual country policies regarding work and schooling are useful for researchers in deciding what ages to consider and how to group those ages. While work laws tend not to be enforced in most current developing countries (more on this later), they are useful at providing insight into country specific views on the ages at which work is a concern. Researchers have to be careful, however, not to let subjective policy statements about "harmful" work drive what types of ages they consider as whether work is harmful ultimately depends on understanding why a child participates in it. Research needs to be particularly concerned about schooling ages, and grouping children based on the category of schooling they would normally attend for their age can be prudent (especially when drop out rates at schooling transitions are high).

For example, observing a seven year old who worked without attending school in a country where schooling typically begins at age 8 might reflect something very different than if the child were at a country where schooling begins at 5. Likewise observing a thirteen year old out of school in a country where thirteen year olds are usually in primary school may imply something different than in a country where thirteen year olds are in secondary school. Moreover, in many settings, the elasticity of child time allocation to factors in the environment appears to be increasing in age at young ages, and explaining child time allocation at pre-school ages is a challenge. Hence, country specific attention to the appropriate age grouping of the data seems merited. Worst forms of child labour The ILO's SIMPOC estimates that a total of 8.4 million children are involved in child trafficking, in forced or bonded labour, are soldiers, are prostitutes or involved in pornography, or participate in illicit activities (ILO 2002). 68 percent of these children are in bonded or forced labour.

An additional 170.5 million children are in hazardous activities. The definition of a hazardous activity varies from country to country. In implementing C182, the ILO has been active in assisting countries in assessing the prevalence of worst and hazardous forms of child labour as well as in developing plans for the eradication of these activities. Nepal was one of the first countries to initiate one of these "Time Bound Programs," and the findings from the baseline work for this program are illustrative of the types of activities that governments label as hazardous and the prevalence of worst forms in a very poor country. These estimates are from ILO (2001). There are approximately 8 million children below the age of 16 in Nepal, and approximately 1.5 percent of these children work in these worst forms of child labour. Child porters and domestic works are the two most common types of "worst forms" of child labour. Among child porters, there are two main types: short distance porters that work in urban markets and bus parks and long distance that work in the countryside.

The ILO estimates that typically long distance porters stay and work with their families while short distance porters have often migrated to find work. Estimates are that there are about 42,204 long distance porters and 3,825 short distance porters. 88 percent are boys. Domestic workers are most prevalent in high status urban households, though domestics typically come from rural areas. In Kathmandu, 1 out of 5 households employ children. The ILO estimates that 43 percent of employers of child domestics are government or non-government service holders. Domestics are believed to be evenly split between paid (to parents) and unpaid (more correctly, paid in a lump sum) workers. The other children included because of the nature of their employment are children in mines, in the carpet sector, and rag pickers, who pick recyclables and other rubbish out of garbage dumps for resale. Bonded laborers and trafficked children both fall under worst forms of child labour as well. Bonded children in Nepal are in bondage either because parents took out debts against the child's future earnings or because they were used as collateral on loans.

The ILO estimates that some 17,152 children in bondage in Nepal, although this estimate is controversial because it does not include children whose parents are bonded in a system of bonded labour that pervades western Nepal. Child trafficking is particularly hard to measure and evaluate. According to the ILO (2001), 12,000 girls are trafficked into the commercial sex industry each year in Nepal. By and large, these girls work in brothels in India. Unfortunately, because of the relative rarity of these activities and the challenges of capturing them in randomized surveys, little research exists on whether these activities are rightly viewed as a type of child work (where human rights is more obviously an issue) or whether they should be viewed as some other type of activity altogether. One difficulty with classifying some activities as hazardous and including them as a worst form of child labour is that children can face hazards in the most common kinds of labour, too. Especially as children get older, they become active in all aspects of agriculture, and it is not unusual to see reports of injuries in operating farm machinery in child labour surveys.

The self-reported injury rate from child labour surveys of children working in agriculture is actually higher, at 12 percent, than the 9 percent injury rate in manufacturing. Agriculture can also be hazardous for children because of exposure to dangerous chemicals such as chemical herbicides or pesticides, exposure to heat or weather, repetitive work injuries, and threats posed by animals, reptiles, insects, parasites, and some plants. Hence, even though in principal, the distinction between hazardous child labour and other types of activities seems less vague than the distinctions some draw between child labour and light work (where "child labour" is labeled as work that is somehow known to be harmful to the child), in reality, a case can be made for looking at some of the more common forms of child labour even if one is only interested in activities that might fall under C182. The next section discusses the case for attention to child activities further. Are worst forms different? In the following sections, this chapter reviews evidence on why children work.

This evidence is culled almost entirely from work that would not be considered hazardous or a worst form of child labour under C182, because the relatively rare worst forms of child labour are difficult to capture with randomized surveys. Hence, before turning to that evidence it is worth reviewing theories as to why selection into worst forms might be different. Three views about differences in the selection process into common forms and worst forms of child labour seem to dominate the academic literature. In one view, worst forms are no different than other types of work from the parent or child's perspective, and factors that drive children to select into worst forms are the same factors that drive them to work in the first place. A variation on this view notes that the work may be more unpleasant but this unpleasantness may be fully compensated through higher wages. In this case, the link between worst forms and income will be the same as that of more common forms of child labour, and the resulting policy prescriptions will be the same. In a second view, worst forms of child labour are partially compensated so that they pay more.

Thus, the entry process is similar to other types of work except that poorer households are more likely to select into worst forms, because the marginal utility for the additional income exceeds the disutility coming from the particular type of work. In a third view, children in worst forms of child labour enter because of poor information about what the work entails. Thus, ex-ante children select into the work under the assumption that it is similar to other types of work, and there are barriers to exiting. This explanation is most often voiced to explain selection into prostitution, but it may be equally substantive for other worst forms of child labour. In reality, because of inference problems with rare events, research on why children select into worst forms and whether selection is driven by characteristics that differ from those discussed below is in its infancy.

2

The Problem of Global Child Labour

From at least as far back as 1802, when Robert Peel's Factories Act was passed in Britain, there has been serious effort to root out child labour. In these two hundred years the world has seen economic growth and the rise of prosperity that, even till fairly recently, would have been beyond the human imagination. If despite that, today, at the time of celebrating the second centenary of the Factories Act of 1802, the world has an estimated 186 million child laborers. This is a failure of stunning proportions. The activism and economic progress of the nineteenth and early twentieth century saw some sharp reductions in child labour in industrialized nations. What may not have been realized then was that some of this problem had merely been exported to the developing countries, which already had their own child labour problem. Partly thanks to the difficulty of collecting data on child labour, and partly because most child labour is integrated with other family work, its dimensions remained unknown for a long time.

Then, as recently as the nineties, and following the Convention of the Rights of the Child (1989), a confluence of factors, such as globalization, increased awareness of what is happening in distant countries and the collection of systematic statistics by the ILO, the World Bank and individual nations, the world became aware that from a global point of view the situation in many countries was not much better than during the industrial revolution, that large numbers of children have been working shockingly long hours in this pertains to the year 2000, the latest for which global data are available (ILO, 2002). But it is worth factories and sheds that are frequently ill-lit, squalid and a hazard to workers' health. One concomitant of this has been an outpouring of writing, research and concern regarding child labour over the last decade or so.

Recent research has given us an understanding of the phenomenon and the consequences of alternative policy interventions that earlier governments and international organizations did not have access to. This raises hope that one can conceive of a time-bound plan for putting an end to child labour and raising the level of well-being of children the world over. The aim of this chapter is to pull together the recent research and help think about policy to deal urgently with this unnecessary problem of our times.

THEORY

Basic Model

Two crucial assumptions that were used in some of the early models and have been subsequently used in a wide range of analyses, from dynamics to the modeling of social norms are the so-called 'luxury axiom' and 'substitution axiom'. The luxury axiom asserts that households send their children to work only when driven to do so by poverty. In other words, child non-work (which would, typically, consist of schooling and leisure) is a luxury good: Households whose non-child labour incomes (or, in brief, adult incomes) are very low cannot afford to indulge in keeping children out of some productive activity. It is only when adult incomes begin to rise that mentioning here that of all children, up to age 17, 5.7 million are in forced and bonded households take children out of the labour force.

Implicit in this assumption is an altruistic view of the household: parents or guardians do not like to make their children work unless compelled by circumstances. The evidence seems to us to largely confirm this axiom, though of course there will be exceptions, or what looks like exceptions, and we turn to some of these in a later section. The substitution axiom asserts that adult and child labour is substitutes, subject to some adult equivalency correction. More specifically, it means that adults can do what children do. There used to be a certain presumption in the folk literature on the subject that there were certain tasks specific to children. Expressions like 'nimble fingers' to describe child labour tended to perpetuate this belief.

The substitution axiom expresses a contrary view on this. And a careful study of the technology of production involving children by Levison et al (1998) lends strong support to the substitution axiom. They show that adults in India are as good if not better in producing hand-knotted carpets as children. So from a purely technical point of view it is possible to replace child labour with adults. But of course adults cost more and for that reason firms may be reluctant to make the transition to adults-only labour. The basic idea behind the theory that emerges from these axioms is simple. Suppose, for simplicity that the economy consists of N households and each household consists of one adult and M children. Production takes place using labour alone. By doing a full day's work each adult can supply one unit of labour and each child ã (#1).

This assumption formalizes the substitution axiom for our use. Child labour is a substitute for labour, 1.8 million in prostitution and 0.3 million in armed conflict adult labour, subject to an equivalent scale correction. Let the wage rate for a full day's work by an adult is w and the wage rate for a full day's work by a child be w. Clearly w= (w. Each household decides what is the minimum tolerable level of consumption for the household. We shall call this 'subsistence consumption' and denote it by s, though this may well embody 'social' notions of what is considered an acceptable level of consumption. Adults work full time. If an adult finds that by working full time, income falls short of the subsistence consumption, then and only then are children sent to work (the luxury axiom).

Assuming, for simplicity that adult labour supply is perfectly inelastic, we have AB as part of the labour supply. As w drops below s, children are sent out to work in an effort to reach the target acceptable level of income. Hence, as w keeps dropping further below s, total labour supply keeps increasing. This continues till there is no further labour to supply. Then labour supply becomes inelastic once again. This explains the shape of the supply curve ABCF. The essential feature of the supply curve here is its backward bending section. Beyond this we can get many variations under different assumptions. The stretch BC can be a segment of the rectangular hyperbola under the assumption that the household uses child labour exactly so as to achieve a total income of s. This however may not be reasonable if it is the case that a small amount of child labour makes it impossible to go to school.

Then once a child is made to work the household may decide to make the child work quite a bit, thereby making the BC segment more elastic. But as long as we have the backward bending segment, the possibility of the demand curve for labour intersecting the supply curve more than once is a reality. In this case the labour market has three equilibria, E, E, and E. Of these, E and E are stable and we shall focus on these. At E wages are high and there is no child labour, while at E wages are low and a high incidence of child labour. The same economy can get caught in any of these equilibria.

If such an economy is stuck at the 'bad equilibrium', that is, one with high child labour, it pays to have a legal intervention banning child labour, for this will deflect the economy to the 'good equilibrium'. It should be stressed that this does not automatically amount to a case for legal intervention, whenever we see child labour. In a very poor economy, it is entirely possible that the demand for labour is so low that the only intersection of the demand curve with the supply curve occurs on the segment CF. In that case a ban on child labour can backfire, leaving the children and their parents' impoverished and even risking starvation. In the above model, child labour is driven by poverty. This is not to deny that it can have other causes, some even beyond economics.

There are important writings, notably by Zelizer (1985), which point to the changing 'social conception' of childhood and, relatedly, the value of the child. How important are these social factors in explaining child labour? Zelizer is right in asserting that, in the nineteenth-century (shocking though this may seem to us today), child labour was often commended as necessary for building character and discipline, and valuable for industrial competition. However, one must be cautious in not interpreting every opposition to legislation banning child labour as reflecting such views and supporting child labour. Even in contemporary times many economists oppose coercive legislation (in some contexts, so do we), but this usually reflects their view of how the labour market works and how legislation is likely to affect children; it need not be an indicator of any normative difference or difference in the conception of childhood and the worth of children.

What one can take away from Zelizer is that social norms matter and these can be in very concrete ways, as demonstrated by Lopez-Calva (2003), following the models of Lindbeck, Nyberg and Weibull (1999). In a nutshell the argument is as follows. For simplicity, assume that each household i has one child and child wage-rate is fixed at w. The benefit from having the child work is given by w. To decide whether child labour is worth it, from the benefit one must deduct the cost of having the child work. Let c (i) be the leisure cost of child work as perceived by household i. Without loss of generality, assume that c (i) rises monotonically with i. But suppose there is another cost of sending the child to work, namely, the social cost or the cost of stigma, (Following standard arguments, for instance, Granovetter and Soong (1983), we shall assume that this cost depends on how many others send their children to work. So if it is expected that n children are working then the stigma cost of sending a child to work is given by ((n), where ('(n) < 0, suggesting that one becomes more brazen if more people are doing the same. Hence, household i will send its child to work if and only if w c - ((n) $ c(i).

Now define 4(n) as the critical household that will send its child to work when it is expected that n children are working in the aggregate. Hence, w c - ((n) / c (4(n)). Since, when n is the expected size of aggregate child labour, all households i # 4(n) will send their children to work, it follows that the actual amount of child labour will be equal to 4(n). Evidently, n* is an equilibrium amount of child labour (in the sense of rational expectations) if n* = 4(n*). Hence, child labour can depend critically on social norms, in particular on the stigma costs of sending a child to work. It is also easy to see that the function 4(n) is a monotonically increasing function. Hence, social norms can be compatible multiple equilibria.

Two innately identical societies can socially engineer themselves into different levels of child labour, which, once in place, tend to persist. Also, given that social stigma may vary depending on whether a child works in a factory, farm or at home, the basis and extent of different kinds of child labour may vary between urban and rural areas and between factories and homes. It is possible to go beyond poverty and social stigma and look for yet more causes of child labour. Child labour could depend on the quality and availability of schools and the transactions cost of child work. These variables can, in turn, be further disaggregated.

Moreover, there is evidence that some of these variables affect fertility, which would make m endogenous. Relatedly, the incidence of child labour will respond to incentives given by government to make schooling more attractive, such as giving children food for attending school, or giving parents of school-going children incentives such as cash transfers. The relation between child labour and schooling can be captured theoretically in a somewhat different way by a political economy model. Such models are quite new in this area and their full implications remain to be evaluated. But a brief account of such a model is provided in the next sub-section.

CHILD LABOUR, SCHOOLING AND POLITICAL ECONOMY

Political economy models in this area are, as yet, rare. These models give us some nice insights into child labour and schooling, and endogenously explain why some nations ban child labour and others do not. In Tanaka's model government does not legislate against child labour. Instead, it collects taxes and runs schools and, by making the schools sufficiently good, tries to wean children away from labour to education. Hence, in this model, as the tax rate is raised, as long as a household does not send its children to school, it is worse off; but once it decides that the schools are good enough to take the children out of the labour market and send them to school, its welfare responds to the tax rate like an inverted-U, since an increase in the tax rate improves the quality of schools. Households differ from one another but their broad contour of preference is as just described. This means that preferences are not single-peaked but they are nevertheless of the kind that may satisfy the conditions for the use of the median voter theorem.

Tanaka then imposes the necessary technical restrictions and uses the median voter theorem to predict the tax rate (and therefore the quality of schooling) that the government will choose. This in turn determines the incidence of child labour that occurs in the economy. In his model a rise in the tax rate results in a decline in child labour. But in the end the tax rate itself is deterministic. He shows that, if inequality is high, in the sense of the median income being much lower than the average income, then the tax rate will be low and child labour will be high. Like in the model of Swinnerton and Rogers (1999), inequality is closely related to the incidence of child labour, though the causation is very different.

In an elegant model, which they then calibrate to fit Britain's experience in the nineteenth century, Doepke and Zillibotti (2002) endogenize the very act of restricting child labour. In their model, households with many children and less wealth tend to oppose legal restrictions on child labour (for reasons similar to ones investigated above). They however recognize that the number of children that a household has and the amount of human capital that it possesses would, in turn, depend on whether there is a legal ban on child labour or not. They first model the steady state that occurs in the presence of a legal ban and the one that occurs in the absence of it. Interestingly, in the presence of such a restriction the steady state is characterized by greater equality and more social mobility.

The most interesting feature of their model is the part where the restriction itself is endogenously explained. They show that there may be multiple steady-state equilibrium in the economy. We can have an economy in which fertility is high, per capita wealth is low and poorly distributed and opposition to legal restrictions so high that government does not legislate against child labour and the above description persists through time. The same economy could alternatively be caught in a steady-state equilibrium where household size is low, equality high and public opinion strongly in favor of a legislative ban. One exogenous change that can shift an economy from the former equilibrium to the latter is a rise in the productivity of education.

Theoretical Extensions

In the discussion thus far, barring the last few paragraphs, dynamics received little attention. As soon as we show an interest in this and to what happens to children when they grow up, it becomes essential to, minimally, break up children's activities into three categories: leisure, schooling, and work. This allows us to ask meaningful questions concerning what happens to human capital formation over time and whether child labour helps or hurts in the accumulation of human capital. Also, there are important questions to be asked about the relation between child labour and schooling. If a child's total time is broken up between labour and schooling, a rise in child labour will, by definition, imply a fall in schooling. But bringing in leisure as a separate category allows us to look for more complicated relations between labour and education.

Finally, an explicit modeling of schooling permits us to inquire into what happens to child labour over time. There is fortunately, now a small literature that analyzes the dynamics of child labour. This literature assumes that a person, who receives more education as a child, grows up to have a higher human capital. It is possible to add qualifications to this by noting that child work can at times take the form of apprenticeship, which enables the child to learn some craft or acquire some other form of human capital, or that in acquiring human capital it is not only the amount of time spent on schooling that counts but also the amount of money spent on education. While these are possible, it seems reasonable to assume that there is a positive link between the amount of schooling and human capital acquired. Now, under normal conditions in capital and labour markets, a higher human capital will mean a higher labour income.

Hence, if a child supplies more labour and gets less education as a child, he or she will grow up to be poorer as an adult. Therefore, the kind of logic used in the model, would mean that this person, when he becomes an adult, will, in turn, send his or her child to work, thereby perpetuating child labour across generations. Child labour can thus be thought of as a 'dynastic trap'. A child laborer tends to have children who are child laborers by virtue of their dynastic history. Likewise, once a child manages to go to school, which will typically mean escaping labour, it is likely that he or she will have a larger income as an adult and therefore have no need to send his or her progenies to labour. Hence, there is once again the possibility of multiple equilibria: two otherwise identical dynasties can be such that one is caught in the dynastic child labour trap, whereas in the other nobody works as a child.

This gives rise to a host of possible policy interventions, including the provision of loans, bans on child labour and the provision of subsidized schooling or simply information campaigns about the adverse effects of certain types of child labour (this could raise awareness of the parents and urge them to weight more strongly the long-run costs of child labour, which amounts to increasing the benefits of schooling in their perception). The interaction between child labour and the nature of the capital market has been studied in a multi-period model by Baland and Robinson (2000).

They construct an interesting model in which it is Pareto efficient to ban child labour. It is possible to develop the above sketch of dynamics further by modeling explicitly the household's fertility decision. Hazan and Berdugo (2002), building on the work of Galor and Weil (1996) do this and show how economies can be caught in a trap where fertility is high, as is child labour, and output per capita is low. Technological progress increases the wage differential between adults and children. This lowers the benefit from child labour and leads to a lowering of fertility. In their model, banning child labour hastens the transition process to low fertility and sustained growth steady-state equilibrium, which is Pareto-dominant.

Over the last few years the theoretical analyses of child labour have been extended in various directions, analyzing the formation of social norms and the role of 'tipping points', the relation between child labour and trade, the relation between income distribution and child labour, the effect of minimum wage legislation on child labour, the worst forms of child labour, efficiency wage and child labour, Nash bargaining and child labour, and the inter-connections between child labour and fertility. We shall not enter these myriad subfields of inquiry but move on instead to survey some of the empirical findings of the rapidly growing literature on child labour and then examine what we have learned about policymaking in this area.

Definitions and Estimates

According to the latest estimates put out by the ILO there are 211 million children in the age group 5 to 14 years who are 'economically active' and 186.3 million who are 'child laborers'. These figures have to be treated with caution; there are problems with both under-counting and over-counting. The ILO collected this data by tracking the children's 'work status' over the previous week. It is, however, well-known and has now been documented by Levison et al (2002) that children's work is notoriously intermittent (for example, seasonal or as needed). That is, they take up and leave jobs much more frequently than adults. So the fact that a child did not work the previous week does not mean that the child has not worked during the previous month or the previous year.

To correct for this, Levison et al have worked out an "intermittency multipliers", which allow them to guess at the number of children who do some work from the estimated number based on one week's record. Their work using Brazilian data shows that the real number will be higher by 72% to 94%. Hence, applying the intermittency multiplier to the ILO estimate would give us a figure of economically active children somewhere between 365 to 409 million. Secondly, there is the problem of under-counting the labour of the girl child. The ILO clarifies that, as with most organizations engaged in collecting data on child labour, it ignores the unpaid and not-for-market work that is done in the household, such as household chores. It is not surprising that boys turn out to be doing more labour than girls, not only in this new ILO data but in nineteenth century British data as well.

Girls do a disproportionate amount of household work—often for absurdly long hours making schooling impossible—and, if this is ignored, girls' work appears to be less. As Burra points out in her exhaustive study of child labour in India, much of female child labour appears "invisible to the casual observer." But when we do carefully estimate child work, including unpaid household work, it turns out that girls do more labour than boys. Burra provides evidence of specific industries and rural work where girls easily outnumber boys Research by Cigno and Rosati (2000), using data collected by the National Council of Economic Research, which includes statistics on household work, shows that girls do 33% more work than boys. Hence, ignoring household work encourages gender injustice and also gives an erroneously low figure of incidence of child labour. If this correction of 33% is made to the above estimate of economically active children, the number goes up to somewhere between 425 million and 477 million. This would mean close to 40% of the world's children are economically active.

Though this number seems high, both corrections are reasonable. What may have gone wrong? In trying to answer this we come up against the opposite problem, to wit, that of over-count. The ILO treats a child as economically active if the child did one hour or more work in the previous week. Surely that is too generous a definition and would tend to include too many children in its ambit. And this is so not only for developing countries but also for industrialized nations, where children do often deliver newspapers and baby sit and, at times, work in (declining) agricultural activities.

THE DETERMINANTS AND CONSEQUENCES OF CHILD LABOUR

Over the last ten years, thanks to a large number of multi-purpose household surveys, a few surveys explicitly focused on child labour, and a substantial amount of econometric research based on these statistics, economists are beginning to map the causes and determinants of child labour and acquire an understanding, which, even though far from complete, is far-reaching Some of the causes identified by this recent research corroborate what many may have expected intuitively. But there are also findings which are either unexpected or concern the matters on which we may not have had a prior opinion. One of the most expected and at the same time contentious determinant of child labour is poverty. This was introduced as the "luxury axiom" in the theory section, above.

The role of poverty has been the cornerstone of a lot of thinking regarding child labour. Casual empiricism seems to confirm its significance. Even in very poor nations, where child labour is widespread and all human beings are subject to the same laws, one, nevertheless, does not find the children of doctors, lawyers, professors and, in general, the middle classes, to be laboring. A recent study by Nagaraj (2002) on the *beedi* industry in Tamil Nadu and Karnataka, India, show that the number children in the age-group 5 to 14 years, attending school, rises strictly monotonically as the household monthly per capita expenditure rises from the category "Less than Rs. 120" to "Rs. 455 to 560" with nine intermediate categories of increasing expenditure. In the absence of other data, Nagaraj treats schooling as a kind of complement of child labour.

This may not be completely valid, but it does seem to broadly confirm the hypothesis that rising income takes children away from work and into schooling. At a more macro level, we know that as nations have become richer, the incidence of child labour has tended to fall. In China, the sharp decline in child labour began in the 1970s and has persisted till now. Thailand in the decade 1985-1995 experienced average annual growth of 9% and the participation rate of children aged 14-15 years (for whom comparable information exists) was halved to 21%. In India, also, the participation rate of child labour has declined since the 1970s though less sharply than China.

In the case of China we know that the growth rate of GDP has been particularly high since the seventies; India's growth rate has been higher through the 80s and 90s compared to the previous decades, though not as high as in China. While all this suggests that the luxury axiom is probably valid empirically, we would be justified in not accepting these broad-brush descriptions as 'proof'. Fortunately, there are now micro studies that seem to reinforce the role of poverty. Vietnam is a country that has witnessed rapid growth through the nineties. It also happens to be a country for which there were two household surveys done five years apart, in, respectively, 1992-93 and 1997-98.

And of the 4,800 households covered in the first round, 4,305 were part of the second survey, thereby providing us with a convenient panel data set. In a recent paper, Edmonds (2001) does a persuasive analysis of 3,436 of these households that were classified as rural. During these five years, Vietnam's

GNP per capita grew at the rate of 6.5% per annum and child labour, between the ages of 6 and 15 years, fell by 26% over the five years. The question that Edmonds asks is whether this decline in child labour can be attributed to the rise in the standard of living. Urban households are kept out because of the complexities caused by the great heterogeneity in the types of labour done by children and also because they are relatively much less important a contributor to the nation's total child labour. Many alternative explanations are considered and attention is paid not just to child labour in the aggregate but to different kinds of child labour, such as in agriculture and in 'family businesses.

Some early research found that the effect of adult income was often negative but small (and at times insignificant) after controlling of the other variables. Most likely this is the result of measurement errors, failure to take into account the role of wealth (especially land), inappropriately controlled endogeneity, and arbitrary functional forms used in the estimation. Edmonds develops a new, non-parametric variation of the Blinder-Oaxaca decomposition approach in order to determine the extent of the decline in child labour that can be attributed to the decline in poverty. He first runs a nonparametric (locally linear) regression to map the cross-sectional relation between the incidence of child labour and household income (measured by household expenditure per capita) using the 1993 data. This cross-sectional relation is then used to predict the amount of child labour in 1998 taking account of the large increase in per capita expenditure that occurred during this interval.

He finds strong corroboration of the hypothesis that it is raising living standards that cause child labour to decline. In particular, he finds that increase in household income can explain 94% of the decline in child labour for households at the poverty line. The axiom that poverty causes child labour has, however, not gone unquestioned. There are empirical studies (for example, Ray, 2000a, in his study of Pakistan) that have failed to find a positive relation between poverty and child labour. But it is arguable that the income that a household targets as minimum acceptable may not coincide with the nation's or region's official poverty line. So if we use the head-count ratio based on the official poverty line to measure poverty, this may not explain the incidence of child labour.

Another critique of poverty-based explanations of child labour has come from Bhalotra and Heady (2002), who have tried to show, using data from Pakistan and Ghana, that households which own (or operate) larger amounts of land tend to make their children work more. Since a larger land-holding would typically mean greater wealth, this seems to suggest that greater poverty does not lead to greater child labour. The main reason why greater land ownership may contribute to higher child labour is, as Bhalotra and Heady recognize, that, in the absence of a properly functioning labour market, owning or controlling land amounts to having the opportunity for more productive use of the household's labour, including child labour. Hence, if two households are equally disinclined to send their children to work but one has more land, then that household may choose to make the children work simply because such a household finds that child labour is more rewarding than the other.

So it is not surprising that, on the margin, land-ownership makes a difference. It is interesting to note that Edmonds and Turk (2002) found something similar in the case of Vietnam. Households that start their own business are more likely to send the children to work. The reason must be the same. A household that starts its own business is like a household with a lot of land. It has greater opportunity to use its own labour more productively. This does not mean that poverty is not a determinant of child labour, but simply that child labour, like all other inputs, responds also to incentives and opportunities. Our hunch is that if we had sufficiently disaggregated data for households, ranging from those that own no land to those that have very large quantities of land, we would find a non-linear relation with child labour first rising, as land ownership rose and eventually falling.

The latter would be because, beyond a point, the wealth of the household would kick in as the dominant factor, causing child labour to decline. The story gets even more complicated when we begin to study the relation between human capital formation and child labour, and the intergenerational dynamics of child labour. Let us first begin by examining the relation between child labour, schooling and human-capital formation. Does child labour hurt education and the acquisition of human capital? Most of us, when we act as parents and not professional economists or sociologists, take the answer to this for granted. We presume that child labour is inimical to education and the growth of a person into a productive human being. But what we aspire for our children is very different from what a person living on the edge of the poverty line can even think of.

Hence, it is entirely possible that for those living such a precarious life there is indeed a tradeoff between education and well-being, at least in their perception. For the child of a poor craftsman, the proposition that it is better to learn the parent's craft than go to school is not something that can be dismissed out of hand. Hence, there is a case for investigating that the data tells us. The existing literature seems to support the view that, though some work can help in acquiring human capital, by teaching individuals the skills and attitudes needed to. This is a topic with a rapidly growing literature. See, for instance, Rosenzweig and Evenson (1977), Maitra and Ray (2002), Ray (2002), Deb and Rosati (2002) and Rosati and Rossi (2002) work well as adults and, at times, by enabling them to earn the money that is needed to go to school, in general child labour impedes the acquisition of education and human capital.

This comes out quite clearly from an analysis of three rounds of data, 1982, 1988 and 1996, of the Pesquisa Nacional por Amostragem a Domicilio (PNAD) from Brazil. Emerson and Souza's (2002a) regression analysis using this data shows that starting to work younger results in foregone earnings as an adult and this is true for men and women. If we break up the starting age for work into three categories: below 9 years,

10 to 13 years, 14 to 17 years, it is found that the loss of earnings is greatest for the first category, followed by the second and that followed by the third. For reasons that are not altogether clear, starting work earlier is relatively more costly for girls than for boys. This needs further investigation since another study that we know that looks at this—Swaminathan (1997), using data from Bhavnagar, Gujarat—finds the opposite result, namely, that boys lose out more by joining the labour force early.

Are these foregone earnings caused by the fact that child labour interferes with schooling? Here an interesting difference shows up between those who start work as children (that is, below the age of 13 years) and those who begin work as adolescents (14 to 17 years). If we run the regression with and without the person's own education as an explanatory variable, these two categories show up differently. In particular, Emerson and Souza (2002a) show that for the adolescents the wage foregone is a direct outcome of education not acquired (that is, time spent away from school, at work). On the other hand, for children, there are negative effects over and above, the loss caused by lack of schooling. Child labour (as opposed adolescent labour) thwarts the acquisition of human capital by causing a loss of education and through other channels, for instance, by damaging health or affecting attitudes. One intriguing relation between child labour and education occurs across siblings.

As noted earlier, while for a particular child (barring some small exceptions) work cuts into education, across siblings in poor families, work and education often seem to go together. That is, one child's labour may make it possible for another child to go to school. While this phenomenon—let us call it "sibling complementarity"—is, at one level, quite obvious, it has not received enough attention in this literature. An exception is the paper by Emerson and Souza (2002b) which analyzes Brazil's 1998 PNAD data and establishes systematic relationships between birth-order, on the one hand, and propensity to go to school and work, on the other. They show that the last-born male child is less likely to work than his other siblings. This seems to be quite universal. Almost as widespread is the fact that the first-born female child is less likely to attend school than others. Of course, this sibling complementarity will show up in households which are moderately poor, since in rich households typically all children will be out of work and in school and in very poor households it will be the reverse.

What the fact of sibling complementarity suggests is that in these moderately poor households some children are kept away from school (and sent to work or made to look after the household) in order to enable other children to go to school. This 'fact' will have important moral and policy questions, especially since birth-order also seems to be tied to gender with the girl child often being used to enable the younger male sibling to go to school. It is not possible for us to say much more about this, since not much more is known. But we wanted to flag this topic as an important one, deserving further research and attention. Finally, let us turn to the subject of inter-generational dynamics. That poverty transmits from one generation to another and this has been the case through the ages is known and documented.

What they show, in addition, is that downward shocks not only leave families worse off but can affect adversely the formation of human capital among the descendants of the family. They reach this conclusion by studying a very unusual nineteenth-century data set. The Marine Society was established in Britain in 1756 to recruit poor, unemployed boys for the Navy. From 1770 to 1861 the Marine Society kept detailed records of the boys interviewed, including their socio-economic background. Horrell, Humphries and Voth use this data set to show that poverty in one generation transmits to future generations in the form of lower human capital. This causes dynastic poverty traps. They also try to show that this pernicious effect of poverty can be countered by having systems of social security, by demonstrating how Britain's Old Poor laws did have a mitigating effect on this process.

Turning to contemporary times and to the specific question of child labour, we find evidence of dynastic traps. Wahba (2002) analyses the 1988 Labour Force Sample Survey of Egypt, which involves a nationally representative sample of 10,000 households. Her analysis is based on 10742 children of the age group 6 to 14 years for whom full information on schooling work and parental characteristics are available. It is worth noting as a digression that she finds strong support of the axiom that it is hardship that makes parents send their children to work. She finds that a 10% rise in the market wage rate for illiterate men results in a decrease in the probability of child labour by 22% for boys and 13% for girls.

Wahba develops a bivariate probit model, allowing for the decision regarding schooling and work to be simultaneous and interdependent. She finds that a parent who was a child laborer has a higher probability of his or her child being a laborer. The probability of a boy working rises by 10% if the boy's mother worked as a child and by 5% if the boy's father worked as a child. The same phenomenon has been modeled and empirically tested by Emerson and Souza (2002) using PNAD data for Brazil. They actually go onto ask a further question. If a person works as a child, would this result in a rise in the probability of his or her child working by more than that can be explained by the fact that the person will be poor as an adult (by virtue of having been a child worker) and therefore compelled to send the child to work?

The answer is yes. Hence, they surmise the presence of social factors, which cause the perpetuation of child labour through non-income channels. It is, for instance, possible that having been a child laborer oneself affects ones social norms and attitude to child labour such that one is more prone to send ones own child to work. One may question whether there may be genetic channels through which these propensities, such as the one to seek education, transmit from one generation to another. The answer however seems to be no, based on an ingenious study of comparing orphans with non-orphans in sub-Saharan Africa by Lloyd and Blanc (1996).

They find that the guardians with whom the child lives matter more significantly than the child's biological parents. This reinforces the likelihood that it is social factors that Emerson and Souza are capturing in their study. There are two caveats which are worth mentioning to the empirical results cited earlier which also caution about the confidence of generalization which can be made with respect to policies which are discussed in the next session. First, the empirical literature on child labour is relatively young. As a result, many studies report results which are at best treated as preliminary. This can of course be corrected in the course of time but some generic problems, endemic to economic and social research may persist well into the future. Second, cross-section estimates may omit to capture important lifecycle effects, and more generally estimates can be affected by endogeneity or identification problems.

Also, studies which include as explanatory variables the occupation of adults, land ownership or other income variables may be haunted by multicollinearity. The results for control variables (such as household size, relationship of child to head of household, age of child, birth order of children) may be similarly affected. Omission of some variables from the estimation (simply because data are lacking) may also give rise biases. Since many studies examine simultaneously the relationship between child labour and education, there can be unobserved heterogeneity (for example, in the academic ability of children or health/disability) which can be further conflated by the inclusion of parental education (a measure of tastes) or nonlinearities in the returns to education.

Regional effects, community infrastructure (measured in various ways such as availability of water, electricity and transportation), and local unemployment rates can render the results of different studies even in the same country and year non-comparable. There are often disequilibrium effects (such as migration) which evade researchers. The use of dummies in estimation pose additional complications as do non-economic variables (such as social norms), which can be proxied in different ways or altogether omitted from the estimation.

CHILD LABOUR IN TAMIL NADU

The state of Tamil Nadu occupies the easterly portion of the southern tip of India, from the hills bordering the state of Kerala in the west to the Bay of Bengal in the east. The capital city is Chennai (Madras), situated on the coast close to the north east boundary of the state. The projected 2001 population was 62.2 million of whom 40 million were rural dwellers and 22 million urban. Administratively, Tamil Nadu is divided into thirty-one districts.

Child Labour in Tamil Nadu

According to a variety of sources, child labour is a serious problem in Tamil Nadu. According to the Global March Against Child Labour, the following types of child labour can be found in Tamil Nadu:

Table 2.0: Global March Child Labour Data, Tamil Nadu

Sector Children	Location	Type	Proportion of the Workforce that are
Hosiery	Tirupur		
Leather tanning			30-40%
Silk weaving		Bonded	
Flowers		Bonded	
Silver work		Bonded	
Beedi rolling		Bonded	
Prostitution	Chennai		12-15%
Gem industry	Trichy		One sixth

Source: India report on Global March Against Child Labour website.

According to UNICEF, in 1991 there were 3.1 million children of school age (5-14 yrs) not attending school in Tamil Nadu. It is assumed that most of these children were working, either part or full time. Many children work in agriculture, but many also work in industrial occupations. The districts with the highest estimated numbers of child labourers were: Coimbatore (where Tirupur is located), North Arcot (where Ambur is located), Periyar (adjacent to Coimbatore) and Salem.

CHILD LABOUR IN THE TIRUPUR GARMENT INDUSTRY

Amongst all the locations of child labour in Tamil Nadu, Tirupur has been a particular focus of attention because it is the major base of the India garment export business. In 1994, Tirupur exported Rs. 1332 crores out of the India total of Rs. 2933.45 crores, i.e. 45% of the total. In 2000, 60-75% of India's exports of cotton knitwear came from Tiru-pur and surrounding towns. There are many links to foreign retailers, some direct and some through agents or exporters in Chennai, Mumbai, Delhi or Bangalore. Tirupur has grown to this pre-eminent status because it is close to large supplies of cotton yarn, water (necessary for the bleaching and dying processes) and labour, and because of the cumulative learning of Tirupur garment enterprises. The Tirupur industry makes extensive use of local networking, with the manufacturing process broken down into specialised "job work" units, such as knitting, bleaching and dying, printing, cutting and sewing, carried out on different premises.

This structure contributes to widespread non-observance of labour laws and to the endemic use of child labour. This is not the original industrial form but was developed during the expansion phase of the industry over the last fifty years. The initiators of the process were members of the agrarian Gounder caste who dominate the ownership of the industry. Many of the current owners worked in the industry as employees at earlier stages of their careers. According to Chari, one of the main motivations for the decentralised system was labour control. Enforcement of labour laws is reported to be weak, and many factories are not registered with the factory inspectorate.

The knitwear factory is the production hub, sending product out for the various sub-tasks then bringing it back in for completion. This method of labour-service contracts is known as the "job work" system. The term "contract" is reserved for contracting out the entire garment or the final stitching (assembly) stage.

"The industrial form in both domestic and export sectors, which are intertwined to some extent, take the form of a web of units ..."

"Any successful domestic or export company, in all probability, also contracts to several other units of the basic knitwear company ..."

"... the successful exporter in Tirupur must reintegrate and coordinate work across multiple worksites in order to create a cheap garment of the right qualities."

Given that we know that child labour is more likely to occur in outsourced workshops and in places where the domestic and export sectors overlap, ETI will need to enquire carefully about the use of labour service contracts in export garment production. In asking such questions, the term "job work" rather than "contract" should be used, so that there is no misunderstanding about what is being referred to. Estimates of the number of child workers vary from 8,000 to 35,000 out of a total workforce of 300,000+. Most are likely to be in the 10-14 age group, though there are reports of children under ten working in the industry.

The causes of child labour in the Tirupur garment industry include:

- Inadequate facilities in primary schools in Tirupur
- A high primary school drop-out rate
- Low levels of family income and family economic insecurity (debt, unemployment)
- Relatively high levels of parental (particularly maternal) illiteracy

- Limited economic opportunities for members of the "Backward castes" and Scheduled Tribes Communities.
- Employers employing children in preference to adults (at cheaper wages)
- Relatively high wages for child labourers in the garment industry compared with other occupations involving child labour (Rs. 30-70 per day in hosiery compared with Rs. 3 per day in *Beedi*)
- Lack of enforcement of the laws against child labour (and other labour laws)

While it is true as a generalisation that low levels of family income and parental illiteracy contribute to the prevalence of child labour, the relationship is not deterministic. According to a socio-economic survey of child workers in the Tirupur hosiery industry some families of child workers earned over four times as much as others and 75% of the fathers of child workers were literate. Children mainly do work that is ancillary to the main processes, such as carrying stock from room to room, feeding work to adult workers, folding and packing. Some work in dying and bleaching. They work very long days (12-16 hours per day, 6 days per week) in often hazardous conditions. For example:

"In the dyeing section around five to six boys are working and they are definitely younger than 14. The air is so polluted with chemical dust ... that it is difficult to breathe and one needs fresh air quickly. I was shocked by this experience. Children and adults work in this unit 12 to 14 hours per day and also in nightshifts.

The children looked exhausted and their shirts were dirty and covered with paint residues from dyed clothes which they had to carry from one dye-machine to the other with their bare hands. Also their faces and hands were coloured with paint coming from the clothes ... I only saw boys working in this dyeing and bleaching unit. They assisted the adult dyers. I saw the adults ordering the children to run to them quickly and assist them. None of the boys was wasting his time ..."

The children are reported to have a negative attitude towards child labour. They would like to go to school like other children they see in the town, but feel powerless to do anything about their work situation. They have to abide by their parents' decision.

CHILD LABOUR IN THE COTTON INDUSTRY

In looking at the cotton garments supply chain in Tamil Nadu we may need to look beyond the factory clusters of Tirupur and Chennai to the cotton growing and spinning industries, which are extensive in Tamil Nadu and adjacent states. Cotton is grown across the whole of western, central and southern India, with the exception of Kerala. The main producing states are Andhra Pradesh, Gujarat and Maharashtra. Tamil Nadu produced 475,000 bales in 1995-96, 2.9% of the India total. Child labour is reported to be common in cotton production.

The following description refers to children working in cotton production in southern Andhra Pradesh (adjacent to Tamil Nadu):

"Typically, 10-15 children are hired for 100-150 days per acre of cotton-seed production. Children as young as six works from 8:30am to 6 or 7pm and some boys even return to the field again from 9pm to 12am. The cotton seed production calendar has been standardised for the process of certification and marketing and has resulted in the regimentation of work schedules of children who are now continuously employed for 6-9 months in the year. In villages where labour is scarce, children are being 'tied' to contract farmers with advances of cash and grain to parents (typically Rs. 1000) and bonuses (a stainless steel tiffin carrier after two years, for example). Children's labour is extended well beyond the work day by paying them piece rates to de-lint the cottonseeds (Rs.10/bag of 25kgs cotton) and catch pests (Rs.0.05/worm). Physical force and holding back wages if a child's productivity is low are routine labour control practices. Many girls also now accompany their mothers for casual coolie work. They are paid daily wages but the mother must not only do her own work but also help her daughter keep pace.

Consequently, more and more girls are being taken out of school."

So far as the cotton spinning industry is concerned, the major concentration is in Tamil Nadu, which (in 1992) had 440 spinning mills out of a national total of 846, employing 174,326 workers out of an India total of 1,055,020. The major concentration of Tamil Nadu mills was in Coimbatore (189 spinning mills). The cotton spinning industry association - the Southern India Mills' Association - is also based in Coimbatore. There are no published reports to hand of the incidence of child labour in cotton spinning, but Steve Grinter of the ITGLWF says that there is no child labour in the formal (large enterprise) export sector.

INDUSTRY POLICY ON CHILD LABOUR

In the mid-1990s, responding to concerns expressed by foreign importers, two employers' associations made declarations of intent to end child labour. The Tirupur Export Association (TEA) gave an assurance that their members would not employ children below the age of 14 years and the South Indian Hosiery Manufacturers Association (SIMHA) adopted an undertaking not to continue employing children below the age of 14 beyond 1998. According to SIMHA the main causes of child labour were lack of parental education and parental poverty. This undertaking had not been implemented by 1997, but there is recent evidence (September 2000 and June 2001) that child labour may have ended in the top layer of export companies. The same sources say that child labour is still prevalent in medium and small garment factories in Tirupur.

Tamil Nadu Government Policy

Elimination of child labour is official policy in Tamil Nadu. In November 1993, the Government of Tamil Nadu adopted a State Plan of Action for the Child in Tamil Nadu, which included targets for the elimination of child labour. These were: elimination of bonded child labour and child labour in the match and fireworks industries, elimination of all child labour (up to 14 years of age) in hazardous occupations and elimination of all child labour (up to 12 years of age) in all occupations by the year 2000.

Hazardous child labour was covered by Specific Goal Two, which was expressed as follows:

"Specific Goal Two: Elimination of child labour in other hazardous industries classified in the Child Labour Act as hazardous which are relevant to Tamil Nadu; namely, beedi, match, fireworks, tanning, wool cleaning, cloth printing, dyeing and weaving as well as others which affect the normal and healthy development of a child.

1995: Plan of action framed and initiated, especially for key industies such as beedi, cashew and skin cleaning and wool processing units. 1998: Eliminate child labour of children less than 12 years, 2000: 100% elimination of child labour for children up to 14 years."

Tamil Nadu policy is underpinned by that of the Government of India which has a constitutional mandate in favour of universal primary education. In 1986, the Government of India adopted the National Policy on Education (NPE) which made universal primary education the top priority.

The Supreme Court of India, in a judgement of December 1996, made it mandatory for the States to conduct surveys to gauge the extent of child labour and reiterated the requirement for free and compulsory education up to the age of 14 years. It also directed that the "concerned employer who employs a child in contravention of the provisions of the Child Labour Prohibition and Regulation Act 1986 shall pay as compensation a sum of Rs. 20,000 per child which would be deposited in a fund known as the Child Labour Rehabilitation-cum-Welfare Fund". Where it is not possible to provide a job to an adult family member in lieu of the child, the Government is supposed to make a contribution into the fund of Rs. 5000 for each child emplo-yed in a factory or mine or in any hazardous employment.

There is not as much information as one would like about

child labour programmes on the web site of the Government of Tamil Nadu. For example, one of the Peace Trust documents refers to the "Department of Bonded and Child Labour" but such a department is not listed on the web site. Such documentation as is on the web site indicates that there is a broad government policy of increasing educational provision, raising the literacy rate and reducing the number of child school drop-outs.

Specific programmes include the Girl Child Protection Scheme, School Nutritious Meal Centres and the National Programme of Nutritional Support to Primary Education.

PROGRESS IN THE EDUCATION SYSTEM

A key component in the elimination of child labour is the availability of quality schooling (teachers, facilities, teaching materials and methods) and strict enforcement of the compulsory education requirement. Tamil Nadu has shortcomings in both these respects, but there is an improving trend. The literacy rate in Tamil Nadu rose from 47% in 1981 to 63% in 1991 (male: 74%, female: 51%). In 1991, Tamil Nadu had the third highest literacy rate in India, after Maharashtra (65%) and Kerala (90%). Kerala was in a category of its own, with a male literacy rate of 94% and a female literacy rate of 86%. Literacy in the rest of India was in a range from 44% to 65%.

Expenditure on education in Tamil Nadu increased from Rs. 260 per capita in 1991-2 to Rs. 488 in 1997-98. Tamil Nadu ranks second to Kerala in per capita expenditure on education. Within Tamil Nadu there is a considerable range in literacy rates from district to district. Taking those districts in which ETI sources have been identified (as at 24 January 2002), Chennai, Coimbatore and Madurai had relatively higher literacy rates (Male: 75%+, Female: 51-75%) while Vellore was lower (Male: 51-75%, Female: Under 50%). Thus it should not come as a surprise if we discover child labour in Vellore as well as in the other states.

Enrolment of children in primary schools (ages 6-11)

increased from 5.5 million in 1990-91 to 6.8 million in 1997-98, taking the enrolment ratio to 94%. Over the same period the number of primary schools increased from 29,979 to 30,796. The number of teachers increased from 120,000 to 144,000, lowering the teacher: pupil ratio from 65 to 44. 99% of habitations had a primary school facility within a distance of 1km. However, only 78% of habitations had a secondary school facility within a distance of 5km.

The difference between western expectations and realities in Tamil Nadu is underlined by the following statement from the Government of Tamil Nadu's Social Sector report, 1997-98:

> "While it is gratifying to note that there is no school in Tamil Nadu without a teacher, as many as 3810 are single teacher schools. However, in respect of availability of class rooms it is a matter of concern that 104 schools are functioning without a class room and 7987 schools have only a single class room facility."

While the primary school enrolment ratio was 94%, the drop-out rate was a serious problem. Many students start school, but leave before completing their primary (or secondary) education. This is reported to be a particular problem in Tirupur where families migrate from rural areas in pursuit of work. Children leave the schools in which they are enrolled when the family leaves its home area, but often do not re-enrol in Tirupur, but are sent out to work instead. In 1990-91, the primary school drop-out rate was 18% for boys and 23% for girls. These rates dropped to 14% and 16% respectively in 1997-98. The gradual improvement in the holding capacity of primary education was attributed by the Government to factors such as the implementation of the Nutritious Noon Meal Scheme, free health check-ups, free education, offering of concessions like free bus passes, slates, books, uniforms and general awareness.

The Government has also adopted a policy to reduce gender disparities under the District Primary Education Programme. Interventions include: flexible school timings, gender sensitive curriculum and text books, recruitment of women teachers and improved school facilities (such as new buildings, toilet and drinking water facilities.) This programme is focussed on the districts with the lowest female educational participation. Turning to secondary education, the Government of Tamil Nadu reports an increase in the number of secondary schools from 3151 in 1990-91 to 3765 in 1997-98 and a 32% increase in student strength over the same period. The number of higher secondary schools increased substantially, from 2045 in 1990-91 to 2975 in 1997-98. Enrolment and drop-out rates for secondary education are not given.

The data and commentary presented in the Government of Tamil Nadu's 1997-98 Social Sector report, show that the Government of Tamil Nadu takes the view that the elimination of child labour requires the universal availability of primary and secondary school education of sufficient quality to enable all children to enrol in school and to retain them once enrolled. The Government is making a considerable investment to achieve that goal and the data show an improving trend, though a substantial number of children are still falling through the net.

CHILD LABOUR SPECIFIC POLICY AND PROGRAMS

Given the diverse array of social and economic factors that affect child time allocation decisions, most development related policies can influence child time allocation. In discussing the determinants of child time allocation, we have already reviewed research from micro credit programs, public infrastructure and school construction projects, school quality interventions, and programs to mitigate schooling costs. Risk reduction and management policies, health interventions, and production technology projects all could have large impacts on child time allocation. However, in this section, we consider policies that aim to directly affect how children spend their time. Empirical research on child labour related policies that meets modern scientific standards is extremely limited.

This does not owe to a lack of policy attention. Policies towards child labour can be grouped loosely into six categories: information campaigns, income replacement programs, flexible schooling programs, reintegration projects, restrictions on employment, and conditional cash transfers. Only legislative restrictions and conditional cash transfers have a sizeable academic literature. This research is described below. First, we describe the other four categories of child labour policies. An incredible variety of policies and programs have been directed towards working children, and there are a considerable number of policy documents that describe these activities. ILO (2006b) for example reviews several ILO affiliated programs. This section briefly discusses these types of programs. However, causal evidence that has survived peer review within economics does not appear to exist for any of these programs at the time of writing. Information or awareness campaigns attempt to educate parents, employers, and children that children should not work or should attend school.

The mechanisms for delivery of information vary as does the precise content of information conveyed. Mass media campaigns are frequent, employing radio or TV programs, news reports, or billboards. Community mobilization is also common where activists or community leaders reach out personally to individuals involved with working or out of school children. Another frequent community mobilization approach is to organize community events that draw attention to whatever type of activity is being targeted. In practice, information and awareness campaigns seem to be the most common type of policy directed at working children, and they seem to be motivated in part by assumptions that parents do not know what is best for their children. Income replacement programs attempt to compensate families for the loss of the child's income in the event that the child stops working. Some programs aim to provide alternative sources of income to the household, often to the mother, by providing working capital and training. Implicit in these programs is that parents make decisions about whether children work and that the direct economic contribution of the child's work is a main reason why children work.

Other programs, attempt to redirect children towards work activities that are more compatible with schooling. For example, one program in Brazil gave working children goats, because it is easy to care for goats outside of school hours. These child income replacement programs address the child's agency in work decisions in addition to economic motives for work. Often, income replacements programs contain some conditionality component. For example, conditional cash transfers typically require that children attend school in order receive transfers. Conditional cash transfers are the one type of child labour related program that have received rigorous evaluation. Flexible schooling programs attempt to make schooling and work more compatible. That is, they typically do nothing to influence whether the child works, but instead aim to make schooling compatible with work. In this way, flexible schooling programs mitigate the costs of working. Many different types of programs are prevalent. School hours can be modified to accommodate work schedules. Academic calendars can be adjusted to reflect local conditions. Additional school shifts could be added during off-work times.

Independent study modules might allow students to progress through schooling at their own pace. The assumption behind these programs is that the timing of school causes conflict between work and school. The actual time spent working is not enough in itself to impair human capital accumulation. Some flexible schooling programs also modify the curriculum to increase child interest in the program. Other flexible schooling programs extend the hours in which school or related facilities are available to children. They programs are analogous to daycare programs. For some children, work is just a way to occupy the child's time, and the extended schooling hours provide an alternative, educational way to occupy the child's time. Moreover, this may benefit older siblings who, absent the extend hours available to younger siblings, would have to care for younger siblings. It is straightforward to imagine how programs designed to prevent children from starting to work can influence child schooling, but children who are already working full time need help to reenter school.

Re-integration projects aim to help students return to regular school when students have missed school or lag behind in school because of work. Working children may be unfamiliar with the school environment, be poorly socialized for schooling, and may be significantly older than nonworking children with the same educational background. This makes returning working children to school a challenge. Most reintegration projects include some counseling directed at formerly working children, some remedial education to catch working children up to age in skills, and some bridge program to gradually introduce working children back into the classroom. This emphasis on how to get working children back into school is often neglected in economics discussions, because most theoretical models treat child time allocation as seamless between different sectors of work, schooling, and leisure. Unfortunately, while these policies are pervasive, scientific evaluation of them is not.

This absence of policy research severely limits our ability to design or improve existing policy. To be effective, scientific evaluation needs to be designed into a project from its inception, with control populations selected to be comparable, ideally through randomization. This is rare. It is telling that of the 35 final program evaluations included in ILO (2006b), none of the publicly available research has been peer reviewed by independent researchers. Moreover, while detailed information is hard to come by, it appears that most of the reviews are process evaluations (did the project do what it is supposed to?) rather than impact evaluations (was the project effective? did it improve the well-being of impacted children?). The typical objection to formal evaluation is expense, but the growing body of randomized evaluation of education related initiatives shows that careful, informative, and scientific evaluations can be conducted on modest budgets. Moreover, considerable money is being spent on evaluation.

That research is just not being held to the standards of peer review that are commonplace in other sciences. Hopefully, future scientific research on how these projects influence time allocation can both improve the design of policy and build our understanding of the determinants of work.

RESTRICTIONS AND PROHIBITIONS ON EMPLOYMENT

Prohibitions on employment typically target children in specific activities. Often prohibitions are intended as symbolic gestures, but at times, they may be enforced by industry groups or the governments, Programs of identification and removal of working children from specific activities have occurred throughout the world. Anecdotes abound about what happens to children upon removal from targeted activities, but rigorous statistical research does not appear available at the time of writing. The case for targeting one activity at a time is that it is more manageable to implement and enforce. However, it can lead to some inconsistencies that lead some to question the motives for targeting a particular activity. General prohibitions on work or restrictions on working conditions are also common in low income countries. ILO Convention C138 on the minimum age of employment has been ratified by 141 countries, and nearly every developing country has some formal restriction on the age of employment for certain types of employment. Similarly, most countries have compulsory school ages as well.

Beyond these aggregate laws, many countries have committed to pursue aggressive policies to eliminate child labour from certain sectors and 156 countries have committed to identify and eliminate worst forms of child labour under C182. Yet, despite all this policy discussion, there does not appear to be any study of the effectiveness of restrictions on work that would meet current standards of evidence. Part of the reason for this might be that bans are often not passed with the intention of enforcement. Instead, the motivation for such legislation can be that it helps outreach and education programs change social views about working children.

However, there is a theoretical case that can be made for the enforcement of general bans on child labour. The Basu and Van model is the most common framework used to illustrate the conditions under which enforced prohibitions on child labour may be welfare improving. BV gives multiple equilibriums as such; it allows a role for policy in the elimination of child labour.

One frequently advocated policy is an enforced prohibition on child labour. In this instance, there are two possible stable equilibriums marked E1 and E2. In E2, children work. The presence of child labour depresses wages and hence creates a need for children to work. The equilibrium E1 creates an opportunity for policy to affect child labour supply. If policy can prevent children from working, the equilibrium in the economy can switch to E1. That is, by preventing children from working (i.e. eliminating CD and BC segment of labour supply), market wages increase, eliminating the household's need to send children to work. Obviously, the potential existence of multiple equilibriums is not a sufficient condition for policy aimed at prohibiting child labour. For example, when labour demand is represented by FF, there is little that a ban can do to curtail child labour without improving labour demand (i.e. shifting FF up).

Similarly, policy aimed at curtailing the demand for child labour could have the unintended consequence of moving households from the equilibrium defined by mG2 to the equilibrium indicated by mF if policy lowers labour demand for child labour without the commensurate increase in demand for adult labour. This might occur for example if a consumer boycott drove an industry out of business in a community. Empirical evidence from contemporary low income countries on either the effectiveness of general bans or restrictions on employment is not available. The case that a ban could be welfare improving even for those with working children relies on the existence of the multiple equilibrium in the labour market. This seems hard to imagine as a general proposition given that children are such a small share of total employment in general. While there is no evidence of the existence of multiple equilibrium owing to child labour supply, Doran (2006) finds evidence in Mexico of a depressive effect of child labour on adult wages. The problem with identifying an effect of child labour on adult wages is that one needs something to affect child labour without separately impacting the adult labour market.

Doran argues that the conditional cash transfer program in rural Mexico discussed below (Progresa) withdraws children from work without otherwise effecting local labour market characteristics. Doran observes that in randomly selected Progresa treatment communities less children work during the corn harvest and there is an associated increase in adult wages and adult employment relative to control communities. This raises the possibility that some of the foregone child labour earnings can be replaced by increasing adult wages although Doran does not observe full replacement and the most compelling evidence on the effects of general prohibitions on child labour come from the historical experiences of the developed countries. Several careful empirical studies exploit variation in the implementation of the child labour and compulsory schooling laws across the U.S. states to examine whether these legislative measures were the *driving* force behind the drastic declines in child labour at the turn of the last century and increases in secondary school enrollment and educational attainment between 1910 and 1940.

Moehling (1999), for example, finds little evidence that minimum age laws for manufacturing employment implemented between 1880 and 1910 contributed to the decline in child labour during this period. She compares differences in participation rates of 13 and 14 year olds across states with and without a minimum working age of 14 before and after the enactment of laws. This difference-in-differences–in-differences strategy can distinguish the effects of the law from differential pre-existing trends in child labour across states with and without minimum age limits that could have influenced the implementation of the law. While the participation rates of children covered by the law declined in states that enacted the laws, boys in control groups experienced similar declines. The results for girls suggest that declines in child labour might be driven by endogenous child labour law implementation: states were more likely to implement the minimum age legislation if other labour demand and supply factors reduced their reliance on child labour prior to the reforms. Doepke and Zilibotti (2005) formalize this idea in a model with endo-genous adoption of child labour laws. While the overall contribution of child labour laws to child labour declines may have been small in the U.S., there appears to have been some marginal contribution.

A number of studies have emphasized this. For example, Lleras-Muney (2002) documents an association between schooling completion rates and increases in the age at which children can apply for a work permit or reductions in the school entrance age in the U.S. in the early twentieth century. She finds some evidence of an effect of school continuation laws among white males but no other demographic group. Manacorda (2006) uses this variation in education owing to work permit ages to look at spillovers to siblings from child labour supply, and a number of studies have used this variation in educational attainment to evaluate the returns to education. Overall, however, Goldin and Katz (2003) emphasize that all these legislative measures combined can explain at most 5 percent of the increase in high school enrollment and subsequent educational attainment between 1910 and 1939.

TRADE SANCTIONS AND LABOUR STANDARDS

Popular discontent in developed economies about child labour in developing countries have lead to numerous calls for harmonized labour standards, trade sanctions against countries with high levels of child labour, and consumer boycotts of products made with child labour. While empirical evidence directly on any of these issues is non-existent, it is worth reviewing the issues raised in the theoretical literature. More rigorous surveys of the theoretical work in this area are in Maskus (1997), Basu (1999), and Brown (2001). Calls for harmonized labour standards typically envision a regime where some international arbitrator would oversee adherence to certain core labour standards. One common argument is to incorporate labour standards into the WTO. Either the WTO or ILO would monitor compliance with these standards. Violators would be punished via trade sanctions.

In fact, the idea of core labour standards is already enshrined in the ILO, and the abolition of child labour is one of the ILO's core four labour standards that many argued should be followed independent of level of development. Moreover, harmonization is argued to be necessary to avoid a race to the bottom, where governments lower their standards to attract business and gain competitive advantage. In fact, one can theoretically show that coordi-nated bans on child labour *might* be more effective in reducing child labour than a national ban when capital can easily move across countries, but one cannot show that this outcome is necessarily the case. Others have suggested the use of unilateral trade sanctions by the rich countries as a stick to fight child labour. Such policies have often been debated in the U.S. For example, the Child Labour Deterrence Act (the Harkin Bill) aimed to prohibit imports of products into the U.S. that are manufactured by child labour. While this legislation has yet to pass, the Sander's Amendment to the 1930 Tariff Act passed in 1997. It prohibits imports of goods produced by forced or indentured child labour. The 2000 Trade and Development Act restricts eligibility for trade benefits to countries that the Secretary of Labour certifies as showing progress to eliminate the worst forms of child labour.

Consumer boycotts of products produced by child labour have become popular in rich countries. Consumers who do not wish to consume goods produced by child labour can do so by purchasing products labeled as "child labour free" at a premium. Visible examples of such policies include RUGMARK-approved hand knotted rugs and "FIFA approved" soccer balls. Davies (2004) considers consumer boycotts in the context of a model or Bertrand competition with product differentiation. The threat of boycott allows for the creation of a profitable niche for adult-labour firms which in turn implies the creation of an analogous niche for child-labour firms. Moreover, he shows that even in the case of monopoly, a monopolist can segment the market by offering different product lines and then price-discriminate to increase profits. It is very difficult to show that this sort of product line specialization will be welfare improving for children. Basu and Zarghamee (2005) think about product boycotts with a focus on labour supply rather than demand. They emphasize that when wages are set locally, a product boycott can depress child wages. When children work only to help families meet subsistence needs, a decline in child wages can cause more children to need to work.

Boycotts can increase child labour. Brown (2006) argues that donation labels where monitoring agencies denote some fraction of the purchase price to child welfare would be a more efficient way to reduce child labour. That said, empirical scientific evidence on the impact of boycotts on children is entirely absent. The potential for unintended consequence is not limited to consumer boycotts. In general, it is not clear what types of policies these sanctions, threats, or boycotts are trying to affect, and it is hard to distinguish whether they reflect a genuine interest in the wellbeing of children in poor countries or are forms of hidden protectionism with all of these policies. When policies aim to restrict the employment options open to children, they can in turn have a depressive effect on child wages.

If bans are not completely successful in eliminating or affecting enforced policies to prevent child labour, they may make child labour worse in two ways. More children may need to work to compensate for lost income, or children may be reallocated to sectors where monitoring is more difficult. It is not obvious that children are better off working in non-export sectors or underground. Scientific evidence on what happens to children displaced from export sectors is essentially nonexistent even in the most publicized prohibitions on the employment of children owing to the threat of sanctions involving Bangladeshi Garment industry and Pakistani soccer balls. In the case of Bangladesh, some suggest that most displaced child laborers went to work for lower wages in garment factories that did not produce for export while others describe children displaced into prostitution and stone crushing. However, it is unclear on what scale these diversions occur and whether they might be offset by improvements in other children's lives.

CONDITIONAL CASH TRANSFERS

A number of countries have adopted policies designed to discourage child labour and increase schooling by lowering the cost of schooling via educational subsidies. Examples include PETI and Bolsa Escola in Brazil, the Midday meals program in India, and the Progresa program in Mexico. The idea of these programs is to condition transfers on household's taking certain desirable actions such as attending school. Consequently, they both lower the relative costs of schooling while raising family incomes. PETI appears to be the only conditional cash transfer program at present that explicitly targets working children, and it is novel in that it requires after school activities for children as a way of mitigating the number of children who work and attend school. Most other conditional cash transfers only affect work as a by product of the cash transfers or as a result of the schooling requirement embedded in the program. The Progresa program is particularly important, because it embedded scientific evaluation into the design of the program at the start.

Consequently, it is the most researched of the conditional cash transfer program, and it is the most emulated. Schooling incentives in Progresa increase with the age of the child in order to compensate the household for the older child's greater opportunity cost of schooling. In addition, at secondary school ages, girls receive larger cash payments for attending school than do boys. Because of the conditionality of the program, it is not possible to separate the effects of changing household income from changes in schooling costs. Nevertheless, the evaluation data on Progresa is extremely encouraging. Schultz (2004) finds a significant reduction in wage and market work associated with eligibility for Progresa. Skoufias and Parker (2001) also document declines in domestic work for girls. Similar findings have been found in other countries as well. Schady and Araujo (2006) for example document declines in market work in Ecuador's program. Interestingly, grants in Ecuador's cash transfer program were not conditioned on schooling, but it appears that a significant number of recipients believed them to be.

The advantage of this type of positive program that indirectly discourages child labour through increasing schooling is that it also addresses the agency problems, credit market imperfections, and difficulty in monitoring most forms of child labour that may interfere with the efficacy of other child labour related interventions such as child labour bans, compulsory schooling laws, etc. Of course, the effect of these schooling incentives on child labour may be small relative to their effects on schooling, as Ravallion and Wodon (2000) found in their evaluation of Bangladesh's Food for Education program which pays students in rice for attending school. It is also worth emphasizing that the idea that conditional cash transfer are in some (imprecise) way the optimal policy tool to combat child labour or encourage schooling is largely without formal justification. Moreover, it assumes that it is worthwhile to encourage schooling.

That is, it presumes the availability of quality schools that are advantageous to the child relative to work. This point is emphasized in Jafarey and Lahiri (2005) who point out that improvement in education quality may be more effective relative to (unconditional) cash or in-kind transfers when credit markets operate. The recent boom in empirical work on child labour has substantially improved our understanding of why children work and what the consequences of that work might be. This survey aims to assess what we currently know about child labour and to highlight what important questions still require attention. Child labour research needs to carefully define exactly what measures of time allocation are being considered. Studies that consider too narrow a scope of activities are apt to generate misleading conclusions.

Children are active in a wide variety of tasks and appear to substitute between them easily. Thus, if a child is observed working less in one task (like wage work), one cannot assume that she is working less. Moreover, though wage work appears less likely to be associated with simultaneous schooling, differences in schooling associated with variation in hours worked are much greater than those associated with location of work. Work is typically classified as market work or domestic work. Domestic work (often labeled "chores") is too often ignored in child time allocation studies. For a given number of hours worked, domestic work appears as likely as work in the farm or family business to trade off with school. Hence, studies of child labour need to consider as wide a range of activities as the data permit.

There is considerable scope for learning about total labour supply or schooling changes by looking at changes in participation in various disaggregate activities. Policy interest in child labour in today's rich countries arose during the late 19th century because of what Zelizer (1994) terms the "sacralization" of children's lives. She writes: "The term sacralization is used in the sense of objects being invested with sentimental or religious meaning". This view is behind much of policies and the public's interest in child labour in developing countries today. This issue arises within economics because of concern about whether child labour is driven by agency problems –do parents fully consider the tradeoffs and costs of work when sending their children to work? However, despite some suggestive evidence, the primacy of agency problems in determining child labour supply has yet to be established. Instead, most contemporary research in economics on child labour is interested because of the impact of work on human capital accumulation.

There are a finite number of hours in a day, so at some margin, there must be a tradeoff between work and schooling. However, work and schooling are simultaneous outcomes of a single decision-making process. Identifying a causal relationship between the two seems likely to be an uninformative exercise. Moreover, work is not the residual claimant on child time outside of school, and the incidence of children who neither work nor attend school appears highest where schooling is the lowest. Consequently, it is somewhat problematic to motivate interest in commons forms of work out of a concern for schooling. Studies of schooling should consider child labour supply in attempts to understand schooling variation, but the existing evidence is insufficient to motivate studying of child labour alone without considering schooling if human capital is the researcher's only concern. Researchers have considered several other consequences of working that might go beyond the child's time constraint and agency problems such as whether there are health consequences, externalities, effects on attitudes and values, occupation choice, fertility, or local labour markets.

Much of this work is in its infancy. The interconnection of child labour and poverty seems intuitive, but evidence has been more difficult to establish. This is because the assertion that child labour stems from poverty is often taken to imply that the only reason children work is because of high marginal utility of income. The data are inconsistent with this extreme view in general. In fact, a more general description of the child labour problem is that the child works when the utility from working today is greater than the utility associated with not working. This raises several issues that the literature has considered about why children work. Perhaps the most important issue is the least researched: who makes child labour decisions -that is, whose marginal utility matters? There is some evidence that child time allocation is influenced by the net return to schooling. While estimating the return to schooling is a challenge, there is suggestive evidence that it influence child time allocation.

Several studies document a correlation between the employment opportunities open to children inside and outside their household and child time allocation. Hence, there should be situations when work is the most efficient use of child time, and there is nothing in the literature which precludes this. The fact that work can be optimal does not exclude the possibility that child labour's prevalence owes less to its efficiency but more to the family's need for the child's contribution to the household. There appears to be a fairly broad consensus that credit constraints force families to make child labour decisions without fully considering future returns to education, and several studies document that declining poverty is associated with rapid declines in the fraction of children who are working, especially in market work. For this to be true, there needs to be both credit constraints among the very poor and substantive changes in the marginal utility of the child's contribution as the family exits poverty.

However, while transitioning out of poverty may be associated with declining economic activity levels, higher income households are apt to have more employment opportunities both outside and inside the household. This creates a difficult econometric problem for researchers if both labour supply and labour demand change in opposite ways with rising income. A failure to understand this has caused many to assert that there is little link between poverty and child labour. Fortunately, as research progresses, there has been increasing attention to all of the different factors that can influence child time allocation. While the quantity and quality of research on child labour has been increasing dramatically in recent years, there are several omissions in the literature that need to be resolved (beyond the agency issues we have already mentioned). Policy appears to be largely operating in a vacuum from research.

Namely, rhetoric is increasingly directed against "worst forms of child labour," but I am not aware of any current empirical work on why children select into worst forms that has survived peer review in a contemporary mainstream economics journal. Moreover, outside of conditional cash transfer programs, policies targeted at these worst forms and more common forms of child labour are not being evaluated in a scientific way as far as I can find. This is unfortunate. Not only could more effective policies be designed but fundamental questions about why children work could be answered in the process. Hopefully, future work on child labour will aim to combine rigorous research on these unanswered questions with formal evaluation of child labour policy.

Some types of work make useful, positive contributions to a child's development. Work can help children learn about responsibility and develop particular skills that will benefit them and the rest of society. Often, work is a vital source of income that helps to sustain children and their families. However, across the world, millions of children do extremely hazardous work in harmful conditions, putting their health, education, personal and social development, and even their lives at risk. These are some of the circumstances they face:

- Full-time work at a very early age
- Dangerous workplaces
- Excessive working hours
- Subjection to psychological, verbal, physical and sexual abuse
- Obliged to work by circumstances or individuals
- Limited or no pay
- Work and life on the streets in bad conditions
- Inability to escape from the poverty cycle – no access to education

The problem:

- The International Labour Organization estimates there are 218 million working children aged between five and 17 (2006)
- 126 million are estimated to work in the worst forms of child labour – one in every 12 of the world's five to 17 years olds (2006)
- 74 million children under 15 are in hazardous work and should be "immediately withdrawn from this work" (2006)
- 8.4 million children are in slavery, trafficking, debt bondage and other forms of forced labour, forced recruitment for armed conflict, prostitution, pornography

and other illicit activities (2002)

- Girls are particularly in demand for domestic work
- Around 70 per cent of child workers carry out unpaid work for their families

CHILD TRAFFICKING

Trafficking involves transporting people away from the communities in which they live, by the threat or use of violence, deception, or coercion so they can be exploited as forced or enslaved workers for sex or labour. When children are trafficked, no violence, deception or coercion needs to be involved; it is merely the act of transporting them into exploitative work which constitutes trafficking. Increasingly, children are also bought and sold within and across national borders. They are trafficked for sexual exploitation, for begging, and for work on construction sites, plantations and into domestic work. The vulnerability of these children is even greater when they arrive in another country. Often they do not have contact with their families and are at the mercy of their employers.

Children work:

- Most children work because their families are poor and their labour is necessary for their survival. Discrimination on grounds including gender, race or religion also plays its part in why some children work.
- Children are often employed and exploited because, compared to adults, they are more vulnerable, cheaper to hire and are less likely to demand higher wages or better working conditions. Some employers falsely argue that children are particularly suited to certain types of work because of their small size and "nimble fingers".
- For many children, school is not an option. Education can be expensive and some parents feel that what their children will learn is irrelevant to the realities of their everyday lives and futures. In many cases, school is also physically inaccessible or lessons are not taught in the child's mother tongue, or both.

- As well as being a result of poverty, child labour also perpetuates poverty. Many working children do not have the opportunity to go to school and often grow up to be unskilled adults trapped in poorly paid jobs, and in turn will look to their own children to supplement the family's income.

Children work **:**

- On the land
- In households – as domestic workers
- In factories – making products such as matches, fireworks and glassware
- On the street – as beggars
- In Outdoor industry: brick kilns, mines, construction
- In bars, restaurants and tourist establishments
- In sexual exploitation
- As soldiers

The majority of working children are in agriculture – an estimated 70 per cent. Child domestic work in the houses of others is thought to be the single largest employer of girls worldwide.

CASE STUDIES FROM AROUND THE WORLD

Dieusibon - Haiti

"When I first moved to Port-au-Prince I cleaned dishes, the house, everything. My 'aunt' would beat me whenever I didn't get water. I worked so hard that my body ached and I couldn't move, but she would beat me if I didn't do more work. Her three children went to school...One day my aunt sent me to fetch water. I refused, so she took a pot of boiling water and threw it at me and burned my face and slammed the hot cooking pot on my hand."

Dieusibon, 14, ran away and found help from a shelter in Haiti.

Mohen and Nihal–Pakistan

In Pakistan, brothers Mohen and Nihal began working on

carpet looms when they were four and five years old in order to help their family meet their basic needs.

"The health hazards caused to us are that our fingers are trimmed and we have to work all day long. Often for a couple of days in a week, we have to work for the whole day and night.

Mohen often gets miserable and fatigued with the long hours or work and he tries to escape. Then the master weaver keeps a strict watch on him and never lets him move for three or four days."

Ahmed – United Arab Emirates

When Ahmed was five years old he was trafficked from Bangladesh to the United Arab Emirates to be a camel jockey. He was forced to train and race camels in Dubai for three years.

"I was scared .... If I made a mistake I was beaten with a stick. When I said I wanted to go home I was told I never would. I didn't enjoy camel racing, I was really afraid. I fell off many times. When I won prizes several times, such as money and a car, the camel owner took everything. I never got anything, no money, nothing; my family also got nothing."

Ahmed was only returned home after a Bangladesh official identified him during a visit to Dubai in November 2002. Our local partner Bangladesh National Women Lawyers' Association provided him with the specialist support and help he needed to resume his life with his family.

CHILD DOMESTIC WORKERS SPEAK OUT

From May to October 2004, Anti-Slavery International and its local partners undertook consultations with more than 450 current and former child domestic workers in nine countries in Africa, Asia and Latin America. Consultations took place in Benin, Costa Rica, India, Nepal, Peru, Philippines, Sri Lanka, Tanzania and Togo reflecting the reality of child domestic labour in many countries.

The majority of those who participated were female – but more than 100 boys also took part. Cutting across cultural and language divides, the child domestic workers who were consulted had some clear messages about the best kinds of assistance to protect them from the daily abuse and exploitation that many of them endure. Their common appeal for those who seek to help them are:

- To provide opportunities for education and training which allow them to move on from domestic work;
- To assist them in seeking redress from abusive and/or exploitative employers;
- Not to alienate employers, but to make them part of the solution to their problems;
- To provide more services which cater specifically to the needs of child domestic workers (since their needs are often quite different from those of other child workers);
- To develop longer-term interventions, i.e. not to develop services for them and then pull-out after just one or two years;
- To develop interventions which take into consideration some of the issues which most affect child domestic workers, for example, early pregnancy and the effect of HIV/AIDS;
- More awareness raising about their situation, and to ensure that this awareness raising goes hand-in-hand with concrete services for child domestic workers;
- Assistance in accessing government and state infrastructure that can help them; for example, in obtaining birth certificates, enrolling in school, in accessing health care, in locating families and returning home.

Perhaps the strongest message to emerge from the consultations was the importance of those providing assistance to talk to the children themselves about what they need. The work of Anti-Slavery International's partners in this area has shown that the most effective interventions are those which systematically involve child domestic workers themselves in the planning and implementation of their projects and programmes.

Child Soldiers

There are about 300,000 child soldiers involved in over 30 areas of conflict worldwide, some even younger than 10 years old. Child soldiers fight on the front line, and also work in support roles; girls are often obliged to be sex slaves or "soldiers' wives". Children involved in conflict are severely affected by their experiences and can suffer from long-term trauma. The *Optional Protocol to the Convention on the Rights of the Child on the involvement of children in armed conflict* entered into force on 12 February 2002, which encourages governments to raise the age of voluntary recruitment into the armed forces and explicitly states that no person under the age of 18 should be sent into battle.

The United Kingdom, which has the lowest minimum recruitment age in Europe at 16, ratified the *Optional Protocol* on 24 June 2003. The Government, however, added a declaration to reserve the right to send under-18s into hostilities "if there is a genuine military need" or "due to the nature or urgency of the situation". This clause is in direct conflict with the spirit of the Protocol, which urges that states "take all feasible measures to ensure that members of their armed forces who have not attained the age of 18 years old do not take a direct part in hostilities".

ACTION AGAINST CHILD LABOUr

International Law

International law forms the basis of our work against the worst forms of child labour. The Conventions of the International Labour Organization, the 1926 and 1956 Slavery Conventions and the *UN Convention on the Rights of the Child* are the major tools we use.

- Article 32 of the *UN Convention on the Rights of the Child* (1989): *"State Parties recognize the right of the child to be protected from economic exploitation and from performing any work that is likely to be hazardous or to interfere with the child's education or to be harmful to the child's health or physical, mental, spiritual, moral or social development."*

- Convention 182 of the International Labour Organi-zation (1999): The main aim of Convention 182 is to eliminate the worst forms of child labour. It stresses that immediate action is needed to tackle the worst exploitation of children and that measures taken by the authorities should start as soon as the government is able following ratification. The main provisions of the convention are to clarify which situations should be classified as the worst forms of child labour, and to specify what governments must do to prohibit and eliminate them.

Anti-Slavery International's Work on Child Labour

Anti-Slavery International is not a funding body, but works with organisations around the world which work specifically in the field of child labour. Anti-Slavery International has worked on child labour since the early 1900s. We have been systematically working on child labour issues since the 1970s, mainly in research and international advocacy. Relevant ILO and UN standards underpin all Anti-Slavery International's work on child labour. We work collaboratively with other NGOs, inter-governmental bodies and trade unions, and focus on the worst forms of child labour and slavery-like practices.

Anti-Slavery International currently works in partnership with local partners on:

- Developing specific expertise on the subject of children in domestic service. This has involved: publishing hard evidence about the situation of child domestic workers in several countries; developing good practice tools on research and advocacy for use by NGOs and others at national and local levels; consolidating and building an international network of NGOs sharing information and expertise about child domestic work issues; and identifying and promoting good practice in programme interventions, particularly those which best protect child domestic workers from abuse and exploitation.
- Campaigning for the adoption and implementation of

legislation in Gulf States prohibiting under 18s being trafficked and used as camel jockeys, and the prosecution of those involved.

- Increasing understanding and raising awareness of other issues, including children in the cocoa industry, forced child begging, and the health and psychosocial effects of the worst forms of child labour, particularly children in domestic service.

Anti-Slavery International also founded a Sub-Group on Child Labour of the Geneva-based NGO Group for the Convention on the Rights of the Child, and remains an active member.

3

Comparative Analysis of Child Activities in South Asia and Sub-Saharan Africa

While South Asia has the largest number of working children, Sub-Saharan Africa has the highest incidence of child labour. Child work participation rates are 41% in Africa as compared with 21% in Asia and 17% in Latin America. Comparative work is a first step in gaining an insight into the universality of the problem of child work. South Asia and Sub-Saharan Africa are clearly very different environments, their common ground being that the average household, at least in rural areas, is poor. We compare the determinants of child labour in the two countries, including household living standards, household human capital and demographics, and community-level data on schools and infrastructure. The data describe prominent differences in the environment that children grow up in. We then present a summary of the determinants of the variation in child work across households within each country. Interesting contrasts across country and gender are highlighted.

There have been a number of empirical studies of child labour in recent years. However, as Basu (1999) points out, there remains considerable scope for good empirical work in this field. At this stage, patterns are only just beginning to emerge among the variety of results in the literature, corresponding to the vast variety of regions, types of child work, and empirical specifications. The main contribution of this chapter is that it uses comparable micro-data on two countries where child participation rates in work are currently very high, in an attempt to determine whether any patterns can be discerned amidst the vast (observed and unobserved) heterogeneity in household conditions. Existing beliefs about the causes and consequences of child labour have tended to be shaped by case studies. These typically interview working children. An advantage of using large scale representative household surveys, as is done here, is that we have comparable information for children who do not work.

A PROFILE OF CHILD ACTIVITIES

In this section we present empirical evidence on school attendance as well as on the prevalence, intensity, and nature of child labour in rural areas. We discuss the extent to which school and work are combined by children, and we highlight the fact that a substantial proportion of children, especially girls, are neither in school nor at work (though they may well be engaged in domestic work). Interesting inter-country and gender differences in child activities emerge.

The Data

The data are drawn from the Ghana Living Standards Survey (GLSS) for 1991/2 (wave 3) and the Pakistan Integrated Household Survey (PIHS) for 1991. The GLSS contains 4552 households, with an average household size of 4.5 members, giving a total of 20403 individuals. Almost 50 per cent of males and 45 per cent of females are aged under 15. The Pakistan Integrated Household Survey for 1991 contains 4795 households. On account of a much larger mean household size of 7.5 members, we have a sample of 36,109 individuals. About 43.5% of males and 45.5% of females in the sample are aged under 15.

The GLSS collects data on employment for persons 7 years or older whereas the cut-off is at the age of 10 in the PIHS. While there are important differences in the two datasets, their structure and coverage are sufficiently similar to allow some interesting cross-national comparisons.

Participation Rates in School

In rural Ghana, 79% of boys and 72% of girls aged 10-14 years are "currently in school". In contrast, school attendance in Pakistan is remarkably larger for boys as compared to girls of all ages. Amongst 10-14 year olds, 72% of boys and only 31% of girls are in school. Except for girls in Pakistan who appear to withdraw into the household at an early age, school participation is lower in the 7-9 and 15-17 year ranges suggesting late entry and early exit (the latter, especially for girls). Consistent with this, participation in all sorts of work, for boys and girls, tends to increase steadily with age.

Participation Rates in Work

In Ghana, 49% of boys and 44% of girls undertake work on the household farm, about a further 3% of each gender are engaged in household enterprises, while less than 1% report any employment outside the household. In Pakistan, 22% of boys and 28% of girls work on the household farm, about 2% of both genders work in a household enterprise, and 6% of boys and 12% of girls work outside the home.

The striking difference between the two countries is that children in Pakistan engage in wage work outside the household, which Ghanaian children do not. The data show that this is more or less full-time work and that, for girls, it is predominantly seasonal agricultural work, whereas the large fractions of boys who work outside the home are engaged in non-agricultural work.

Data on domestic work, which includes fetching firewood or water, cooking, cleaning, laundry, shopping and child care, were collected for boys and girls in Ghana and for girls alone in Pakistan. Virtually all children participate in domestic work of some sort. In addition, about 5% of Pakistani girls engage in home work for sales, an activity in which boys have no part. It appears unusual for children to be active in more than one type of work though a small fraction of Pakistani children do combine wage work and farm work.

Hours of Work

How hard do working children work? Mean hours increase with age for all groups other than Pakistani girls working for the household. Work intensity for the household is similar among girls and boys in Ghana. Pakistani girls exhibit lower intensity work, while boys in Pakistan work harder than the other sub-groups. Indeed, many children combine farm work with school attendance. On the other hand, wage work, which is restricted to children in Pakistan, is more or less full-time work. Boys work on average 45 hours a week while girls work about 30 hours a week.

Competition between Work and Schooling

Of Ghanaian children who work on the household farm, almost three in four boys and girls are at the same time in school. Combining farm work and school would appear to be less easily done in Pakistan, where almost half the boys but only one in ten farm-working girls manage it. Similarly, in Ghana, virtually all boys and almost half of the girls combine working on the household enterprise with going to school while, in Pakistan, this is rare amongst the boys and unknown amongst girls. Child wage work is virtually absent in Ghana but in Pakistan, where it occupies about 6% of boys and 12% of girls, it clearly interferes with schooling: less than 1% of children combine wage work and school. Overall, in all its forms, child work in Pakistan is much more evidently in competition with school attendance than is the case in Ghana.

A remarkable fact is that, in both countries, a substantial proportion of children neither work nor goes to school. In Pakistan, this is 35% of girls and 10% of boys and in Ghana; it is 14% of girls and 8% of boys. These fractions are especially large among girls. Therefore, if the main concern is with low educational attainment (and the gender gap therein), then policies designed to discourage child labour may be rather less important than policies that directly promote school attendance.

POTENTIAL DETERMINANTS OF THE VARIATION IN CHILD WORK

In this Section, we discuss the variables that both theory and existing evidence suggest have an impact on child labour. This underlies the empirical analysis in the remainder of the paper. Bhalotra and Heady present a theoretical model of household choice relating to the supply of child labour. The key issue is the allocation of child time between work and school. This time allocation will depend on the relative advantages of work and school, both in the short-term and in the long-term.

The main quantifiable short-term advantage of work is the wage that is received. In the context of working for the household, which showed to account for most of the child labour in Ghana and Pakistan, the wage will typically not be explicit. Instead, it is necessary to look for variables that determine the marginal product of child work. These include child characteristics such as age and sex, household characteristics such as land at the disposal of the household as well as household size and composition, and community level characteristics such as local infrastructure and indicators of local labour demand (for example, the region of the country or recent changes in local economic well-being). The main quantifiable measures of the short-term attractiveness of schooling are the access to schooling and quality of schooling, both of which are defined at the level of the community.

The long-term advantages of work and schooling depend on their ability to raise the child's future earnings. This is hard to measure in itself. However, there are observable variables that affect the relative weight that households put on the short-term and long-term advantages. In a perfect capital market, the relative weights will just depend on the rate of interest, but this is an extreme assumption. In reality, it is reasonable to think of households having differential access to credit and thus placing different weights on current and future benefits. As access to credit typically varies with income, this corresponds to the popular belief that children are more likely to work the poorer the households they come from. We therefore include household income in the analysis, proxied by the natural logarithm of per capital food expenditure.

In addition, household assets such as land and the availability of local risk-sharing institutions may influence households' access to credit, and thus their ability to keep their children out of work. These economic considerations will be modified by household and community attitudes to the importance of education and the appropriate treatment of children. This might depend on the age and sex of the child and whether he or she is the child of the household head. There is also evidence of birth order effects on the distribution of household investments across children (e.g. Das Gupta (1987), Butcher and Case (1994)).

Attitudes to education will depend on the education of the child's parents, although it is important to distinguish the effect of parental education on attitudes from its effects on household income. Attitudes will also depend on which ethnic and religious groups the household belongs to. Many of these variables have been shown to play a role in determining children's labour market participation by studies based on similar household surveys, such as Canagarajah and Coulombe (1998), Jensen and Nielsen (1996) and Patrinos and Psacharopoulos (1997)

VARIABLES BETWEEN GHANA AND PAKISTAN

Child Work on the Household Farm

Henceforth, the discussion will concentrate on farm work which employs by far the largest proportion of chil-dren in both countries and which is comparable across them. The vast majority of working children in developing countries, whether in Brazil or Pakistan or Ghana are engaged in agricultural work. Yet, this work is severely understudied as compared with the more visible forms of work in Latin America and Asia, which involve children in labour-intensive manufacturing.

Contrasting Environments for Children in Ghana and Pakistan

The discussion here is a summary of the broad magnitudes relating to some interesting contrasts between the rural regions of the two countries in the environments in which children work. Recall that children in Ghana are 7-14 and in Pakistan are 10-14 years old. Approximately half the children in each sample are first-born children and something like three in four are children of the household head. However, cross country similarities stop at child characteristics. It is not uncommon in Ghana for a household to own more than one plot of land, but this is unusual in Pakistan. In Ghana, households appear to have access to freely available or village owned land, which is not the case in Pakistan. Sharecropping is much more prevalent in Pakistan than in Ghana, involving almost 40% of households as compared with about 7%.

The most remarkable contrasts between the countries appear with respect to household structure. Average household size is about 7 in Ghana and is closer to 10 in Pakistan. A striking difference between the countries is that almost 30% of households in Ghana have a female head as compared with less than 3% of households in Pakistan. Another difference of enormous magnitude is that approximately 35% of fathers and 25% of mothers are absent from the home at the time of the survey in Ghana but in Pakistan only 1 or 2% of households report at least one parent absent. This is also reflected in the household composition variables which show that the proportion of males 20-59 years old in the home is about 10% in Ghana as compared with about 16% in Pakistan. A further difference in household composition that may have a story to tell is that, while the proportions of elderly men in the two countries are similar, the fraction of elderly women (over 60) in Pakistani households is about half the corresponding fraction in Ghanaian households. This suggests that life expectancy for women is especially low in Pakistan.

Educational attainment of the adult generation in rural areas is considerably greater in Ghana as compared with

Pakistan, and this is true for men and women. In Ghana about 65% of mothers of our 7-14 year olds have no formal education and in Pakistan this fraction is about 96%. Close to 20% of mothers in Ghana have completed their secondary school as compared with less than 1% in Pakistan. Less than 50% of men in Ghana have no formal education as compared with about 65% in Pakistan. This is reflected in levels of education too. The percentage of fathers that have completed secondary education is about 40% in Ghana and less than 10% in Pakistan. Turning to community-level infrastructure, the vast majority of communities in both countries have a primary school but while about 65% of rural communities in Ghana have a middle school, in Pakistan, only about 40% have a boys' middle school and less than 30% a girls' middle school.

Working and Non-Working Children

Unless particularly stated, the effects discussed are similar across boys and girls. The average age among workers is about a year greater than among non-workers. Being the first child makes it more likely that the individual, girl or boy, will work; as does being a child who is not the child of the household head. It is of some interest to note that about three in four of 7-14 year olds are children of the head. Households with working children are poorer (by 7% for boys and by 12% for girls), as measured by their per capita food expenditure. This is in spite of the fact that child work will contribute to raising expenditures.

In the analysis, this feedback effect, running from child work to p.c. expenditure is controlled for. What, at first glance, may seem contradictory to the expenditure effect, is that children are more likely to engage in household farm work if the household owns a larger acreage of land and has a larger number of farms. Land owning would therefore appear to reflect the marginal productivity of family labour rather than wealth. In the regression analysis that follows, we will be able to look at the land effect holding constant food expenditure, which should reflect household wealth. Boys are more likely to work if the household rents land but the converse is the case for girls.

Access to freely available land increases the probability of child labour while access to village-owned land decreases it. Whether the household sharecrops does not appear to have any impact on child work. The effects of parents' education are complex. Mothers' primary education appears to increase boys' work and reduce girls' work, but their secondary education has the reverse effect for both boys and girls. Fathers' education has a smaller effect that mothers' education at the primary level, but a larger effect at the secondary level. Household size does not appear to have much explanatory power, although working girls would appear to come from relatively small households, contrary to common perception. Children, and especially girls, are clearly more likely to work if they come from female-headed households.

The regression analysis will confirm whether this is the result of the greater poverty of female-headed households or whether there is a further effect after controlling for poverty levels. Working children are more likely to be found in households where a parent is absent. This suggests that migration, for example, can be costly for children. Turning to the age and gender composition of the household, the female-male ratio is not correlated with child labour. The presence of elderly (over 60) women in the household appears to increase child work, especially for girls. The presence of elderly men also increases the likelihood that 7-14 year old girls work on the farm. The presence of a relatively large fraction of adults (20-59 year olds) has some beneficial effect on boys but does not display any tendency to reduce the work of girls. The variables measuring access to school and the quality of local schools do not show the expected patterns.

There therefore does not seem to be any overwhelming case, in looking at the data alone, to suggest that child labour on household farms in Ghana is primarily determined by weak school infrastructure. As indicators of availability of work, we have the response to subjective questions about whether life was better now and about whether it was easier to find work now than a decade ago. The latter has a weak positive relation with girls' work but, on average, children were seen to work more in communities where life was said to have improved. An indicator for the presence of a farmers' cooperative in the community may have been expected to reflect opportunities for consumption smoothing that would remove the need for child labour to operate as an insurance mechanism. However this variable appears to be associated with higher rates of girls' work. Similarly, there is a mild positive correlation of child labour with the existence of a bank and (for girls) with fertilizer use.

More positive findings of some interest are that in village communities that have electricity, or irrigation facilities, or that report relatively good rainfall, children appear less likely to work. There are dramatic variations in the rate of child work by region. Thus the Central, Volta and Ashanti regions exhibits high child labour participation while the East and West regions exhibit very low rates. Child workers are disproportionately from the Akan group while the Gaadangbe ethnic group has low rates of child labour. Children from households following the animist religion appear to work less than other children.

Pakistan: Working and Non-Working Children

Unless otherwise indicated, the remarks here apply equally to boys and girls. Working children are only marginally older than non-workers. As observed for Ghana, working children are more likely to be first-born and less likely to be children of the household head. The per capita food expenditure of households with working boys is smaller (by 8%) than that of households without working boys, suggesting that they are poorer on average, in spite of the economic contribution of the child. This is not the case for girls, from which it would appear that the work of girls must be explained by factors other than household poverty.

In households that own large plots of land, children appear more likely to be engaged in farm work and this effect is much larger for girls than for boys. An indicator for whether the household rents any land does not have a strong correlation with child work. However, in households that sharecrop land, the incidence of child farm work is considerably larger. The illiteracy of parents ("mother none", "father none") increases child work participation and the effects are larger on daughters than on sons. The effect of mother's having completed between 1 and 5 years of education (primary or less but more than zero) on daughter's work participation is striking, reducing it fourfold; the effect on boys is much smaller.

In no household where mothers have acquired more than primary (middle/secondary) education, do either their sons or daughters participate in work. The broad pattern is seen with fathers' educational levels as well but the differences, especially for father's secondary education, are less striking. Working children come from households that are smaller by more than one individual (or by about 10%). The female-male ratio of the household and the age of the head has no impact on child work participation. However, children are about three times as likely to work if they belong to female-headed households. There is a weak tendency for the absence of one or both parents to increase participation by boys and to decrease it for girls.

An increase in the proportion of 20-59 year old males and females in the household would appear to have a small beneficial effect for girls but none for boys. In households with a relatively large fraction of 5-9 year old boys, the 10-14 year old boys that we consider are less likely to work. Access, within the community, to a boys' primary school is associated with lower participation in work by boys but, interestingly enough, higher participation by girls. Inconsistent with expectation, we find that communities with a primary school for girls exhibit a higher participation rate of girls in work. The indicators for middle schools are uncorrelated with child work. The presence of local transport reduces the work rates of girls but increases those of boys. The presence of a canal is associated with considerably greater participation in work, especially for boys.

Labour would, on average, appear to be a complement to irrigation water in the farming technology of these regions. Communities which have a market show lower child work participation rates but the presence of a post office has no such beneficial effect. Compared with Punjab, the largest province in Pakistan, child participation is relatively low in Baluchistan and NWFP and it is relatively high in Sindh. As compared with Christians and other Non-Muslims, Muslim children are less likely, on average, to be engaged in work.

Tobit Estimates of Influences on Child Work

This section is based upon Bhalotra and Heady (1999), who estimate tobit models to explain the weekly hours of child work on the household farm. The data on workers and non-workers are pooled within country and gender group, so as to determine the extent to which the variables considered above can explain the inter-household variation in child work. While comparison of summary statistics was restricted to looking at participation rates (by virtue of comparing the samples of workers and non-workers), this section generalises the discussion to look at the effects of different regressors on the participation and hours of work of children. Child hours of work exhibit substantial variation.

The analysis here also progresses in looking at the effects of every variable holding all other relevant variables constant, and controlling for any simultaneity. For theoretical underpinnings and for details of the empirical specification, including a discussion of instrumentation of household income, refer to Bhalotra and Heady.

Results for Ghana

Child characteristics have broadly similar effects for boys and girls. Child work increases with age though this effect is quadratic. Dummies indicating highest birth order and relation to household head are insignificant. Household poverty, as (inversely) represented by the natural logarithm of per capita food expenditure, appears to be orthogonal to boys' hours on the family farm. For girls, we observe the expected negative relation, significant at the 13% level.

We find a strong positive effect of the number of farms operated on hours of work for boys and girls. Since this result obtains when controlling for acres of land operated by the household, it suggests not a size effect but an effect associated with the subdivision of land. This merits further micro-level research. Total acres of land utilised by the household has no impact on the farm labour of boys or girls. Household size is insignificant for boys and girls. Boys work is uncorrelated with household composition but there is a weakly negative effect on girls' hours of the proportion of boys under seven in their households.

The absence of the father from the home has a significant positive effect on girls' farm work but no effect for boys. The effect of a female household head is insignificant. The finding that land size and household size are insignificant suggests that the hours of child work on the family farm are not very sensitive to the household-specific marginal product. This might be because while more land means more fruitful work opportunities for the household, it also signifies greater wealth and it may therefore be picking up the effect that we expect per capita expenditure to fully capture. It might also be a result of Ghanaian families being able to adjust the size of their landholdings to fit their desired labour supply.

Parents' education impacts on child work and since these effects are at given levels of household living standards they would appear to reflect preference heterogeneity rather than resource constraints. The only clearly significant effect is that the sons of mothers with secondary-level education work less. There is a negative effect of mothers' primary education on girls' farm work, significant at 18%. Fathers' primary education has a weakly significant (at 11%) positive effect on girls' work. This does appear odd but might be explained by a chain of intra-household substitutions which the current analysis does not explore. The impact of fathers' education on boys' work is insignificant and has a negative sign.

Regional differences are significant and have larger effects for girls. Religion has no systematic effect on boys' work but Christian girls work significantly fewer hours on average than animist girls, who work less than Muslim girls. Ethnicity is insignificant for girls, but Ewe Boys are significantly less likely to work. The effects of community variables are very different between boys and girls. The one variable that has a very similar and negative effect for boys and girls is the age of the secondary/technical college in the village. For both boys and girls, dummies for the presence of primary, middle and secondary schools in the cluster take the expected negative signs but their effects are poorly determined. Variables that have a significant negative effect on boys' work are indicators for electricity in the village, and for whether there was more rainfall in 1991-2 than in the preceding year.

In households where the respondent judged life to be better than it was ten years before the survey, boys were found to be more likely to be in work. A positive effect for girls flows from a similar subjective question asking whether it was easier to find work in 1991-2 as compared with 1981. For reasons that are not evident, girls' work hours are positively correlated with the existence of a cooperative society and the age of the local primary school. A strong negative effect of the existence of public transport in the village on girls' work is consistent with the hypothesis that distance to school may deter the attendance of girls more than it does that of boys. Irrigation, tractors and fertilizers do not have significant effects on child work, nor does the presence of a village bank.

Overall, among a range of variables in the model, those that display a significant relation with hours of child work on the household farm are child age, the number of farms owned, mothers' education, region, ethnicity, religion, the age of the local primary school, availability of public transport, rainfall, electricity, and the dynamism of the region as reflected in subjective assessments of life and work opportunities having got better in the last ten years. Among variables directly manipulable by policy are maternal education, school quality (arising from age of local school), public transportation in the village, electricity and irrigation (arising via the significance of rainfall).

Results for Pakistan

The child's age has a positive effect on hours worked, which is much larger for boys than for girls. There are no birth order effects. The 10-14 year olds who classify as children of the household head are more likely to be employed on the farm than other young people in the household including grandchildren, nephews, nieces and siblings of the household head. This effect is significant for girls but only marginally so for boys. Household living standards have a highly significant negative effect on boys' hours of work. The corresponding effect for girls is also negative but about a fifth of the size and insignificant.

The stronger effect for boys is consistent with the much greater participation of boys in school, as compared with girls in rural Pakistan: In the cross section of households in the sample, those with relatively high incomes (expenditures) are better able to afford to send their children to school and, in this, boys have priority over girls. In contrast, variation in child farm work in Ghana appears to be independent of household income for boys and girls alike. This is consistent with the apparently greater facility for combining work and school in Ghana as compared with Pakistan. In contrast with our findings for Ghana, farm size and household size are significant and take the expected signs in Pakistan. Acres of land operated by the household have a positive effect on girls' work, while it is insignificant in the boys' equation.

For girls, it would seem that any (negative) wealth effect of acres is captured by household food expenditure and the observed (positive) effect is a "wage" effect. Household size has a negative effect on child work which is significant for both genders but considerably larger for boys than for girls. Existing studies of child labour in other contexts tend to find positive effects of household size (for example, Patrinos and Psacharopoulos (1997)). However, where the discussion pertains exclusively to child work on household farms and farm sizes are relatively small, the negative effect of household size on child work is exactly what theory would predict. Our results therefore caution against hasty generalisations to the effect that the wellbeing of children is inversely related to the size of their households.

At given household size, there are some fairly complex effects of the age-gender composition of the household on child hours of work. Both girls and boys in the 10-14 year age group do significantly less farm work in households with a relatively large fraction of boys aged under-10. Boys are also less likely to be in farm work, the larger the fraction of 15-19 year old boys or girls in the home. Girls, on the other hand, are significantly less likely to work on the farm in the presence of elderly females (over 60) or adult males (20-59 years) in the home. The overall proportion of females in the household has a negative effect on child work, significant at about 10%, suggesting that child and female labour are substitutes. Children of both genders who come from female-headed households are more likely to be in farm work.

This suggests there are aspects of ill being in female headed households that a household income measure does not pick up. Work intensity for girls is, at the 15% significance level, a positive function of age of the household head, possibly an indication that young adults (or parents) are better able to "protect" their daughters from work than older adults. Parents' education is represented by a set of dummies for up to-primary, middle, and secondary education, with "no education" being the benchmark (the omitted dummy). Since only 0.1% of mothers have secondary-level education, this group is combined with middle-level education for mothers. There is a significant negative effect of fathers' secondary education on the work hours of their daughters, while fathers' education is not a significant predictor of boys' work. Mothers' education to the level of middle or secondary school has a strong negative effect on child work that is a bit bigger for boys than for girls.

Comparing with Ghana, the broad tendency is for mothers' education to reduce child labour in both countries and for both genders, with fathers' education having no effect in Ghana and a benign effect restricted to girls in Pakistan. The presence of a primary school for girls reduces the farm labour of 10-14 year old girls and, possibly because of sibling competition for resources, the presence of a primary school for boys increases girls' farm labour. These school access variables have no effect on boys' work. Dummies for the presence of middle schools are insignificant for boys and girls.

Other cluster specific variables which have a significant effect on boys' work include positive effects from a market and negative effects from a telephone, a bus route and a canal. The presence of post office and tractor do not have significant effect. For girls, community-level variables are altogether much less significant and the only effect to speak of is a negative one associated with a bus route. Might the bus route effect common to boys and girls, denote mobility away from the household farm, whether for outside work or for school. Province and religion dummies affect girls though not boys. Amongst girls, those from Baluchisatn work less. Christian girls work significantly less than Muslims, who work significantly less than other Non-Muslims. Christians constitute 1.5% of the population and other non-Muslims (mostly Hindus) account for another 3.6%; the vast majorities are Muslim.

This chapter has shown that there are substantial differences between the Ghana and Pakistan in relation to child labour. It has shown that, although work on the family farm is the most common form of child labour in both countries, only Pakistan has significant child work outside the household. Also, the difference in both labour force participation and schooling is fairly similar for Ghanaian girls and boys, but very different for Pakistani boys and girls. The paper also shows that there are important differences between the countries in variables that might be expected to influence the incidence child labour. The most important are the larger family sizes and lower parental education in Pakistan than in Ghana.

However, the difference in child labour patterns between the two countries is not simply due to differences in these variables. The factors that determine child labour participation in the two countries are also different. For instance, any impact of household poverty or household size on child farm work is context-specific. The one striking tendency that seems to hold across gender and country is that the children of relatively well educated mothers are less likely to be engaged in work. Since this effect persists after controlling for household income, it would appear to reflect the impact of female education on preferences and the power of women in household decision making.

In Pakistan, raising household income per capita appears to reduce boys' hours of work, the effect for girls being insignificant. The magnitude of the effect for Pakistani boys is rather large: An increase in food expenditure of 10%, ceteris paribus, reduces the probability of work by 6 percentage points and, conditional on working, it reduces hours of work by 1.28 hours. However, there is no evidence for Ghana or for girls in Pakistan to suggest that increasing living standards will, on its own, reduce the incidence or severity of child labour on the household farm. There is some evidence that both school quality and access to school affect child labour.

The significant positive effect of female-headed households on child work in Pakistan, even after controlling for household income, is consistent with these families facing tighter capital market constraints than others and thus finding it harder to ensure survival without child work. The negative effect of a canal on boys' work in Pakistan and the negative effect of increased rainfall on boys' work in Ghana may indicate the importance for child labour of reducing income fluctuations. The size of the household farm has no impact on child hours of work in Ghana, where land is relatively abundant. In Pakistan, it increases hours of girls' work, with no effect for boys. Household size has no effect on child labour in Ghana but it decreases hours of farm work performed by children in Pakistan.

This is probably a reflection of the relative scarcity of land in Pakistan, the average household farm being smaller than in Ghana. There are some interesting effects of household composition in Pakistan: the greater child work in female-headed households has already been noted, and children tend to work fewer hours if they have male siblings younger than themselves. These effects are very large. There are no household composition effects for Ghanaian children. Our results contradict evidence from other regions. Existing work has tended to implicitly think of large size as creating large consumption needs and therefore greater labour supply to meet needs. This neglects the fact that household assets are often constrained, at least in South Asia, and that this may drive the marginal productivity of family labour to levels that are too low to compensate withdrawal from school, leisure, or other alternative uses of time.

Father's secondary education significantly reduces girls' work in Pakistan but has no effect on the labour of the other three groups. Mother's education tends to reduce boys' hours of work in Ghana and the hours of work of both boys and girls in Pakistan. The magnitude of these effects is so large that policy aimed at eliminating child work is best targeted here.

THE CASE FOR ATTENTION TO WORKING CHILDREN

Few issues in developing countries draw more attention in rich countries than child labour. This attention is typically motivated by human rights concerns. Horrific newspaper issues of children burned to death while chained to their job in garment factories in Bangladesh or forced into prostitution in Thailand drives much of this concern. These human rights concerns are well grounded, but, as most working children are from poor families and are helping in their family's activities, the typical working child is not in a situation where the human rights issues are obvious. As such, much of child labour related policy is not directed at worst forms of child labour but instead at the more prevalent forms of child labour in developing countries. This section considers the academic case for attention to the more prevalent forms of work.

Child Labour in International Policy

Researchers for years have studied adult labour supply with great interest, but the research interest in child labour is augmented by policy's interest in the topic. Consumer boycotts and student protests against products with some child labour component during production are relatively frequent occurrences. One often reads of protests in American universities over the involvement of children in the production of athletic clothing. Outrage over the involvement of children in producing soccer balls hit a fever pitch in the late 1990s when it was learned that FIFA licensed products contained a considerable child labour component. Beyond boycotts, labeling campaigns such as the Rugmark campaign to label hand-knit carpets as "child labour free" garner considerable popular support.

This consumer activism has been matched by legislative interest. For example, the U.S. Congress has repeatedly considered legislation that would prohibit imports into the United States of all products made with child labour. Under threat of such sanctions, export oriented garment factories in Bangladesh released more that 10,000 child workers under the age of 14 in the mid 1990s. More recently, the U.S. House of Representatives has deliberated the "Child Labour Elimination Act" that would impose general trade sanctions, deny all financial assistance, and mandate U.S. opposition to multilateral credits to 62 developing countries with a high incidence of child labour. This threat is implicit in a 2002 act of the U.S. Congress that mandated a study by the Department of Labour's Bureau of International Labour Affairs about the relationship between military and education spending in countries with a high incidence of child labour.

Under current law, the U.S. can withdraw a poor country's eligibility for trade preferences under the Generalized System of Preferences (GSP) based on a country's poor record on child labour. Moreover, the 2000 Trade and Development Act restricts eligibility for trade benefits to countries that the Secretary of Labour certifies as showing progress towards eliminating the worst forms of child labour. This policy interest in child labour in developing countries is a relatively recent issue, and corresponding to it is growth in the academic literature that seeks to understand why children work and measure the short and long term consequences of work.

Work and Schooling

Is schooling attendance lower for working children? There are fixed number of hours in a day. As such, time spent working necessarily trades off with other uses of child time such as play, study time, or time in school. Despite their importance for child development, especially at young ages, very few researchers consider play and leisure in efforts to measure the opportunity costs of working. Concerns about play were at the forefront of concerns about child labour in early 20th century U.S. In contrast, the extent to which work affects schooling attendance, performance, and attainment is perhaps the second most researched question in the child labour literature (second, to the income elasticity of child labour supply).

The Minimum Working Age Convention (C138) in part necessitates this interest in that it permits light work in children as young as 12 provided it does not interfere with schooling. When and how does work interfere with schooling? The main challenge in this literature is that schooling and child labour decisions are joint outcomes out of a single time allocation problem. Hence, the interpretation of any found correlation between labour status and schooling is controversial. Do children work because they are not attending school? Do children not attend school because they are working? Do other economic or cultural factors simultaneously influence both schooling and work decisions? Before turning to the problem of establishing causation, a simple description of the association between schooling attendance and work in the MICS countries will be useful.

First, children can work and attend school. In fact, in the under 10 population, working children have slightly higher schooling rates than non-working children although this reflects age trends in both the start of schooling and work. Second, of different categories of activity, schooling attendance rates are lowest among children in market work outside of their household. Third, children who work only in market work without any domestic work tend to have lower schooling rates than children who work in domestic and market work. These two pieces of evidence are often cited as justification for only looking at wage work or market work respectively, but they may proxy hours worked and have little further implication. Children who only work in market work without any domestic work are typically working substantive hours, and children that work outside the household tend to spend more time working than those who help in the family business.

Total hours worked are highest among children that work outside their household in market work and lowest among children that only perform domestic work. In general, girls work more than boys (despite having similar school attendance rates), except among children that participate in market work only. If the lower schooling attendance rates of children who work in market work alone or work outside the household reflects hours worked, this would imply that the decline in schooling attendance with total hours worked should be steepest in the neighborhood of 30 hours worked as is typical for those who only work outside the household. School attendance rates appear relatively flat with respect to total hours worked until about 8 hours worked. The probability of observing a working child attend school declines gradually between 8 and 29 hours, then the rate of decline increases dramatically starting around 30 hours per week.

This is not surprising as it implies that it becomes most difficult to work and attend school simultaneously when the child is working full time. One clear difficulty in assessing the tradeoff between hours worked and schooling attendance is that the tradeoff depends on how one defines work. Hours worked are largest and schooling attendances rates are lowest for children working outside of their home. However, a failure to consider work within the household or work in domestic work can create a misleading picture of the trade off between schooling and work, especially for girls.

Assaad et al (2003) observes that the low attendance of Egyptian girls relative to boys appears to be associated with a substantial domestic work burden of girls. Because boys do not face the same work burden within the home, they face fewer barriers to schooling such that in the Egyptian data, they do not observe a tradeoff between working and schooling attendance for boys. The sensitivity of attainment to work also depends on the definition of work. Levison and Moe (1998) using Peruvian data and Levison, Moe, and Knaul (2001) in Mexico document that whether there is a tradeoff between schooling attainment and work depends on whether work includes domestic work, especially for girls.

In fact, school attendances rates do not appear to vary significantly with whether hours worked are in market or domestic work. 95 percent confidence intervals are also pictured, and there is significant overlap in the confidence intervals. Beyond 10 hours of work, the school attendance rates associated with time in market work are slightly below that of time in domestic work. However, the differences are never statistically significant, and the shape of both curves looks that work in one type of activity (e.g. market work) is associated typically with some work in the other activity (e.g. domestic work). In contrast to market and domestic work, schooling attendance rates associated with hours worked inside and outside of the household appears very different.

Between 12 and 53 hours per week, a child who is working a given number of hours outside of their household is less likely to attend school than is a child who is spending the same amount of the time inside of the household. A large part of the reason for this apparent difference between work inside and outside of the household is that children working outside of the household typically also work significantly more hours inside the household. In the MICS data, each hour in work outside of the household is associated with an additional nine-tenths of an hour work inside the household on average. In contrast, each hour in work inside the household is associated with one tenth of an hour work outside the household. Hence, the total hours worked for a child working 20 hours a week outside of the household is 38 hours.

A child working 38 hours has a school attendance rate of slightly above 80 percent, within the confidence interval of the observed schooling attendance for a child working 20 hours a week outside the household. Thus, the difference between schooling attendances rates for children working inside and outside of the household appear to owe more to differences in the resulting total hours worked by the child rather than something else intrinsic to work outside of home.

Is schooling achievement and attainment lower for working children? If lower attendance is meaningful for human capital accumulation, it should translate into lower schooling attainment. Moreover, beyond attendance, work may undermine human capital accumulation by interfering with learning as evident in test scores or schooling comp-letion rates. Panel data on child labour histories is rarely available, so studies typically compare current labour supply to current attainment.

This is hard, because current work status necessarily depends on past education and work histories as these affect the value of child time and whether it's optimal for the child to work. This makes interpretation difficult, but studies typically find that attainment is lower for working children. Ray (2003) observes that an additional hour of wage work in Ghana is associated with more than a year's less completed educational attainment. Psacharaopoulos (1997) notes that children in wage work in Bolivia have nearly a year less completed schooling than non working children and that working children in Venezuela have almost 2 years less attainment. Beyond the obvious challenges of inferring causation from these correlations, another difficulty in interpreting evidence on attainment is that standards for advancement vary across schools and may be correlated with factors of interest. For example, it is not difficult to imagine that passing in a poor quality school in a poor area might reflect a different knowledge level than passing in a very good school in a rich area. However, work is also correlated with worse performance in other measures of academic achievement.

For example, Akabayashi and Psacharopoulos (1999) note that working children spend less time studying which is reflected in both math and reading test scores in their Tanzanian data. Heady (2003), using the same Ghana data as Ray, notes that reading and mathematics test scores are substantially lower among wage working children than non working children. *Is there a causal relationship between work and schooling achievement and attainment?* Causal studies of the impact of child labour on schooling face the challenge of isolating some factor that affects child labour without simultaneously affecting schooling. This is difficult, because child labour, schooling, and leisure decisions are jointly determined; it is hard to imagine how one can be affected without all other decisions being affected. Consider the analytical model of equation 1.1. Choices of schooling, leisure, and all types of work depend on the shadow value of child time which is, in turn, a function of choices of schooling, leisure, and all types of work.

Hence, without directly observing the shadow value of child time, there is no way to identify a causal impact of one type of activity on another without additional assumptions. Studies typically rely on either modeling assumptions or on legal variation in child labour or schooling regulations. A common modeling assumption is that some factor only effects whether a child works without otherwise effecting how the family values other uses of the child time. Legal variation is typically assumed to be one such factor. These studies face two difficulties. It is typically hard to imagine the exclusion restriction of how factors that influence work decisions would not simultaneously influence other household decisions, and variation in the value of child time or regulation is apt to be correlated with latent socio-economic characteristics of the child's environment. Hence, authors estimating the causal impact of work on schooling face a considerable challenge. Instrumental variables estimates of the effect of child labour on schooling tend to produce a stronger association between child labour and schooling than in the raw data.

This is not surprising as the instruments typically capture variation in the child labour-schooling relationship that is more variable than the full variation in the data. For example, instruments that work through the value of child time are then using variation in child labour that owes to the families need for the child's contribution or the relative return to work rather than school. It is not surprising to learn that this variation leads to a greater elasticity of schooling with respect to child labour relative to alternative reasons for child labour such as social norms about working, the absence of accessible quality schooling, etc. Legal variation is likely correlated with institutional quality and thereby living standards. Hence, for similar reasons, as the value of child time, these instruments, when valid, might be capturing variation in child labour which is inherently more apt to trade off with schooling.

Do changes in the price of schooling affect child labour supply? Several studies implicitly consider the link between schooling and child labour by examining how child labour and schooling reply to a change in the relative price of schooling. In general, they find that cash or in kind transfers that are conditioned on school attendance increase schooling but have a much smaller effect on child labour. For example, Ravallion and Wodon (2000) consider market work participation and schooling attendance responses to the Food for Education Program (FFE) in Bangladesh in which families receive food rations as long as they send their children to primary school. They observe that households who participate in this program have higher school attendance. Market work participation declines with this school attendance although the decline in market work is about a third of the increase in schooling.

A similar finding is in Cardoso and Souza (2004) who compare market work and schooling attendance in families that receive cash transfers as a part of Brazil's Bosca Escola program to similar families that do not receive the payment. Bosca Escola conditions cash transfers on school attendance, and Cardosa and Souza find larger increases in schooling than declines in market work. Endogenous program participation is a concern in any study that compares program participants to non-participants. Ravallion and Wodon address this by instrumenting for program participation with whether the program is present in a child's village, and Cardosa and Souza use propensity score matching to create a control group with similar observable characteristics to program participants. There is a debate about the implications of the finding that changes in the price of schooling lead to larger changes in school participation than in work *participation*. Some argue that this implies the absence of a connection between either schooling and child labour or poverty and child labour.

There are several reasons to doubt this interpretation. First, if one observed changes in the consumption of two goods (leisure and schooling in this case) with a price change in one of the goods, but the quantity of one good changed more than another, would one conclude that there is no budget constraint? Second, this finding might reflect that there is more of an intensive margin with work than school. School attendance is a rather discrete thing. That is, when a child attends school, that typically means they attend a full days of classes (which is often in the neighborhood of 4 or 5 hours a day). However, market and domestic work are much more flexible. In response to attending school for 4 hours a day, a child could have a precisely corresponding change in total hours worked (indicating a 1 for 1 trade off) but yet still work.

In fact, in a much smaller sample with detailed time use data, Arends-Kuenning and Amin (2004) document that the decline in hours worked among FFE participants is similar in magnitude to the increase in time in school. Third, if children are working because of poverty, schooling subsidies may induce a substitution away from play and leisure to schooling, rather than work. In faet, Arends-Kuenning and Amin (2004) argue that before the FFE program arose in Bangladesh, children on average were not working so many hours that their labour burdens prohibited schooling. The idea that children work because of the family's poverty does not imply that children can have no leisure, especially in a setting where parents care about their child's welfare. Hence, it seems difficult to argue that a movement into schooling without a corresponding change in participation in market work can be interpreted as evidence against a child labour-schooling connection.

Modeling the joint determination of schooling and other time allocation decisions

Most researchers generally treat the analysis of schooling and work separately. That is, they estimate some limited dependent variable model (linear probability, logit, probit) for schooling and work separately. This is attractive for several reasons. First, it is transparent and the properties of these estimators are well understood. Second, it will lead to results that are consistent and comparable to studies that only consider schooling or only consider types of child work. However, because schooling and time allocation decisions are joint, studies frequently adopt empirical methods designed to model the correlation between schooling and work decisions. The bivariate probit is probably the most common alternative to the single variable models. Conventionally, it is similar to a SUR regression in that it allows for correlations in errors between the schooling and child labour regressions.

It can be efficient when bivariate normality of errors is correct, although this is not universally true when the same covariates are included in each regression. If there were viable exclusion restrictions, the model can be used to infer the effect of change in one endogenous variable on the other (that is, a type of work's effect on schooling), although there is still the difficulty of finding plausible exclusion restrictions. Moreover, there are several limitations that researchers need to consider. The bivariate probit has the standard probit problems (need to evaluate the cdf to compute a marginal effect that will vary with covariates, need for large samples per fixed effect to recover fixed effects, inconsistency under heteroskedasticity), and two important additional issues. First, when there are two outcomes of interest (child labour and schooling), computing the effect of a change in any covariate on child labour and schooling requires evaluating the joint density rather than the univariate density as in the standard probit.

Second, when children are classified as either working or in school, the error distribution will become degenerate. Thus, the bivariate probit is not appropriate for data where most children either work or are in school so that the product of the two is zero in expectation. Hence, application of the bivariate probit approach requires some caution on the part of researchers. Another frequent approach to modeling child labour and schooling is a multinomial choice model such as the multinomial logit (MNL) or probit (MNP). These models are especially attractive for structural models of time allocation. They are, however, inherently difficult for evaluating causal effects, because computing marginal effects of some covariate on the choice of schooling and work combination is not straightforward. Typically, the different choices in a multinomial model are different activities that children may perform, and this approach seems broadly consistent with the simultaneous nature of decisions about time allocation.

The computational simplicity of the MNL and the ease with which one can estimate fixed effects make it the more popular than the MNP. However, the MNL relies on the assumption of the independence of irrelevant alternatives (IIA). What does IIA mean in the case where children can participate in multiple tasks? Consider a setting where a child chooses between wage employment and the family farm. IIA implies that if a third choice is added (schooling or work in a family business), the third choice should not affect the probability the child chooses wage work over work on the family farm. IIA would be violated if the third choice drew children disproportionately out of either wage work or work on the farm.

For example, a family business might draw more from

the family farm than wage work. Schooling might draw more from wage work than working in the family farm. Alternatives to the MNL that do not rely on IIA are available. If choices could be ranked and ordered, a nested logit might be feasible. However, given the joint nature of time allocation decisions, this seems problematic. Perhaps it might be feasible in cultural settings where there is strong qualitative evidence to support a particular nesting in familial decisions. The multinomial probit (MNP) does not require a hierarchy of choices, nor does it require IIA. However, it is used less frequently for several reasons. First, the model needs to estimate the entire covariance structure. Hence, the number of parameters that need to be estimated can be extreme. This requires large sample sizes and the model often has difficulty converging. Second, the MNP is flat near its optimum, and this can lead to parameter estimates that are arbitrary but within the tolerance of the optimization routine and hence difficult to detect. A hierarchical choice model such as the sequential probit (SEQP) is also popular.

Modeling typically proceeds by first modeling the choice of whether to attend school or work, then proceeding to model the choice of different types of work, conditional on surviving the previous choice of types of work. That is, the SEQP is essentially a selection model where the researcher uses the results of lower sequenced choices as corrections for selection into higher sequenced choices. When the same covariates are used in each step of the sequence, the SEQP should be identical to the MNP (assuming no misspecification). Hence, the purpose of the SEQP is to allow different variables to affect different choices. The logic behind this approach is not obvious. The shadow value of time for the child reflects the opportunities open to the child, and hence it seems impossible to imagine a sensible exclusion restriction. Moreover, when the included variables differ in the sequence of choices of activities, estimates will depend on the order of the sequence in addition to the exclusion restrictions and functional form of the selection correction. Perhaps qualitative evidence can make the case for some ordering and a set of exclusion restrictions in a particular country context.

Overall, though, given the difficulties with all of the alternatives, it is not surprising that univariate models are the predominant tools for examining work and schooling choices. *Are there future consequences of working?* Because of the conceptual difficulty in isolating some exogenous factor that affects either schooling or child labour, most studies of child labour and schooling tend to focus on economic factors that influence both child labour and schooling without explicitly trying to parameterize the path through which participation in one activity affects participation in the other. However, another alternative is to exploit timing differences in when the adult or older child is observed and when child labour occurred. Factors that have changed over time but were correlated with whether the individual worked as a child can be used as instruments.

Much of the work on the effects of child labour in childhood on adult labour market outcomes comes from Brazil, where the 1996, large-scale PNAD household survey asks individuals at what age they entered the workforce (which is likely interpreted as beginning fulltime market work) Ilahi et al (2000) observe that adults age 18 and older who started fulltime work before age 13 have adult wages that are 13-17 percent lower than adults who entered the workforce later. Emerson and Souza (20044) extend the analysis of Ilahi et al by addressing the endogeneity of the age at which an adult started working as a child with state-time variation in the number of schools. Does the finding of lower adult wages for child laborers reflect anything more than lower educational attainment? It appears to.

Early entry into the labour force lowers the return to a year of education by roughly 20 percent in Ilahi et al's data. Interestingly, in individuals with no education, they observe slightly higher wages for children that start working earlier, conditional on the adult's age. This might reflect an experience premium as without any education and conditional on age, earlier entry means more time to accumulate experience.

Alternatively, starting work at an early age requires having employment opportunities, typically with the child's own family. Hence, this relationship could also reflect something about family background. Emerson and Souza (20044) speculate that the tradeoff between returns to experience and education depends on what sector the individual works in as an adult and child.

The tradeoff between additional experience and education is considered explicitly in Beegle, Dehejia, and Gatti (2005). Using panel data from Vietnam, they evaluate how the labour status of children influences their education, wages, and health five years after they are observed working. In their analysis, they focus on children who are enrolled in school and compare enrolled in school and participating in market work children to children enrolled in school without market work. They impose this sample selection rule in order to isolate the effects of market work itself without confounding the effects of working with the effects of not being in school. Thus, their attention is only on the effects of working per se; they do not capture how the future of children who work exclusively is affected by their work.

When they correct for the endogeneity of market work participation as a child with economic conditions in the base year of their data, they find that each additional hour of work as a child while attending school is associated with a nearly 3 percentage point decline in the probability the child is in school 5 years out and a 0.06 year decline in grade attainment. The mean hours worked for a working child in the base year of their data is 24 hours per week in market work. Hence, going from 0 hours to the average is associated with a more than 90 percent decline in the probability the child attends school and a nearly 20 percent decline in completed schooling five years after the child is observed working while in school. They also observe that the probability the child engages in wage work and the child's wage earnings conditional on participating in wage work are increasing in the child's hours worked. Beegle et al calculate that over a relatively short horizon (as might be appropriate in poor, credit constrained families), the value of increased earnings and the return to experience will outweigh the opportunity cost of foregone education.

WORK AND HEALTH

Is the health status of working children worse? The consequence of child labour may extend beyond schooling attendance and attainment. Woodhead (2004) surveys the psychological ramifications of work as a child, and it is not obvious how one should view the psychosocial impacts of child work. Research has focused more on the effects of child labour on child health. Much of the literature focuses on the injury and morbidity risks associated with the child's work environment. For example, Graitcer and Lerer (1998) list morbidity, injury, and hazard risks faced by children in different occupations and industries. While manufacturing draws a lot of popular attention, family work, including work on the farm, also poses risks. Moreover, Forastieri (2002) points out that the increased nutritional needs associated with arduous work may exacerbate malnutrition, leaving the child stunted and impairing the child's productivity into adulthood, and Parker (1997) emphasizes that children who start work at a young age will be exposed to environmental hazards in the work place for longer, perhaps at a time when the effects of these hazards on development are more substantive. However, working does not necessarily impair a child's health.

To the extent that child labour brings additional resources to the child, this may improve health and nutrition (especially in the destitute populations where work is most prevalent). The benefit of this additional income to the child may be greater than other sources of family income as the child may retain greater control over her own earnings. Further, the fact that the child is a productive, contributing member to the household may affect the child's ability to capture other family resources or influence how they are spent in ways that benefit the child. These types of gains to the child must be balanced against any lost education (and its returns to health) as well as the consequences for malnutrition, morbidity, and injury. Several studies attempt to gauge the net effect of child labour on child health. Evidence that working children have worse health at the time of their work is generally absent from the literature.

O'Donnell et al (2002) look at data from 18 developing countries and observe that across these 18 countries self-reported health status looks unrelated to whether the child participates in market work, is in school, both, or neither. Francavilla et al (2003) look at data from 6 developing countries and find no evidence of a connection between domestic work and self-reported morbidity or BMI either. It is unclear whether the absence of evidence reflects a lack of any relationship, the countervailing factors discussed above, measurement problems, or heterogeneity in the effect of working on health. For example, children working outside, in the family farm in the summer might be no worse off because of their work while children working 12 hours a day in a tannery might be substantially worse off. However, because the former is much more common that the later, there is no apparent relationship on average in the data. *Does child labour affect future adult health?*

There are two basic classes of mechanisms through which a child's labour status may influence adult health. First, physical injury at work may lead to health problems that survive into adulthood. Second, psychological stress or trauma at work in childhood may lead to health problems in adulthood. Speculation about this second mechanism owes to the psychology literature which shows a strong correlation between stress in childhood and the persistence of mental disorders such as depression, anxiety and panic disorders, and schizophrenia or even health problems such as diabetes, heart disease, and immune disorders. There is a debate over the interpretation of this evidence as there is a strong correlation between severe stress in childhood and stressful life events in adulthood, but some argue this association reflects that childhood traumas induces a vulnerability to the effects of stress later in life.

Most of this research focuses on stresses like the loss of a parent and severe physical abuse at very young ages, so whether this evidence is relevant for typical child labour is an open question. Blattman (2006), for example, considers the psychological impacts of forced abduction into the military among children from northern Uganda, and he finds little evidence of sustained psychological distress after the end of conflict in child combatants relative to non-combatants. Three recent studies consider whether child labour impacts future adult health. Kassouf et al (2001) observe in Brazilian data that individuals who start work earlier have worse self-reported health status as adults. They observe that the younger a person starts working, the greater the probability that the individual reports being ill as an adult. This finding may reflect something about the impact of child labour on child health and how that persists into adulthood, the impact of education on adult health, the impact of income on adult health, or something about the child or adult's environment associated with both youthful work and adult health.

Two papers using Vietnamese panel data employ instrumental variable strategies to consider the effect of working as a child on young adult health outcomes five years later. O'Donnell et al (2002) compare the BMI, selfreported morbidity, and height in 1998 of children who worked in agriculture in 1993 to those that did not. They instrument for a child's participation in agriculture in 1993 with labour market and education conditions in the child's community in 1993. They find that children working in 1993 have higher self-reported morbidity rates in 1998. Using the same data but a different identification strategy and a subset of the sample, Beegle et al (2005) observe similar patterns to O'Donnell et al but the patterns are not statistically significant in Beegle et al.

While O'Donnell et al look at rural children 6-15 in 1993, Beegle et al consider rural children 8-13 who attend school in 1993. Beegle et al also relate self reported health status to variation in total hours worked, using a different source of variation. While the two papers are not directly comparable because of data and identification differences, it is not surprising that there don't appear to be detectable marginal effects of working one additional hour while working vs. not appears to have more substance for long term health. Evidence on specific mechanisms through which child labour might propagate through to adulthood seems to be largely speculative.

4

General Equilibrium Considerations of Child Labour Externalities

The ramifications of a child's working status may extend well beyond the child. First, as the working child is supporting the family and its members, there may benefits to siblings of having a working child. Second, there may be intergenerational implications of a child's labour status, a so-called child labour trap. Third, they may be general equilibrium ramifications of a high prevalence of child labour that merit attention. *Do working children support their siblings?* When most working children are helping in their family, it is very difficult to quantify the economic contribution of working children to the household as their compensation is often not in monetary terms.

Further, concerns about surplus labour or training aspects of the child's contribution to the household complicate distinguishing the child's marginal product from her average product. Nevertheless, efforts to value the child's contribution to family income typically guess it to be substantial. Psacharopoulos (1997) observes that income earned by working Bolivian 13 year olds amounted to 13 percent of total household income on average. Menon et al (2005) attempt to compute the value of child's own farm labour to largely subsistence farm households in rural Nepal. They estimate that children contribute roughly 11 percent of the value of total agriculture production in Nepal or about 9 percent of GDP.

To what extent do siblings benefit from the economic contribution of their siblings? There are several possible mechanisms. In poor households additional income or output, may help maintain the consumption of family members. A number of studies, discussed below, document a role for child labour in how households cope with shocks. Beyond shifting out the budget constraint, working older siblings may provide money that is directed explicitly towards younger siblings. Alternatively, working older siblings may provide additional labour services to the household which lower the productivity of younger siblings, thereby encouraging their education. Direct evidence on the influence of a child's income on the activities of siblings is rare. One often hears assertions, especially in the South and East Asian context, of older sisters working to support their sibling. Parish and Willis (1993) discuss this literature in detail, although they find little support for this hypothesis in Taiwanese data. Instead, they argue that early marriage is a more important channel through which older girls help their siblings.

In contrast, Edmonds (2006b) finds some evidence that older siblings help their siblings through their work. He argues that one possible channel for this support owes to older siblings comparative advantage in working in both market and domestic work. In data from Nepal, he documents that older siblings are more likely to work than younger siblings, and their time allocation depends on the sex composition of younger siblings. In particular, time spent in market working is increasing in the number of younger boys in the household. Edmonds speculates that this additional market work is to help afford schooling and other investment expenditures that younger boys are more apt to command, but he lacks direct evidence of this. Perhaps the most direct evidence of older siblings working to support younger siblings is in Manacorda (2006) who finds strong evidence of externalities towards siblings in early twentieth century U.S. He considers the relationship between a child's school attendance and participation in wage work and the fraction of co-resident children that are active in wage work.

To address the obvious endogeneity concerns in correlating siblings' labour supplies, he uses state variation in the minimum age of employment laws and the age at which work permits become available. That is, consider a 10 year old child with siblings age 14 and 15. Across U.S. states in 1920, there is variation in whether 1, both, or neither sibling can work in the formal wage labour market. Thus, whether the older sibling is able to bring in wage income to the household will vary with the sibling's age and the state of residence. He finds considerable sharing of resources across children. The greater the fraction of siblings who works, the lower the child's own labour supply. Moreover, Manacorda observes a rise in schooling with the fraction of siblings who can work that is about equal to the decline in work and no substantive change in idleness. However, the benefits of having children work appear to largely accrue to children. He does not observe any substantive change in either the labour supply of mothers or fathers as the fraction of working children increases. One important note is that his identification strategy works off variation in wage work that is constrained by child labour laws. Hence, affected families are apt to be those where child income is most needed to support siblings. As such, it might be isolating variation where externalities are largest.

Are working children more likely to have working children? The most obvious mechanisms for intergenerational persistence of child labour are through child labour's impact on education. Barham et al (1995) develop a model where financing for education is obtained from within the family. Hence, low educational attainment leads to lower income leads to lower educational investments in the next generation, an educational poverty trap. Beyond the effects of income, lower parental education might affect child health and nutrition which in turn feeds back to the relative productivity of schooling and work.

Another option is that a parent's own experience growing up affects their attitudes about child labour. In turn, then, work experience at a young age might cause a parent to feel that such work is appropriate. As discussed earlier, several studies document an effect of child labour status on future adult income. Using the same Brazilian data as Ilahi et al (2000) used to examine the effects of child labour on adult income, Emerson and Souza (2003) look at whether the child labour status of a parent affects the child labour status of the child. 17 percent of children whose father began working before age 14 are employed. 6 percent of children are working whose father did not. Mother's child labour status shows similar patterns with differences that are slightly larger in magnitude. Further, this intergenerational correlation in child labour persists even when they control for the educational attainment of both parents and family income. Possible explanations for this include measurement error in both parental education and family income that is correlated with parental child labour status or omitted socio-economic factors that persist over time that would be correlated with past and current child labour supply.

These factors might include local or family labour market conditions, school quality, latent relative talent for work or school, or social norms / parental attitudes that are correlated with child labour status. Lillard and Willis (1994) try to disentangle the reasons why educational attainment is correlated across co-resident generations in Malaysians. They estimate that about two-thirds of the impact of parental education on children's educational attainment is through direct and indirect effects of parental schooling. Omitted factors appear to account for the remaining third. However, more research is necessary to disentangle the mechanisms behind the observed intergenerational transmission of child labour. *Does child labour promote high fertility?* While the long-run implications of high population growth are often debated, a relatively common view is that high fertility rates are a source of long-run poverty traps. Emerson and Knabb (2003) for example is formal theoretical treatment of the idea that higher fertility can create a poverty trap, in their case through child labour: because families expect children to have to work, they have lots of children.

Then because families have lots of children, they need them to work. Do poor families have children in order to put them to work? The "wealth flows" theory of fertility posits that families have children, because they expect positive net transfers from the child, while the "evolutionary" view posits motives such as altruism, genetic survival, the consumption value of children, etc. A necessary condition for the "wealth flows" view is that the net flows from child to parent are positive. A number of studies find a connection between child employment opportunities and fertility. Rosenzweig and Evenson (1977), using data from rural India, find evidence of a connection between the economic contribution of children and fertility, child labour, and schooling decisions. Family attributes positively associated with the pecuniary returns to market work (size of landholdings, farm productivity, child wage rates) are negatively related to schooling and positively related to fertility and market work.

Examining data from the U.S., Rosenzweig (1977) argues that the declining value of children as assets in agriculture is an important factor in declining farm birth rates for post war U.S. A number of accounting studies attempt to directly compute whether the net return to children is large enough to motivate fertility. The most cited evidence from this is from Mead Cain (1977). In a village in north central Bangladesh, he estimates that male children become net producers as early as age 12 and compensate for their own cumulative consumption by age 15. However, whether his findings generalize is an open question. In subsequent work in other Asian countries, Cain (1982) found that the individual earnings of boys exceeded consumption at far older ages, and Kaplan (1994) in data from a forager-horticulturist group in Peru, finds that Cain's observation is not robust to considering a larger basket of consumption goods than Cain examined.

In fact, a more common finding is that it seems unlikely

that parents are repaid all of the costs associated with children. Stekelov (1999) for example finds that the annual rates of return on children in Cote d'Ivoire are between -6 and -10 percent. Two challenges throughout this work, however, are what discount rates to consider and whether and how to value the insurance value of children both as potential laborers in their youth and as sources of old-age security. Together, there appears to be little compelling evidence that variation in child labour opportunities can explain a large portion of the high fertility rates in developing countries. *Does child labour affect local labour markets?* In their seminal study, Basu and Van (1998) point out that if children and adults are substitutes in production (the "substitution axiom"), the prevalence of child labour depresses adult wages. Basu and Van focus on the implications of this depressive effect of child labour on the prevalence of child labour. In particular, they posit what they term the "luxury axiom:" children only work when parental income is below subsistence levels.

With the combination of the luxury and substitution axioms, Basu and Van argue that child labour depresses adult wages which in turn makes child labour necessary. Multiple equilibriums in the labour market are then possible. Because of this study's importance, a slightly more formal presentation is useful. A number of additional assumptions are necessary to keep the present exposition transparent. First, assume that the household consists of one parent and one child. The parent chooses whether the child works. Second, there are N one parent, one child households that may differ in what they perceive as their subsistence needs. Third, parental labour supply is perfectly inelastic. The adult daily wage from working is m. Fourth, when children work, they earn a daily wage of w. Define an indicator c that is 1 if the child works. Finally, all household consumption is financed by adult and child labour. Households do not have assets that may contribute to household income and do not have access to credit markets.

Define as the subsistence level of expenditure, above which parents no longer have children work. The luxury axiom implies that if m>s, children do not work and household income is m. Effective labour supply for a household is 1 when children do not work. If parental income does not cover subsistence (m<=s), children work and household income is m+w. The substitution axiom implies a strong relationship between child and adult wages. Namely, if one child's labour is equivalent to a (a<1) units of adult labour, then the wage children are paid is w=am. Similarly, then, when children work, effective labour supply for a household is 1+a. Market labour supply is then N*(1+a). Market labour supply is the sum of all individual household labour supply functions and is marked ABCD. When daily wages are above the highest subsistence level s H, no children work, and the market labour supply function is defined by the segment AB.

If wages are below the lowest subsistence level s L, all children work. The segment BC is drawn to be downward sloping (rather than the discontinuous horizontal line that each household perceives) to acknowledge that the subsistence level of expenditure *s* may vary across households based on household and community attributes as discussed below. Market equilibrium adult (and thus child) wages are given by the price at which the supply of effective units of labour equals the demand for effective units of child labour. In the depicted equilibrium, labour demand is sufficiently high, that there is no child labour in the economy. Because adult wages are high, no children work. The effective employment in the economy is N and adult wages are indicated by m*. Note that if labour demand is very low (so it intersects labour supply along the CD segment but not along the AB segment), the economy is very poor and all children work. Does the prevalence of child labour depress adult wages?

Evidence which is broadly consistent with the luxury axiom and the substitution axiom will be discussed in greater detail below. However, while this is a critical question in the child labour literature, direct evidence on whether child labour affects adult labour markets is scarce. The reason for a lack of evidence is the joint determination of adult and child wages, especially when the substitution axiom holds. However, it is reasonable to ask how plausible it is that child labour, which is mostly outside of the formal labour wage market, can suppress adult wages. In countries where children form a substantial share of the active labour force, this effect seems more plausible than countries where it does not. First, children are a larger share of the economically active population when their economic activity rates are higher. This could be mechanical if population is independent of economic activity rates. Second, children constitute a very small share of the total economically active population, even in countries where economic activity rates of children are very high.

There are only two countries in the world where children are more than a hundredth of a percent of the economically active population. Is it possible that variation in the activities of less than a hundredth of a percent of the economically active population can influence equilibrium wages in the labour market? Questions such as this are largely unanswered in the literature. If child labour depresses adult wages in the local labour market, then the implications of child labour may extend much further than the working child. Ljungqvist (1992) for example develops a model where the prevalence of unskilled labour suppresses the wage of the uneducated workers relative to the educated. This causes the cost of education to be high relative to the labour earnings of an unskilled worker. Unskilled workers with few assets then choose not to obtain an education, because the marginal utility of foregone consumption during education is greater than the family's valuation of the return to education. Banerjee and Newman (1993) emphasize that depressed wages coupled with capital market imperfections can constrain entrepreneurship, leading to a stagnant, low wage economy. Thus, to the extent that child labour suppresses adult wages, this may have long run implications for growth and development.

DETERMINANTS OF CHILD TIME ALLOCATION

Academic research on the determinants of child time allocation is often categorized as either labour demand or labour supply. Loosely defined, labour demand is typically concerned with the availability of employment whereas labour supply focuses more on questions related to willingness or ability to work. The distinction between the two is often difficult in the context of adult labour in high income economies. Despite the absence of formal tests of the separation hypothesis for child labour, the general assumption among researchers is that distinguishing between demand and supply is especially arbitrary for children in low income countries where most children work with their parents in a family activity.

Take for example, the literature on how household composition influences child labour. On one hand, the presence of younger children may raise the return on child time in domestic activities (labour demand), but on the other hand, younger children may also raise the marginal utility of income and thereby change labour supply. Should this research be classified as labour supply or demand? Nevertheless, this section is organized by mimicking the labour demand and supply dichotomy. The first subsection focuses on what might be considered labour demand. What direct influence do local labour markets have on the activities of children?

This includes evidence on how production technology, environmental factors, the industrial composition of local labour markets, the employer composition of local labour markets, and internal and international trade affects the employment opportunities open to children. The second subsection considers research on family factors that influence the activities of children. This includes research on agency problems, adult and child labour supply interactions, and the interaction of siblings. These factors are easily viewed as both labour demand and supply, and hence merit their own section. The third and fourth subsections consider issues that are typically considered as labour supply. Modern researchers tend to focus that the returns to schooling as the main opportunity cost of work, and surveys the literature on how returns and costs of schooling affect on decisions about how children work. No topic has garnered more attention that the relationship between children labours and poverty, and considers this literature.

LOCAL LABOUR MARKETS AND CHILD TIME ALLOCATION

Most of the work on why children work focuses on why families send their children to work. Comparatively few papers consider child productivity in the family or the wage market. This lack of research reflects that very few children are employed in the formal labour market and that suitable data for examining labour demand in the formal labour market is extremely limited. Most researchers work with household surveys which are generally not suited to modeling the formal employment sector and which will rarely have power to analyze the comparatively rare event of wage employment. Establishment surveys with detailed data on child labour appear to be non-existent.

Production technology

How is child labour influenced by the technology used in production? Put another way; are there certain types of production that are especially apt to draw in working children? Marx argues that a supply of children and women is critical for the early stages of industrialization, because they are both cheap and suited to affine tasks that require little fingers. A similar argument is in Goldin and Sokoloff (1982). With data from early 19th Century U.S., they emphasize that comparative advantage appears to be the explanation for high female and child labour participation rates in early industrialization.

The proportion of the northeastern manufacturing labour force composed of females and young males seems to have grown from about 10 percent at the start of the 19th century to 40 percent by 1932. The low relative productivity of women and children in the North's agriculture sector (hay, dairy, grains) kept the opportunity cost of their labour low relative to that in the South. In fact, Goldin and Sokoloff (1984) argue that this may partially account for why manufacturing industries were disproportionate in the northeast. Because most working children are by their parent's side in the family farm or business, an emphasis on industrialization to explain the high rates of working children around the world is clearly unsatisfactory. Moreover, in a contemporary setting, very few studies even document a link between changes in the activities of children and either the industrial composition of local labour market or the types of employer in a community. Edmonds (2003) is one exception.

Using both cross-section and a household panel in Vietnam, he considers both the association between the activities of children and the types of industries and employers in the child's community. He observes that domestic work is more prevalent and market work less prevalent in locations where handicraft industries are located but observes very little association between the activities of children and variation in other types of industries (over time or between locations) including manufacturing. For type of employer, Edmonds observes that children are less likely to be engaged in market and wage work in locations where state or large private employers are more prevalent, while hours worked is slightly larger in communities with significant small employer presence. However, the endogenous placement of industries and employers is a serious concern and it is not addressed, and his findings cannot be taken as more than suggestive of future avenues for research. Are there tasks that might be important in industrialization that require children for anything other than cheap labour?

The literature on child development suggests possible ways in which children might have an advantage in several activities. Sloutsky et al (2004) showed color pictures of animals for memorization to a small number children around age 5 and young adults around 20. Children appear more effective at memorization of details because of differences in their approach to memorization. The young adults memorized by categorizing the animals whereas the children appeared to memorize by comparing each new animal to a reference animal. When the experimenters asked the young children to categorize animals for memorization, their performance deteriorated. Other work has found that children perform better than young adults in comparing visual objects and in drawing spatial analogies. Studies that compare young adults to older individuals suggest that the tendency towards categorization and thereby false analogy grows stronger with age. Research like this might imply that children would have an advantage at detailed work requiring pattern memorization such as carpet weaving or knitting.

The most detailed case-study we have on child productivity in manufacturing focuses explicitly on an industry where these developmental advantages should be most important: the hand-knitted carpet industry. Levison et al (1998) find little empirical support for the "nimble fingers" view. Adults and children tend to work on the same types of carpets and that children are 21 percent less productive in hand-knitting than adults (productivity is measured in square inches knit per hour). This case seems consistent with the overwhelming empirical fact about child labour in today's developing countries: formal sector wage employment of children is extremely rare. If children were critical for the early stage of industrialization, then its low prevalence would be a surprise. That said, our understanding of labour demand would clearly benefit from additional work like Levison et al (1998). While it is unclear whether there are activities for which children have an absolute advantage in, there must be activities in which children have a comparative advantage.

It is this comparative advantage that Goldin and Sokoloff appeal to in order to explain north-south differences in the employment of women. When the return to these activities in which children have comparative advantage is high relative to other uses of child time, we expect children to work everything else equal. Interestingly, Galbi (1997) argues that the nature of the child's comparative advantage in early English cotton mills was that adult laborers did not know how to be factory workers. In fact, he argues, that children were replaced in English cotton mills when the children became adults, trained and socialized for factory work. Collection activities are often mentioned as activities where children will have comparative advantage. For example, Nankhuni and Findeis (2004) note that children in deforested areas of Malawi spend significantly more time collecting wood for fuel than do children in less deforested areas, and this collection time is associated with reduced schooling participation.

Several studies document a connection between variation in access to water facilities and child schooling. For example, Psacharopoulos and Arriagada (1989) find that schooling is higher in Brazilian households with piped water; Cockburn and Dostie (forthcoming) note that work time is lower and schooling higher in Ethiopian households with better access to water; and Guarcello and Lyon (2002) observe in Yemen that households connected to a water network are more likely to send their children to school and less likely to report their children as idle. While these studies do not address the non-random nature of water access, they are suggestive of how important the return to child time in activities other than schooling can be for child time allocation. Several recent studies note that children work more in households with more self-employment activities, and Wydick (1999) notes a correlation between work and household involvement in a micro credit program.

For example, using detailed time use data from Botswana, Mueller (1984) documents that the more productive capital the household has, the more productive work its children perform. Using Mueller's data from Botswana, Chernichovsky (1985) observes that this association between market work inside the household and the presence of productive capital varies depending on whether substitutes for child labour are present in the household. Cockburn and Dostie (forthcoming) go into further detail in Ethiopian data. He notes that small livestock and land appear to be market work increasing whereas oxen, bulls, ploughs, land quality, and again, proximity to water are child labour decreasing. Shafiq (2006b) points out that, while greater assets may lead children to report working more because of the availability of employment opportunities, the human capital ramifications of this are unclear. In his data from Bangladesh, children work more in the presence of productive assets, but they are also more likely to attend school.

Some closely related evidence also illustrates how technology changes that replace the types of activities typically done by children can alter schooling and the activities of children. For example, Brown et al (1992) documents technological changes in the U.S. Fruit and Vegetable canning industry that lead to a shift to adult labour. Levy (1985) shows a relationship between the mechanization of Egyptian agriculture and the decline of child labour in cotton. Two important technologies he emphasizes are the spread of tractors and irrigation pumps. Dessy and Pallage (2005) emphasize the importance of technology in child labour formally in arguing that one way to view child labour is as the result of a coordination failure between parents and firms investing in skill intensive technologies.

Technology changes can also affect child time outside of the formal wage labour market. Fafchamps and Shilpi (2004) observe that in Nepali data, there appears to be greater household specialization as proximity to urban areas increases, and Fafchamps and Wahba (2006) argue that children are more likely to attend school and not work as specialization increases with urban proximity. Interestingly, they note that while work in the household is reduced with urban proximity, there is a rise in child labour outside of the household although it is not enough to offset the total decline in hours worked.

Trade

One frequently reads popular anecdotes about children working in export industries, and it is often asserted that the ability to trade with high income countries causes children in developing countries to work. Put another way, this argument implies that trade creates work opportunities for children that would otherwise not be present. Maskus (1997) is a formal presentation of this idea. In his model, the poor country produces an export good that is labour intensive and an import-competing, capital intensive good. The export sector subcontracts to the informal sector which employs children.

The demand for child labour then depends on product demand for the export good. An expansion of the export sector then increases child labour through higher equilibrium child wages. A number of studies have examined data on cross-country trade flows to consider whether there is any evidence of a link between trade and child labour in aggregate statistics. They typically document a negative correlation between child labour and openness which is defined as the sum of exports and imports as a share of GDP. Edmonds and Pavcnik (2006a) is one such study that explicitly attempts to account for the endogeneity of openness. They instrument for openness with trade based on geography. The main identification assumption in this approach is that trade which is driven by geography does not affect working children except in its impact on total trade flows. They also observe that economic activity rates for children are lower in countries that trade more.

Moreover, addressing the endogeneity of trade nearly doubles the magnitude of the elasticity of child economic activity rates with respect to openness. What explains why children work less in countries that trade more? Edmonds and Pavcnik find that the negative association between openness and economic activity rates mostly reflects the well documented positive link between trade and income. Once they condition on a country's income, they find a very small and statistically insignificant relationship between trade and child labour. This result holds in the full sample, when they split the sample into different country groups, consider only trade between high and low income countries, or focus on exports of unskilled-labour intensive products from low income countries. Thus, the cross-country data provide no support for the claim that trade perpetuates high levels of child labour in poor countries via the labour demand channel. Given that most children work in agriculture and family businesses, it is perhaps unsurprising that there is no evidence of a labour demand effect on economic activity rates through trade in the cross-country data.

More detailed industry or within country data on changes in industrial employment with growing trade is promising for shedding more light on how international markets might affect the activities of children. Edmonds and Pavcnik (2005b) examine the relationship between market work, domestic work, and trade using panel data on rural Vietnamese households. Vietnam liberalized its rice export quota during the 1990s and lifted restrictions on trade in rice across Vietnamese regions. Subsequently, from 1993 to 1998 the price of rice increased on average by almost 30 percent relative to the consumer price index, and rice price changes varied widely across communities of Vietnam. Edmonds and Pavcnik relate market work participation to regional and intertemporal variation in rice prices. Despite the growth in labour demand associated with a booming rice sector, they find that market work and domestic work decrease by more in communities that experience greater increases in rice prices. The declines in working children are greatest in households that were net rice producers prior to market reform.

Part of this decline in work owes to an income effect, but part also owes to a rise in household specialization that Edmonds and Pavcnik (2006b) document in the context of these rice trade liberalizations. Land and labour are the two primary inputs into rice production, and overall both are sufficiently equally distributed in Vietnam that most households are well positioned to enjoy the additional income stemming from this trade liberalization. Of course, it is possible that a growth in trade could have opposite effects when the income gains are not distributed to those whose employment opportunities are rising. For example, Kruger (2004) observes that during the coffee boom of the mid-1990s in Nicaragua, there is an overall increase in market work that is especially large in poor households in coffee producing areas. Her findings mirrors what Alessie et al (1992) observed with cash crop price increases in Cote d'Ivoire: increases in cash crop prices are associated with more children working in the cultivation of those crops.

One explanation for Kruger's findings is that because of the concentration of land in coffee (and the resulting market power in local labour markets), poor laborers have received increases in income that are minor compared to the growth in labour demand, and hence market work has increased. Another interpretation of these findings is emphasized in Kruger's (2007) study of the coffee boom's effects on working children in Brazil. In that context, she emphasizes that when booms are expected to be transitory, households should seize temporary employment opportunities, especially if it is easy to make up for lost schooling time in the future. Her findings are then consistent with evidence of delaying schooling or temporary withdrawals from school in response to macroeconomic crisis. In the Vietnam rice price case, much of the affected population is exiting poverty while such improvements in living standards are not evident in Kruger's coffee data. Edmonds, Pavcnik, and Topalova (2007) look at the connection between trade policy, child labour, and poverty directly in their study of schooling and child labour responses to India's trade reform in 1991.

They observe that children who were in areas with a concentration of heavily protected industries prior to liberalization are more impacted by tariff cuts. They do not experience the same increases in schooling and declines in work without schooling evident elsewhere in India over the 1990s. This pattern of rising work without schooling and declining schooling relative to the national trend does not appear to be explainable with falling returns to schooling (they appear to be increasing) or rising unskilled wages (which appear to be falling). Rather, they reflect the relative rise in poverty in areas that experience a larger decline in protection. Further, they argue that the avoidance of schooling costs lies behind this trade policy–child labour- schooling connection. This combination of micro-studies emphasizes how multidimensional the interaction of trade and child labour can be and that the effects of international trade on the working status of children will be context specific.

CHILD LABOUR AND THE FAMILY

Unitary models of the household are typically used in the child labour literature. The model is one example with its single decision-maker. Implicit within these is an assumption of either unanimity of preferences within the family or a dictatorial household. Typically, parents are viewed as the primary decision-makers for child labour supply and schooling. This raises the classic parental agency problem. While parents may make child labour decisions, they do not fully internalize the costs of these decisions. Moreover, this assumption that parents make child labour decisions has led many to assert that child labour supply is evidence of parental callousness and indifference to their children. Specifically, if parents make decisions about child labour supply and do not consider either the current or future welfare in so-doing, then they will select higher levels of child labour than the child would choose or than governments would consider socially optimal. "Nimble Fingers" theories of child labour take this parental agency problem to an extreme.

They posit that parents always take advantage of employment opportunities open to children and therefore that labour demand is the dominant determinant of whether and how children work. In recent years, more attention has been paid to the fact that there is typically not one decision-maker in the household, and empirical studies uniformly reject the unitary household model. Decisions about child time allocation will be influenced by mothers, fathers, extended family, and perhaps even children themselves. Edmonds and Sharma (2006) consider an extreme example of how child time allocation can be affected by multiple decision-makers. In studying a population in Western Nepal with a high intrinsic risk of bondage, they argue that child labour is increased and schooling reduced in part, because parents, children, or bondholders have security over the returns to investments in children. They argue their case can be read as an extreme representation of the classic parental agency problem.

Several recent studies examine deviations from the unitary household model in more conventional situations. A common question is how parental characteristics affect the activities of children. Emerson and Souza (2007) for example observe that the elasticity of child labour supply with respect to parental education is greater for fathers than mothers and that it is more important for the son's labour supply than the daughter's. Whether this reflects something intrinsic to education, relative earnings ability, actual incomes, type of occupation, or some omitted geographic characteristic correlated with child labour and schooling decisions is outside the scope of the study. A perennial difficulty in tests of the unitary household model is to find characteristics that are associated with variation in the influence of different family members but that do not simultaneously affect child labour and schooling decisions, but Emerson and Souza's findings are suggestive that researchers may observe patterns in child labour that is consistent with what other studies of intrahousehold allocation have found.

Similar findings for education are surveyed in Strauss and Thomas (1995), and they argue that the evidence strongly supports effects of parental education that go beyond the effect of education on income. Basu (2006) considers how the status of women in the household affects child labour supply. In his model, both mothers and fathers dislike sending their children to work, but they differ in their preferences over consumption goods. As female status improves, the family opts for less child labour, because it becomes increasingly difficult to agree on other decisions over which there is disagreement. However, as women's status improves and she becomes dominant in the household, child labour may rise as she can exert more influence over consumption choices in other goods. For example, suppose that utility depends on the child's labour status and consumption of two different goods.

Additional consumption of good 1 does not improve the woman's utility, and additional consumption of good 2 does not benefit the man (but it does the woman). Thus, as female power increases in the household, first the family shifts to less child labour, then it shifts to more good 2 consumption and more child labour. Thus, the relationship between child labour and female power in the household is predicted to be a U-shape. Basu and Ray (2002) examine this in household survey data from Nepal. The maximal female education in the household as a share of sum of the maximal female and male education in the household proxies female power. The Nepali data are consistent with this inverted U-shape hypothesis. Comparatively little attention has been directed to the child's own role in child time allocation decisions. The focus on parents is driven by the observation that parents have comparatively more power within the household than do children.

The fact that most working children are employed within the household in activities that are apt to confer little in the way of status or economic independence seems consistent with this view. Moreover, work is typically considered in tandem with schooling, and schooling is expensive in ways that may require the parents to finance it. If children cannot pay for alternatives to work, then parents necessarily influence child labour supply. However, there is some evidence that suggests that when opportunities outside of the household are open to children, they may be able to influence household decision making. Moehling (2005) is perhaps the most compelling direct evidence on the ability of working children to influence household decision-making. She examines data from the U.S. collected between 1917 and 1919. She observes that the share of total household expenditures on child goods is increasing in the children's contribution to household income.

Unless the child's work demands this expenditure, it is hard to understand why more income to children increases spending on child goods more so than other types of income without some impact of child's income on family decision-making. Interestingly, Moehling (2006) notes that despite the fact that young children typically turned over their entire pay envelope to their parents, it still seems to be treated differently than other sources of income although her results for younger children may reflect something about the younger children's requirements for work. Basu (2006) also points out that there may be a cycle of power in the household. As children work, their ability to influence household activities increases, and thus they may choose to work more. How important is the child's role in deciding her own labour supply? If she can influence household decision-making by working, it seems the potential is large. However, very little research has considered the child's own role in deciding her own labour supply or schooling. One suggestive piece of evidence is from Iverson (2002).

He interviews child migrants in one location in a rural South Indian district about why they migrated and the extent to which they have contact with parents. He reports that the labour supply of young children and girl migrants seem to be largely determined by parents. However, boys who start working at ages 13 and above, report little contact with parents which may reflect that they are working by their own choice. Iverson speculates that autonomy is an important motivation for this group's migration decision; these early teen migrants may have migrated and work in order to have greater control over their lives. The implications of some child influence over their time allocation can be very important for interpreting evidence that purports to show a link between the labour market opportunities of children and child labour supply. This evidence is often interpreted as parental callousness about the welfare of their children or indifference to education. However, it may reflect more about the child's own valuation of their time.

In particular, if children are myopic relative to adults, they may respond more to changes in their employment opportunities than parents. If this is the case, there may be relatively little scope for anti-poverty policies, etc., to affect the labour supply of this group. Future research understanding the child's own role in her time allocation is perhaps the most pressing need in the child labour literature.

PARENTAL ATTITUDES TOWARDS WORK AND SCHOOLING

One of the key reasons why child labour is viewed as a human rights issue is that parents likely have considerable influence over child time allocation. They may capture many of the benefits of child work while not personally bearing the costs (except in as much as they internalize the child's welfare). As discussed above, it is unclear how important child and parental agency are in child time allocation, but to the extent that parents have influence (especially over young children), then parental attitudes towards work are of potentially great importance. Accusations of parental callousness towards their children and disregard of the costs of work abound in the policy debate and in the academic literature.

The focus of the anti-child labour campaigns in the Progressive Era of the United States was largely on changing parental attitudes towards work. Zelizer (1985) emphasizes the important role changing attitudes towards children played in the changes in schooling and work in the U.S. during the later half of the nineteenth, first part of the twentieth century. Analogous campaigns to stigmatize work for children are pervasive in many developing countries today. There is ample basis for this focus on norms in the treatment of children in qualitative work on child labour and schooling decisions. For example, the Public Report on Basic Education in India (1999) found that 37 percent of parents listed a lack of parental interest in educating their children as an explanation for why boys had never enrolled in school.

However, it is very difficult to disentangle cause and effect in studies of child labour and parental attitudes towards work and school, and statements about motives are often a challenge to interpret. There are a few approaches taken in the econometrics literature to study the influence of parental attitudes on work decisions. One approach is to look at correlations between the parent's background and the child's activities. This evidence has already arisen, obviously attitudes towards work are only one component of how parental background can influence child time allocation. A second approach is to look at some measure of parental attitudes or gender bias within the household and correlate these with child time allocation. These studies are surprisingly rare, perhaps because of the challenge of capturing variation in attitudes or gender bias that is not simultaneous with other factors influencing child work. A third approach is to correlate community average behaviors with an individual household's schooling or work decisions.

The hope is that the community mean reflects local values and not anything else about the community. In reality, the econometric challenges presented by this approach are insurmountable. Several studies assert that regression residuals capture social norms or parental attitudes for child labour decisions. This is strange. By construction, in linear regressions, residuals are mean zero and orthogonal to included covariates. However, it seems unlikely that norms and attitudes towards work have no influence on work decisions on average or that these beliefs would be orthogonal to observable household characteristics. Moreover, regression residuals will be influenced by misspecification of the model, mismeasurement of any included covariates, and the researcher's subjective choice about what covariates to include in the estimated models.

Perhaps the most frequently cited evidence directly on parental attitudes towards child labour is Parsons and Goldin (1989). They consider the association between savings and child wage labour supply among industrial families in the U.S. in the late nineteenth century. They note that the marginal propensity to save out of child income is significantly less than 1 and that there is a positive correlation between asset levels and child labour income. In both cases, child income appears to be treated like adult income in the household. Moreover, Parsons and Goldin observe that child income appears to have little effect on total family income.

Each dollar of child income implies a 9/10 reduction in male household head income. They hypothesize that this reflects family migration toward areas with better child labour opportunities that comes at the expense of adult income. Indeed, Parson and Goldin paint a bleak picture of how parents allocate the time of their children. They write: "These working-class families apparently sold the schooling and potential future earnings of their offspring very cheaply". There are, however, several difficulties with this interpretation of the patterns observed by Parsons and

Goldin. In particular, the source of variation in child income is unclear in their data. Suppose, for example, that parents are altruistic towards their children and only have children work when it is critical to meet basic needs.

In that case, we would expect to observe lower adult earnings as child labour earnings are higher, but the causality runs from adult earnings to child earnings. In this case, child income is compensating for the loss of adult income, so the marginal propensity to save or spend should be similar for each. With imperfect insurance markets, part of the family's basic needs must include a saving component to help cope with future shocks. Hence, the marginal propensity to save out of income is likely to be above 0. The positive correlation between child income and asset accumulation is more of a puzzle, albeit one that can be explained in several ways. It may reflect the same concerns as savings (and may be the instrument for savings); it may reflect the indivisibility of fixed schooling costs (school costs tend to need to be paid on irregular intervals like the start of the school year); or it may reflect a latent correlation between the degree of economic activity in an area and the activities of children.

Recall, that even perfectly altruistic parents send their children to work when the relative returns are highest. Hence, it is very difficult to draw concrete conclusions about the callousness of parents in this data. Future studies of norms or attitudes towards child labour and schooling would be better served in trying to codify or measure such attributes directly. In general, the role attitudes and norms play in child labour is poorly understood. It is clear that child time allocation is in general elastic with respect to the household's economic environment, but it is not clear whether this elasticity is bounded by social attitudes towards work, whether there are some children who are especially vulnerable in this regard, and whether this elasticity reflects changing norms or if norms are just one component of how child time allocation decisions are made. Ultimately, the interest in parental norms is most acute for its implications for the design of policy, and it is unfortunate that so little work has been done to study how policy efforts to change attitudes towards work have influenced child time allocation decisions.

Child and Adult Labour Supply Interactions

Most working children work inside their home. There are several explanations for this. Parents may prefer to have children at home to better monitor their working conditions or simply, because they enjoy their proximity. There may be strong norms against child work outside of the house-hold which lowers the perceived return from having a child work outside of their home. Children may also be more productive workers at home. Parents may be more effective at monitoring or disciplining children. Moral hazard problems may be especially acute with children who may not perceive or care about threats of social sanction outside of the household. There is a literature on the activities of children in family run businesses in developed economies that emphasizes the productivity of children relative to hired in labour. Sanders and Nee (1996) for example consider the role of children within the self-employed immigrant families in the U.S.

They emphasize the importance of child labour within these families because it is both very reliable and continuous over time in comparison to other sources of labour. In her study of Chinese take-out businesses, Song (1999) emphasizes the work of children as translators and mediators in these businesses. Parents rely on their English language skills for assistance and guidance, often freeing the parent for oversight duties of hired in help. Song also emphasizes that parents often prefer family labour, because typically there is not much privacy in the work environment that often starts in the family home. For children to work within their own household there must be a sufficient amount of economic activity and working capital within the household. Hence, many observers emphasize a positive correlation between family asset holdings and work inside the household. When children work outside of their household, there appears to be a strong association between the types of work they do and that of their parents.

Parents may prefer their children to work with them, be more effective at affecting high levels of effort, have better information about job opportunities open to children, and there may be geographic clustering in the types of activities performed. Genicot (2005) also emphasizes nutritional spillovers to children from adult earnings as an explanation for the association between child and adult work. She considers (theoretically) a setting were an employer elects to pay a higher wage to enhance his employee's nutritional status. The worker spends a portion of this higher wage on his child, enhancing the child's productivity. The employer then prefers to hire the child in addition to the parent in order to capture all of this externality. Some of the strongest evidence of complementarities between parent and child in the type of wage work performed comes from U.S. history.

For example, Goldin and Parsons (1981) find that the median schooling of males whose fathers were employed in textiles (where child labour was also prevalent) was 3.3 years less than those whose fathers were not, even controlling for parental income differences. Goldin (1979) observes positive elasticities of male and female child labour supply with respect to the father's wage in nineteenth century Philadelphia, but she does not see this pattern in mother's labour supply. From this, she infers that children (rather than wives) were the most common source of labour income apart from the male head of household. However, in a contemporary setting, there is much more evidence of same sex substitution patterns with respect to adult female labour supply. For example, Skoufias (1993) observes a negative correlation between adult female wages and wage child labour. He theorizes that this connection is driven by children filling in for absent mothers in the households and thereby reducing their work outside of the household (although an income effect is hard to rule out in his case). Wahba (2006) observes that wage work is less frequent for boys in the parts of Egypt where unskilled wages are greater. She emphasizes an income effect explanation.

Further, Katz (1995) and Hazarika and Sarangi (2005) observe increases in girl domestic work as mothers become more involved in home enterprises or microcredit programs. Katz (1995) speculates that the availability of an older girl to substitute for the mother in domestic work could act as a binding constraint on female labour supply in her data from Guatemala. Adult–child substitution patterns can be affected by changes in the returns to activities in which adults or children have comparative advantage. For example, Field (2003) examines how patterns of child and adult time allocation change when Peruvian squatters receive secure titles to their land. She finds that children work less outside of their household when titled and that adults work more outside of the household. Her evidence does not seem to suggest that this is an income effect as their does not appear to be an identifiable income effect of titling.

Instead, she argues that adults have comparative advantage in providing security for their property. Hence with insecure property rights, children work away from home, but adults are freed to work away with titling. Thus, there is support in the empirical literature for both complementarities in wage labour supply and substitution possibilities between child and adult labour depending on the economic environment. *Does parental co-residence influence child labour?* There are many ways that parents might influence child labour supply aside from either complementarities or substitution patterns in child labour. The absence of a parent might either attenuate the employment options open to children or accentuate the need for children to fill in for the parent's work. It is worth noting that these two issues work in opposite directions and are most likely to affect different types of work. Thus, the relationship between child and adult work can be very sensitive to the types of activities considered.

Beyond substitution patterns, the absence of a parent is likely associated with variation in family income (although the direction of this variation is unclear). There is a separate concern from biology that parents might have differential investment incentives in their genetic offspring. This can be modeled by allowing child investment incentives to vary with the biological relationship. Moehling (2004) considers the association between family structure and child labour and schooling in the American South at the start of the twentieth century. Living apart from one or both parents is associated with lower school attendance and greater market work participation, especially for black children. She is careful to note that the variation in child labour and schooling for American blacks that is attributable to variation in living arrangements is small compared to parental literacy, household resources, and school characteristics.

Interest in the relationship between parental coresidence and investments in children has risen significantly in recent years, because of the AIDS crisis in sub-Saharan Africa. Most existing studies find that orphan hood is associated with reduced schooling enrollment. Two approaches are common in the literature. First, many studies compare children living within the same household who differ in whether they have had a parent die. Case, Paxson, and Ableidinger (2004) exemplify this household fixed effects approach in their study of orphan hood and school enrollment in 10 Sub-Saharan Africa countries using data from demographic and health surveys. They find that orphans are less likely to attend school than the non-orphans with whom they live. These within household (household fixed effects) comparisons are complicated by the fact that the orphans and non-orphans likely come from different backgrounds and certainly differ in one important experience: the loss of a parent.

A second approach to study the relationship between schooling and parental death is to use individual level panel data that follow children over time. Evans and Miguel (2005) is one such study. In a panel of 20,000 rural Kenyan children, they find a substantial decrease in participation in school following a parental death and some decline prior to the death. Beegle, De Weerdt, and Dercon (2006) follow a smaller sample of children from the Kagera region of Tanzania for over 10 years, and find substantive, sustained declines in educational attainment and height associated with parental mortality. The effects of parental death on child work are less clear. There does not appear to be any individual level panel studies on orphanhood with detail on child work. Guarcello and co-authors (2004) use some of the same demographic and health survey data as Case, Paxson, and Ableidinger (2004) from sub-Saharan Africa and cannot draw generalities about correlations between parental death and various forms of work.

Throughout this literature, a chronic problem is how to separate different mechanisms for the impact of parental death from the non-random nature of deaths. Are children withdrawing from school to work to substitute for lost parental wages, to fill in for the parent's role in the household? Alternatively, is withdrawal a trauma effect of the loss of a parent? Studying child time allocation seems to be a promising way to better understand the schooling -orphan hood connection, and it is likely to be of interest in its own right. *How does sibling composition affect child labour?* A number of studies document a positive correlation between family size and child labour. This correlation is generally viewed as suggestive of resource and credit constraints on child time allocation. Family size may also influence the shadow value of child time when there are tasks for which it is difficult to hire in help. Many researchers have attempted to better understand why children work by looking inside the household to see how sibling composition affects child labour and schooling.

The reason for this attention is that by looking at differences in how parents treat children, many believe it might be possible to infer the influence of parental preferences in child labour and schooling decisions, although it is not obvious how we can learn about preferences from sibling differences in child labour. Studies typically look at birth order, sibling sex composition, or birth spacing. There are a variety of mechanisms through which birth order may affect investments in children. They can be roughly categorized as mechanisms owing to parent's age, socialization, or resource constraints. Higher birth order children will have older parents who may be wealthier, more experienced at raising children or feel more altruistic but they also face a higher risk of birth defects and twinning. Lower birth order children grow up in a more adult environment, have the experience of teaching their siblings, but have comparative advantage to younger siblings in the wage labour market and in household production.

Higher birth order children grow up in households with more competition for scarce resources such as income and parental time, the present value of returns on investment may be lower because of longer time horizons until the market realization of these returns, or they may benefit from sibling transfers. Ejrnaes and Portner (2004) argue that birth order (conditional on household size) reveals something about the child's latent genetic talent, because they argue that the probability the family stops having children is increasing in the child's ability relative to the family's expectation. While a number of studies document an association between birth order and child labour or schooling, few studies attempt to distinguish a mechanism. Emerson and Souza (2002) observe in Brazil that older boys and girls are more likely to work and less likely to attend school than their younger siblings.

They point out that this could be of credit constraints - older children might be working because poor families are unable to borrow to finance education. Edmonds (2006b) observes similar patterns in Nepal and argues that they may also owe to differences in comparative advantage in household production. He cannot exclude a preference or credit constraints based explanation, but he observes that sibling differences in total hours worked are largest in household production, and that the oldest girls especially spend more time working in domestic work when there are more younger siblings. Parish and Willis (1993) emphasize a similar supportive role of the oldest girl in Taiwanese households. She helps with the schooling outcomes of their younger children by caring for younger children and by bringing in income through wage employment that helps with school fees and allows later entry into the labour force for younger siblings. However, Parish and Willis argue that her most important contribution to the household comes through leaving early and marrying. Two studies stand out in their ability to identify specific mechanisms through which birth order is correlated with child labour and schooling.

First, Manacorda (2006) finds that children are less likely to work when they have older siblings and are in U.S. states where those older siblings can work. Second, Birdsall (1991) emphasizes the importance of constraints on time in generating birth order effects. In data from urban Columbia, she shows that education is lower for later born children. She argues that this is inconsistent with what would expect to see with credit constraints where older children should support younger children. Moreover, she observes that birth order effects are less likely among working mothers in urban Columbia. She argues that this reflects that time can be traded for money in the market so that working mothers can shift in and out of the labour force to keep the shadow value of time equal in all periods. The sibling sex composition literature tends to emphasize sibling rivalry, peer effects, or sex-typing to explain sibling sex composition effects on child labour and schooling.

The sibling rivalry idea is that everything else equal, the child is better off with more siblings who are comparatively less valued in terms of preferences, market opportunities, social status, etc. For this to hold there needs to be some type of a constraint on credit, transfers, labour markets, or household production that cause household investment decisions to depend on the sex composition of children in the household or parental preferences have to vary across children. Peer effects work through the influence of the sex composition of siblings on the family environment. A more masculine environment, for example, may influence a girl's social interactions in the world. Sex-typing occurs when there are certain tasks that are stereotypically male or female but a child goes against type because of the absence of an appropriately gendered individual to carry out the task in the household. For example, a boy raised in a household without girls may engage in tasks that are more typically female in a household.

Peer effects and sex-typing of tasks have drawn the most attention in the developed economy context, but for developing economies, many writers have emphasized sibling rivalry. Parish and Willis (1993) for example emphasize in Taiwan that it is the support available from having an older sister that is critical for schooling. While Parish and Willis focus on the oldest sister, Edmonds (2006b) observes in Nepali data that the probability younger boys and girls work is declining in the number of older sisters. Morduch (2000) finds that moving from all brothers to all sisters raises completed schooling by nearly half a year in Tanzania. Similar patterns are documented in Garg and Morduch (1998) for Ghana, but the result is not as general as Morduch (2000) observes no such pattern in South Africa. Whether sibling rivalry is more intense between sexes or within sex groups may vary across cultures. In Malaysian data, for example, Lillard and Willis (1994) observe that siblings of the same sex appear to be rivals in attracting investment of resources from their parents in the sense that female education is reduced by more girls present, boys by more boys. Much of the attention in the child labour literature has been on sibling sex composition or birth order.

Comparatively little attention has been devoted to issues of birth-spacing. Implicitly, many of the mechanisms for birth order effects on child labour are actually working through spacing. For example, two children close in age are more apt to be seen as substitutes in household production, work, or schooling opportunities. Likewise, the probability of receiving substantive support from an older sibling is likely to increase with the age gap between siblings. While there is some suggestive evidence in Edmonds (2006b) that sibling sex differences in activities are more pronounced when age gaps are small, more research on the implication of birth spacing for child labour and schooling is needed. Several empirical problems plague most of the research into how sibling structure effects investments in children. First, births are typically unobserved. Rather, only co-resident children are observed. This could easily be resolved by surveys that collect complete fertility histories or details about non-resident siblings, but in practice, this appears rare in surveys with detailed child labour data.

Second, household composition is typically endogenous to the household's economic environment (and thereby labour supply) through fostering, mortality, marriage, migration, etc. Akresh (2004) for example emphasizes how important fostering can be to a family's risk management strategy. Third, when households include extended families or when polygamy is prevalent, it may be impossible to even establish resident sibling relationships. Fourth, fertility is endogenous to factors influencing child labour supply. Sex composition may reflect parental preferences about the type of children they would like to have. Birth order, for example, cannot be separated from factors influencing fertility or from household size as higher order birth orders can only be observed in larger house-holds. Several authors address this later problem with specifications that compares birth order effects within household size groupings. However, the empirical challenges dealing with these issues are considerable.

An additional issue is whether to include household fixed effects in the analysis. On the positive side, this controls for common household factors such as current employment opportunities inside and outside the household, parental attitudes that may be correlated with sibling size, and other child invariant characteristics. However, this approach will limit the analysis to children with siblings; exaggerate sibling differences when they are relatively small, and may not address most omitted variable concerns as the effects of factors such as local labour market opportunities or household endowments may vary with age and thereby birth order, age spacing, or sibling sex composition. To the extent controlling for household fixed effects expand within sibling differences, they may make controlling for differences in factors associated with age more difficult. Similarly, within household differences in sibling composition owe to differences in the sex of the child or differences in parents.

Both of which create estimation problems. Hence, while household fixed effects can be useful, they are often viewed incorrectly as a solution to most of the empirical problems that plague the empirical analysis of sibling differences in child labour.

CHILD LABOUR AND THE (NET) RETURN TO SCHOOLING

In the developed country context, a number of authors have emphasized that work is not the main opportunity cost of schooling; rather, foregone leisure is. In the developing country context, researchers tend to view work as the main opportunity cost of schooling. If so, there should be a close connection between work and the relative return to schooling. This section surveys the evidence on a link between the measured or proxied return to schooling and child labour. Note that in the model, it is the relative return to education that matters for child labour supply.

Thus, time allocation between wage work and school depends on the local wage, the marginal utility of income, and the net return to schooling. The net return to schooling is the difference between the marginal utility associated with any future returns to education and the foregone consumption schooling costs require. A major consideration in the literature on the returns to schooling and child labour is what factors could lead to a situation where the returns to schooling do not affect child labour.

A lack of parental altruism or credit constraints are the two most frequently cited explanations. We have considered altruism. Here, we discuss credit constraints.

Credit Constraints and Child Labour

Most recent studies of credit constraints and child labour are based on the theoretical work of Baland and Robinson (BR 2000). BR is a variant on the Ben-Porath model that emphasizes child labour explicitly. BR has a single household decision-maker (a parent) who decides child labour and schooling decisions after making other household income decisions. The parent lives two periods. In the first period, the parent chooses savings *s* and the fraction of child time spent working, *h*. *m* is the household's income each period. Wages from working are normalized to 1.

However, if bequests are zero, then the return to notworking is greater than the household's cost of not having the child work, and child labour is inefficiently high. Without bequests, children cannot compensate parents for the foregone consumption that comes from decreasing child labour. Likewise, if savings are zero, then, the household's marginal utility of consumption in the first period is greater than the marginal utility the household attains from increasing child well-being, and child labour is inefficiently high. Evidence directly on whether credit constraints influence child labour and schooling is relatively rare, because of the difficulty of disentangling credit constraints from other market imperfections. For example, a number of studies that will be discussed below consider the association between child labour and crop shocks, but they cannot in general separate insurance failures from changes in the relative returns to work or from credit constraints.

There is some suggestive evidence at the cross-country level. Jafarey and Lahiri (2001) emphasize that borrowing constraints in the aggregate should decline as access to international credit markets increase and that this in turn should mitigate the need for children to work. Dehejia and Gatti (2002) consider the link between formal financial development and child labour in aggregate cross-country data. They measure credit constraints by the ratio of private credit issued by deposit-money banks to GDP, and call this "financial development." They find that financial development is negatively correlated with economic activity rates. In particular, a move from the 25th to 75th percentile of financial development among low income countries is associated with a 17 percent decline in the economic activity rates of children 10-14.

The BR model and other theoretical writings on child

labour and credit constraints tend to emphasize the inability of families to borrow against the future returns to child education. Testing for constraints on intergenerational transfers or long-term borrowing is generally not feasible in existing datasets. However, if households are not able to move resources over relatively short (and potentially measurable) time horizons, then it seems unlikely that they should be able to move resources over the long-term. Micro-studies of household responses to crop-shocks have attempted to look at credit constraints to see whether there is a correlation between household assets and responses to shocks. Unfortunately, isolating the credit channel in this way seems infeasible given the correlation between household assets and the value of child time in a setting when most children work at home.

An alternative approach is to consider household responses to anticipated changes in their economic environment. For example, Edmonds (2006a) examines the response of schooling and market work to the timing of anticipated income in the context of the social pension program in South Africa. The end of apartheid in South Africa brought the extension of the white social pension program to black South Africans. The pensions are large (125 percent of median black per capita income in 1999), highly anticipated, and primarily determined by age in the elder black population. Edmonds compares market work and schooling in families about to receive a fully anticipatable social pension income to market work and schooling in families already receiving the income. The average rural South African child living with an elder that is not yet pension eligible spends 3 hours per day working. In the data, pension income to an elder male is associated with over an hour less work per day.

These declines in hours worked occur simultaneously with increases in school attendance (to nearly 100 percent for rural boys). These changes in hours worked and schooling with male pension eligibility lead to levels of work and schooling that are similar to what the data report for nearly eligible elder women. Hence, his results suggest a role for credit constraints, but only for elder men. Moreover, unlike the data above that tend to emphasize the economic contribution of children, the South African data suggest that an inability to afford schooling is the primary reason why children are not in school prior to receipt of anticipated income. One interesting appendum to the empirical work on credit constraints and child labour is the theoretical paper by Rogers and Swinnerton (2004) who point out that with credit constraints and an agency problem, rising incomes can increase child labour. In their model, each child is altruistic toward his parent and the savings strategy of a very poor parent includes investing in her child's education in part to induce a voluntary repayment when the child grows up.

To induce repayment, the poor parent realizes that her consumption decisions must be consistent the child's preferences, and as a result she provides more education for her child than she would if not for the "child preference" constraint. As parental income rises, there comes a point when the parent can optimally circumvent the "child preference constraint" by doing her all of her saving directly, rather than in part through the child's education, so that the education meant to induce voluntary repayment stops. At this point, child labour goes up. The interesting dynamics between incomes and intergenerational transfers is a fertile area for further study. *Does child labour respond to the return to schooling?* The presence of credit constraints within a population does not exclude the possibility of the relative returns to education influencing child labour. The major challenge in isolating the returns to education as a causal influence on child labour is that it is very difficult to measure perceptions about the returns to education.

Typically, researchers rely on the assumption that the expected returns to education at the time child labour decisions are made depends on the current return to education or literacy. While likely imprecise, even this approximation is difficult to estimate for two reasons. First, it is difficult to separate variation in the returns to education from confounding factors influencing income in the local community. Hence, an apparent response to the returns to education may just reflect parental income differences. Second, it is often very difficult to measure the returns to education, because child labour is most prevent in locations where wage work is rare. Most production occurs in family enterprises, and there is little specialization. Hence, it is extremely difficult to assign income to individuals in places where child labour tends to be most prevalent, and analysis based only on wage workers may suffer from severe selection bias that is likely to be correlated with child work status. How does one identify returns to education in populations where few individuals work for wages? One option is to measure the returns to education data at some aggregate level. Chamarbagwala (2006) is one example. She observes that Indian children in regions with higher returns to education are more likely to attend school and less likely to work. In addition to the problems of confounding factors and selection mentioned above, an additional difficulty inherent in this aggregate approach is that estimates of the returns to education are essentially a common effect to the level of aggregation with a functional form assumption and the more aggregate the study is, the less variation researchers have to work with. Hence, Chamarbagwala is one of the few published studies using this approach. A second option is to examine whether there are changes in the returns to education and schooling for a common factor rather than directly measuring the link between the two. Foster and Rosenzweig (1996) approach this by estimating a conditional profit function from the adoption of HYV rice in India and capturing the additional profit associated with more schooling in areas where HYV has diffused. They report changes in schooling which are consistent with improvements in the return to schooling (and school construction) by finding the same variables linked to increased schooling.

A related approach is to infer movements in returns to education through observing other behaviors that depend on the returns to education. For example, Edmonds, Pavcnik, and Topalova (2007) infer movements in returns to education in two ways. First, they compare differences in per capita expenditure by head's literacy or schooling completion. Second, they examine changes in adult employment by education status. They assume that adult labour supply is upward sloping and that expectations about the returns to education are based on differences in the wages of literate and illiterate populations with a given geographic area (the district in India in their case). They infer what must be occurring then to returns to education in the labour market by comparing changes in employment of the literate and illiterate populations. A novel set of studies considers how the schooling activities of rural children are influenced by urban labour markets to which they could migrate.

In addition to being a realistic description of how expectations of returns to education are formed, this approach minimizes the problem of a confounding between returns to education and adult income effects and is more apt to be measurable. Kochar (2004) for example finds that urban rates of return influence rural schooling in India, especially among landless who are most apt to migrate to urban areas. De Brauw and Giles (2005) observe that the education of rural migrants does not appear to be rewarded in the city in China. They make use of geographic and time variation in the implementation of national identity cards which make legal migration possible, and find that schooling enrollment declines with the opportunity to migrate. Of course, unlike the above studies that seek to isolate a returns to education effect, these two studies consider more the relative returns to schooling in the rural sector. While limited, it may not be possible to isolate returns to education from changes in labour market opportunities.

An alternative approach to studying the link between returns to schooling and child labour and schooling is to look at whether improvements in school quality affect child labour. Causal evidence on a link between school quality and child labour that would meet modern standards of evidence does not appear in the literature. However, descriptive studies such as those by Lloyd and co-authors (2003) suggest a connection, and evidence on the link between some measures of school quality such as pupil-teacher ratios and schooling attainment is well documented. For example, Case and Yogo (1999) use variation in school quality for blacks in apartheid South Africa to study the link between pupil-teacher ratio, the returns to schooling, and school attendance. Their findings are dramatic. A decline in the pupil-teacher ratio by 10 students is associated with a 2 percent increase in the return to education and an additional 0.6 years of completed schooling. Hence, while the problems with looking at the return to education are considerable, there is some suggestive evidence of a connection between returns to education and schooling which might also be reflected in child labour data provided that the marginal utility of income today is not the dominant causal factor in the decision to have a child work.

School Costs and Child Labour

Further, the relevant return to schooling is the return net of direct costs, and like with school quality, direct evidence on a link between schooling costs and child labour is rare. Several studies document an association between the mitigation of school costs and schooling, and Foster and Rosenzweig (2004) argue that school construction accompanying the green revolution in India facilitated increased schooling and decreased child labour in both landed and landless households although they do not directly observe a measure of child labour in their data. Slightly more direct evidence of a link between child labour and schooling costs also exists. Several studies find a link between measured schooling costs and child labour.

In rural Pakistan, Hazarika and Bedi (2003) observe that children are more apt to work outside the household in communities where schooling costs are higher. Shafiq (2006b) observes that boys are more likely to work and less likely to attend school in Bangladesh in communities where schooling costs are higher. Edmonds, Pavcnik, and Topalova (2007) argue that the avoidance of schooling costs explains the child labour-schooling-poverty association observed in their study of rural India, and they find that the relative declines in schooling and increases in work associated with India's tariff reforms are smaller in areas where schooling is less expensive. Edmonds (2006a) study of credit constraints in South Africa reports some qualitative evidence suggesting that schooling costs are an important part of why there is a link between credit constraints and child labour and schooling. Kondylis and Manacorda (2006) study one dimension of schooling costs, travel time, in rural Tanzania. They observe that children longer travel times induce children to specialize in either schooling without work or work without schooling.

The interpretation of all of these studies is complicated by the fact that the source of variation in schooling costs is not well understood, and it is difficult to separate whether these findings reflect support of other siblings or the child's own schooling, however, as higher costs for one child likely imply higher costs for siblings in the same. Nevertheless, these studies provide some support for the idea that the relationship between child labour and schooling costs and quality is a fertile area for future research.

One important interpretation point often emphasized in the literature is that the relevant return on education for family decision-making is the present discounted value of the future return to education. Thus, differences in discount rates across households can lead to differences in the family's valuation of education or the marginal utility of income and thereby differences in child labour and schooling. Why might discount rates vary across households? Das and Deb model this explicitly as a function of the family's current consumption, the subject to which we now turn.

CHILD LABOUR AND POVERTY

The link between child labour and living standards

Theoretically, there are many reasons why there might be a negative connection between family incomes and child labour. First, child labour may be a bad in parental preferences so that as incomes improve, the family chooses to have children work less. In fact, in the seminal child labour paper by Basu and Van (1998), they posit the "luxury axiom": children only work when the family is unable to meet its basic needs. Beyond subsistence, the luxury axiom posits, families always opt to keep children out of work. In the model, the idea that work might be a bad is captured by families receiving positive utility from child leisure. The luxury axiom is just a particular characterization of preferences. Second, with diminishing marginal utility of income, the value of the marginal contribution of the child's income decreases.

Note that an important part of the child's economic contribution to the family might be through not attending school if direct and indirect schooling costs are high. That said, the economic contribution of working children can be substantial. Psacharopoulos (1997) observes that income earned by working Bolivian children of age 13 amounted to 13 percent of total household income on average. Menon et al (2005) attempt to compute the value of child's own farm labour to largely subsistence farm households in rural Nepal. They estimate that children contribute roughly 11 percent of the value of total agriculture production in Nepal or about 9 percent of GDP. Third, higher family incomes may facilitate the purchase of substitutes for child labour that lower the return to child labour within the household. For example, a washboard, fertilizer spreader, or a combine harvester may replace child labour within the home. In the model, this would be a downward shift in productivity in household work, F (-), and would only reduce work when work outside the household is at a corner solution.

Fourth, the child's productivity in other activities such as schooling might improve because the family might be able to afford better inputs to schooling such as nutrition, textbooks, or uniforms. In addition, market imperfections and other aspects of the family's economic environment (including discount rates) might be correlated with family economic status and also affect child labour supply. The important question for policy is to what extent a family's standard of living is the dominant determinant of whether children work.

Are returns to education or leisure sufficiently high or employment opportunities sufficiently unproductive that children can be expected to transition away from work as incomes improve without additional policy changes? If child labour is an outgrowth of poverty and nothing else, then it is difficult to make an argument for attention to child labour without attention to the factors that create a need for the child to work. On the other hand, if child labour is independent of the family's economic status and if it has long term consequences for child welfare, then there exists a much stronger case for policy attention specific to child labour.

The answer to the question of living standard's role in child labour is obviously context specific and can be expected to vary both between and within countries as well as over time. It is not surprising that there are a wide variety of findings evident within the empirical literature.

The empirical evidence

The cross-country data on living standards and child labour suggests a strong connection between economic status and economic activity rates. Each country observation is pictured as a circle where the size of the circle represents the size of the country's population between ages 10 and 14. While child labour is pervasive in poor economies such as Ethiopia and Nepal, child labour is unusual in a country wealthier than Gabon with a GDP per capita of $8,400. The regression curve shown here is weighted by the population of children aged 10-14 in each country, but the unweighted regression curve is nearly identical.

With this specification, variation in GDP per capita explains 73 percent of the variation in the economic activity rates of children. Countries differ in many ways that may be associated with economic activity rates and GDP per capita. Attempts to address the endogeneity of income as in Edmonds and Pavcnik (2006a) do little to affect the strong correlation between national income and economic activity rates of children. Most within country studies of the link between income and child labour are cross-sectional. They specify a linear relationship between some measure of work and family income, and test the hypothesis that the marginal effect of family income on work is different from zero on average. In general, researchers that compare poor households to rich households at a single point in time in a country find mixed evidence of a link between poverty and child labour. Comparative studies implement the same empirical approach in multiple countries, and the different results observed between countries in comparative studies such as Bhalotra and Heady, Ersado, Maitra and Ray, Psacharopoulos, and Ray (Pakistan and Peru, 2000) illustrate how varied the cross-sectional relationship between economic status and child labour can be.

An intrinsic problem in studies of the link between economic status and child labour is that poor households differ from rich households in many ways that might be associated with child labour. Disentangling these omitted factors from the underlying causal relationship is difficult. Despite the great challenge, there are two basic approaches researchers use to address the endogeneity of living standards. First, many studies address part of the problem by relating child labour to variation in income that excludes the child's income (Dammert 2005, Duryea and Arends-Kuenning 2003, Ray 2000). While this addresses a mechanical source of endogeneity, it does not deal with the joint nature of child time allocation and family living standards. The second approach focuses on the broader endogeneity problem and argues that certain factors affect family income without also affecting the time allocation of children except through family income. Examples include Bhalotra (2000), Bhalotra and Heady (2003), and Ersado (2005).

Note that the assumptions required for identification are often quite strong in these studies, as almost anything that affects the family's economic environment should also influence the value of child time in one activity (schooling, work outside the home, market work in the home, domestic chores). Glewwe and Jacoby (2004) focus on education rather than child labour, but they emphasize the types of structural assumptions necessary to accept many of the common IV strategies. Another approach to address the intrinsic differences that exist between poor and rich families is to track children in the same household (or cohort) over time. Of course, using panel data only replaces the problem of cross-sectional heterogeneity with the problem of explaining differential changes over time. That said, studies tracking families over time almost universally find large increases in child labour with substantive declines in family incomes. For example, in tracking children over a three-year period in rural Tanzania, Beegle et al. (2006) find that children tend to work when households experience unexpectedly poor harvest, and that children stop working when households recover from the bad harvest. Duryea, Lam, and Levison (2007) find that children transition in and out of employment with adult unemployment spells in urban Brazil. Dammert (2006) observes that market work increases in coca growing states of Peru after coca production (and its associated income) shifts out of Peru for Columbia. Beyond endogeneity, another methodological issue is important in the child labour-living standards literature. There are strong theoretical reasons to expect the relationship between child labour and families to be non-linear. In the Basu and Van (1998) model, children no longer work when families can meet their subsistence needs with adult earnings. Hence, variation in income below subsistence should have no effect on child labour, nor should variation in income above subsistence. It is only over the range of incomes that corresponds to the existing heterogeneity in perceived subsistence needs in which Basu and Van would expect to see changes in child labour that are correlated with improvement in living standards. Edmonds (2005) finds support for this idea directly with panel data collected during Vietnam's economic boom in the 1990s.

The data for this figure comes from the 1993 and 1998 Vietnam Living Standards Survey where information on the activities of children is collected in over 3,000 rural households that are interviewed first in 1993 and again in 1998. For households below the 1993 poverty line, participation of children in market work exceeds 30 percent. From 1993 to 1998, real expenditure per capita increased by more than 50 percent for the poorest 10 percent of the population. For Vietnam overall, the incidence of poverty declined 36 percent. Thus, for each point on the per capita expenditure distribution in 1993 (the x-axis), market work participation rates are pictured for the same households in 1993 and 1998. Participation rates drop substantially over time, with the largest declines in market work occurring in households in the neighborhood of the poverty line in 1993.

Edmonds (2005) uses the market work - per capita expenditure relationship in 1993 to recover the implied distribution of subsistence levels across households. He then projects the changes in market work that would be expected in the Basu and Van framework based on the observed improvements in per capita expenditures between 1993 and 1998. He finds that improvements in per capita expenditure and the implied distribution of subsistence levels across households can explain 80 percent of the decline in child labour that occurs in households whose expenditures improve enough to move out of poverty. The strong structure of the Basu and Van model is not the only model that could generate these findings (a simple Engel curve in preferences would as would variable discount rates that depend on living standards).

Moreover, factors other than preferences can generate important non-linearity in the child labour-economic status relationship. For example, one can imagine non-linearity in the household production function that would lead to discrete changes in the value of child time within the household. A family might opt to change its production technology to replace the labour of a child, and this type of shift could generate results as in Edmonds if changes in household production techniques are correlated with exiting poverty. Nonetheless, non-linearity in the child labour - economic status relationship appears very important, as does the correlation between improvements in living standards and declines in child labour. *Can the effect of rising incomes differ from that of declining poverty?* The empirical literature on child labour and living standards largely attempts to estimate whether there is a link, but it might serve policy more by considering why there is a link. Indeed, one suspect that a more nuanced view of the determinants and definition of child labour might resolve some of the apparent inconsistencies observed across cross-sectional studies.

For example, in the Basu and Van model and in Edmonds' data, child labour declines rapidly in the neighborhood of the poverty line, but appears relatively income inelastic elsewhere. Hence, depending on the distribution of variation in income in a population, standard approaches may miss the importance of poverty in child labour decisions. Moreover, depending on the definition of child labour and local economic conditions, it may be that child labour appears to increase with family incomes. Rising incomes might be associated with changes in the types of activities in which children participate. Edmonds and Pavcnik (2006b) for example find that growing trade inside Vietnam is associated with a rise in household specialization which in turn may explain some of the decline in work in the family farm and business that they observe in Edmonds and Pavcnik (2005b).

Fafchamps and Wahba (2006) observe a positive correlation between household specialization and wage work in Nepal as well. Consequently, if child labour is defined as wage work, then it might appear to grow with rising incomes even if the total time spent working when one includes work within the household declines. This might explain the rise in wage employment among children with economic growth that Swaminathan (1998) documents in Gujarat, India or that Kambahampati and Rajan (2005) have observed across Indian states. Moreover, in a setting where the lack of employment opportunities is relevant, child labour may actually increase with rising incomes if they are associated with expanding economic activity or increased employment opportunities for children within their households. Bhalotra and Heady (2003) label the positive correlation between market work participation and household assets or employment opportunities in the household a "wealth paradox."

Ganglmair (2005) shows that this "paradox" occurs in Ugandan data when one fails to control for variation in the employment opportunities open to children and when one only considers types of work directly engaged with the asset. Shafiq (2006b) points out that, while greater assets may lead children to report working more because of the availability of employment opportunities, the human capital ramifications of this are unclear. In his data from Bangladesh, children work more in the presence of productive assets, but they are also more likely to attend school. In fact, several studies find a negative correlation between child wages and child employment and a positive correlation between child wages and schooling. This may be, because children are often substitutes for adults. Rising child wages imply higher adult wages, and child work appears more elastic with respect to adult income than child wages. The finding in Edmonds and Pavcnik's (2005b) study of rice price changes in Vietnam is suggestive of this.

Children are actively involved in rice cultivation, the returns to that cultivation increase, but market work declines. Wahba (2006) is more direct evidence. She finds in Egyptian data from 1988 that a 10 percent increase in the illiterate male market wage *lowers* the probability that a child engages in wage work by 22 percent for boys and 13 percent for girls. In fact, the academic literature on how households respond to macroeconomic shocks tends to emphasize declining child labour with declining income. Thomas et al (2004) examine education responses to the Indonesian financial crisis. They find that poor households coped with the shock in part by reducing educational expenditures and educational enrollment. These declines in education were particularly large for younger children as households appeared to triage to protect the schooling of older children. Interestingly, Cameron (2000) notes that in Indonesia, declines in schooling do not appear to be accompanied by a rise in formal employment amongst children.

This is consistent with Thomas et al's observation that young children were withheld from school to cope with the crisis. In fact, Schady (2004) suggests that as a result of the decline in employment options for children during Peru's 1988-1992 macroeconomic crisis, schooling attainment for affected cohorts has increased substantially. Thus, even if poverty is a key reason children work; it is possible to find child labour rising with incomes. More attention to the reasons why there might be a link between family incomes and child labour can then be important in understanding how child labour will evolve, as countries grow richer.

ECONOMIC SHOCKS, CREDIT CONSTRAINTS, POVERTY, AND CHILD LABOUR

Poor households are more apt to be credit constrained, because their poverty typically means they lack collateral with which to access credit and they often live in locations with poor credit institutions. The poor also are less likely to have access to formal insurance and more likely to face uninsured credit risks. Pouliot (2006) adds uncertainty to the Baland and Robinson model, showing that incomplete insurance markets can lead to inefficiently high levels of child labour even with functioning credit markets. Several studies document a relationship between child labour and schooling and an inability of the household to cope with income shocks that extend beyond any effect the potential for uncertainty has on schooling and work decisions. The adult labour supply literature in developing countries tends to emphasize how individual labour supply is used to buffer income shocks. Kochar (1999) for example observes that Indian men increase their market hours of work in response to unanticipated (weather related) variation in crop profits and that this rise in labour supply explains reduced form results that fail to find a significant effect of crop shocks on consumption. Does child labour supply also act to help cope with shocks? Using the same ICRISAT data as Kochar, Jacoby and Skoufias (1997) find that market work and variation in school attendance is an important part of family self-insurance. They observe declines in schooling and increases in market work in households that experience both idiosyncratic and aggregate shocks.

Moreover, they decompose variation in income using rainfall data to estimate predictable seasonal variation in income and unpredictable variation in income. They find that small farm households adjust schooling and work in response to both predictable and unpredictable variation in income. Hence, they argue that small farms are not well insured ex-ante, and they do not have access to seasonal borrowing and lending. A similar study in Tanzania is Beegle, Dehejia, and Gatti (2006). They correlate self- reported crop shocks with changes in child labour. They observe a significant increase in market work in households that report experiencing a crop shock, and that this shock is larger among households with few assets. One important point in Jacoby and Skoufias is that, despite variation in work and schooling with both predictable and unpredictable income variation, the overall effect of this on schooling attainment appears very modest. de Janvry et al (2006) note that the conditional cash transfers in Mexico's Progresa program were sufficient to protect school enrollment in the presence of agricultural shocks, but conditional transfers appeared to have little effect on the rise in market work associated with the shocks.

As they point out, this is to be expected if child labour supply is part of the household's self insurance strategy. Insurance failures and child labour are not just interconnected in rural agrarian societies. Using a longitudinal employment survey from urban Brazil, Duryea, Lam, and Levison (2007) compare households in which the male head becomes employed during a four month period to household where the head is continuously employed. They find that an unemployment shock significantly increases the probability that a child enters the labour force (by as much as 60 percent) and decreases the probability the child attends school. They do not observe changes in labour supply in anticipation of shocks. Hence, they conclude that the child's labour supply in part compensates for the lack of unemployment insurance. Moreover, unlike the evidence in Jacoby and Skoufias, Duryea et al observe substantial declines in schooling completion with these adult unemployment spells. For girls in particular, it seems that the loss of employment for the male household head often triggers a complete and permanent withdrawal from school. The idea that child labour is part of the household's self-insurance strategy seems broadly supported in the literature. Yang's (2006) study of how Philippine households with overseas members were affected by the 1997 Asian financial crisis is especially useful for framing how to think about the insurance component of child labour supply.

Migrants from the Philippines work in dozens of countries. Thus, the financial crisis was broadly felt in the Philippines, but there is a great deal of heterogeneity in how families were impacted by the crisis depending on what country their migrant members lived. Yang observes that a 10 percent appreciation in the Philippine/foreign exchange rate is associated with a 6 percent increase in remittance flows. Schooling increases, schooling expenditures increase, and work declines in households that benefited from the appreciation. This behaviour is similar to classical permanent income behaviour. Schooling is an investment, and families seem to be "saving" transitory income through increased schooling and less work. Likewise, the temporary (as in Jacoby and Skoufias) or permanent (as in Duryea, Lam, and Levison) declines in schooling and increases in work may reflect similar permanent income behaviour. It is striking that decisions about schooling and work might reflect how households manage transitory income. These findings illustrate the complex set of interactions and response to market imperfections and market failures that are important in understanding the determinants of child time allocation.

5

The Phenomenon of Child Labour

This chapter aims to highlight the main areas of discrimination and how they affect child labour and working children. It is not a comprehensive document covering every possible angle, but aims to stimulate discussion for best possible implementation of ILO Convention 182. It also aims to provide food for thought on integrating children into next year's global report on discrimination, and to encourage research into child labour and discrimination. The discrimination that working girls and boys endure mirrors discrimination in society as a whole. But there is also discrimination directly related to children. We know that discrimination helps cause child labour, and we know that children suffer discrimination as a consequence of the work they do. They also are discriminated against while at work itself – for example, insulted because they are foreign/poor/female, just like their parents. Different forms of discrimination suffered by children may overlap, and one form of discrimination may help cause another, creating a variety of situations with different impacts. This document will try to look at the various different forms of child labour, addressing the impact of each as both a cause and a consequence of child labour.

POVERTY

We know that poverty is one of the major causes of child labour, and that child labour perpetuates poverty. Poverty is one of the most obvious grounds for discrimi-nation, affecting people's access to equal treatment including services such as health and education, and leading to a vicious circle of discrimination, poverty and social exclusion. The children of poor and/or uneducated parents are more likely to be sent to work. Discrimination suffered by parents leads to lower wages, unequal pay for equal work and lack of access to employment opportunities and rights, causing family poverty, in turn making children more vulnerable to exploitation. There is also discrimination against workers with family responsibilities – such as inadequate maternity/paternity protection or lack of job security for pregnant women and mothers. Work done by children which keeps them in poverty and out of education will result in discrimination. Lack of education or skills training denies necessary human capabilities for productive life, excluding children from the benefits of economic growth and from fulfilling their human potential. Education is often the key to accessing other rights, so a denial of education has serious implications for enjoyment of all other rights.

GENDER

The education system reflects the inequality found outside the classroom. Girls the world over are less likely than their brothers to be attending primary school. In some cases, where a decision has to be made about which children to send to school, parents decide to invest in their sons' education rather than their daughters'. This may reflect the fact that upon marriage, daughters in some cultures may no longer contribute to family income and are therefore not seen as worth investing in. However, by contrast there may also be pressure on boys but not girls to leave school and contribute to family income. Certain types of work are gender biased. As a result, boys and girls may face different forms of harm and exploitation. Boys tend to work more in environments away from parental control, or in jobs that are associated with men's work, such as work outdoors or physical labour.

Examples include fishing, wholesale and retail trade, transport, construction, and restaurants and hotels. Girls on the other hand tend to work in the domestic sphere, in what are perceived to be protected environments in or near the home, or in jobs that are associated with women's roles, such as work demanding patience or attention to detail. These include domestic service, home-based manufacturing, family based agriculture and garment work. Discrimination in the workplace may mean that girls have fewer options available to them. For example, girls in slums in Dhaka, now excluded from garment work, may be forced to choose between the few options available - brick-breaking, child domestic work or sexual exploitation. Boys may have more varied opportunities and therefore the option to choose less hazardous work. Girls are also less likely to get equal pay for equal work.

Such less visible work can be more hazardous to children since its invisible nature makes it easier for abuse to go unchecked, and more difficult for the state machinery such as police or labour inspectors to gain access to private premises. Different work is also often given to girls and boys on the basis of their future roles in life, for example, 'the placement of girls in Africa is linked to perceptions that domestic service is a good preparation for marriage, and that girls families' might raise their dowries by putting them to work'. Furthermore, girl children are at a much higher risk of sexual exploitation, commercial and otherwise, in society and also in the workplace. There are several gender discrimination-related consequences of child labour. One of the most obvious are the problems faced by girls who have been sexually exploited. On return to their families and communities, if their situation is common knowledge they may face ostracisation and even physical harm. In cases where girls have worked in industries deemed to have put them at risk of harassment, or to have taken them out of the appropriate sphere, they may face the same difficulties - for example this has affected girls fishing and preparing prawns in Bangladesh.

Such gender discrimination also affects reintegration programmes: are there differences in how people regard girls and boys as being 'victims', or how they are stigmatised? Is there a difference between how ex-child soldiers or formerly sexually exploited children are treated according to whether they are girls or boys? How does this affect that way that supportive activities are designed? How does one reintegrate a girl into a society where she was not integrated to start with, and where gender discrimination was one of the causes of the initial exploitation? Is it desirable to reintegrate girls if there is a risk of further physical harm at the hands of their families and communities?

CASTE

In much of South Asia, the socially imposed segregation of society into a caste hierarchy is an overarching feature of all social and economic relations. The vast majority of bonded labourers, including child bonded labourers, belong to 'scheduled castes' or 'scheduled tribes', and are placed at the very bottom of the social order. They represent the most discriminated against groups. A study of child domestic workers in Chennai, India in 1999 revealed that 70% of the children interviewed were from 'scheduled castes'. Similar segregation of society and its impact on economic activity is also present in other parts of the world, for example in West Africa where it may be traditional for certain ethnic groups to 'serve' others in a variety of ways.

RACE AND ETHNICITY

Those who experience discrimination on the basis of race and ethnicity include: indigenous peoples, tribal groups, refugees and asylum seekers, the internally displaced and migrants. For example, "children belonging to marginalised ethnic groups...are often targeted for trafficking." In Peru, where formal education is taught in Spanish, not in local indigenous languages, indigenous children were discouraged from attending and staying in school where lessons were inaccessible to them. Efforts have now been made to teach in local languages in areas where this is appropriate. This example illustrates how discrimination in education itself and in access to education can result in increased child labour.

DISABILITY/HEALTH

The impact of HIV/AIDS both as a cause and a consequence of child labour is enormous in some countries. The result of illness, morbidity and death of family income earners means that many more families are forced to rely on work done by children. A child suffering from HIV/AIDS maybe discriminated against, affecting the type of work they can do or their access to education. The belief that children do not have HIV/AIDS or can cure those with HIV/AIDS has increased the demand for children in commercial sexual exploitation. There is very little information available about the impact of disability on child labour - research is sorely needed in this area. However, there is evidence of children being intentionally disabled for exploitation such as begging.

Furthermore, it is recognized that disability can be a cause of poverty so disabled children or children of disabled parents are likely to be more vulnerable to poverty-associated risks of discrimination that cause child labour. Anecdotal evidence suggests that like women, disabled children (and disabled adults) are less likely to get equal pay for equal work. Children in hazardous work face risks to their health on a daily basis. If children are disabled through work, they have very, very little chance of gaining any form of compensation, though their chances of a normal adult working life may have been ruined through loss of a limb or permanent damage to their lungs. This in turn increases the risk of poverty and the discrimination associated with it outlined above. The same is true for those who contract HIV/AIDS or STIs or are raped at work - again, sexually exploited children as well as those in armed conflict and domestic work are particularly at risk here. They may be discriminated against and stigmatized on the basis of the exploitation they underwent *and* for the illness/ health problems they now carry, causing extreme difficulty for the rehabilitation and reintegration of affected children.

Child domestic workers are often denied medical treatment when required since they are child domestics, and do not share the same status as the other children in the household. Children who suffer an accident at work may also feel that this is their own fault for being clumsy or bad at their job, and the adults and medical personnel who they encounter may have the same attitude. Work that is particularly traumatic may also cause mental problems for children, ranging from depression and low self-esteem to severe psychological disorders. Child soldiers may be left with especially deep psychological scars. Such conditions are likely to go untreated, the child may gain a reputation as difficult and as a result that it may be hard for them to reintegrate or work.

RELIGION, IDEOLOGY AND CULTURE

Globally, there is a considerable variation in child raising systems, and this is reflected in attitudes towards children's work. While in many Western cultures, childhood is perceived as a time for schooling and play, in other communities children are prepared for adulthood through work activities. Sometimes there is also a belief that children should not remain idle, and where schooling is unavailable, work for children is therefore perceived as a better alternative. Cultural values also vary within cultures. For example, while it may be seen to be totally unacceptable for an 11 year old girl from a middle class background to work, many middle class families employ children from poorer backgrounds to work within their homes.

Religion and ideology may also create situations that result in children being involved in harmful work. For example, many children may be recruited, forcibly or otherwise, into armed conflict under a religious pretext. For example in Northern Ireland, paramilitaries have recently reported increasingly young members joining for ideological reasons. Religious traditions may also play a role in the exploitation of children, such as the *Trokosi* system in Ghana and *devidasis* in India, where young girls are handed over to religious leaders or shrines. It has been reported that the leaders of some Koranic schools (*madrasas*) in some countries, for example in West Africa, have forced their pupils to beg. The working conditions of many children prevent them from practising their religion – those who are never allowed time off cannot frequent places of worship.

LEGAL STATUS AND NATIONALITY

Children who have not been registered at birth are denied official identity, and therefore access to services such as education. Moreover, the cost and complexity of getting a birth certificate in childhood may discourage parents and children from enrolling in education. Migrant children who may have legal identity in their own country may be discriminated against once outside their own country – for example in many Gulf countries, children of migrants are not entitled to free education, whereas citizen children are. As a result, children in all of these categories are more likely to be working. The illegal status of children trafficked across national borders and children of illegal migrants makes them more vulnerable to exploitation and abuse, especially since they cannot attend school.

Children of migrants, refugees, the internally displaced, asylum seekers and minority groups are not only more likely to be working, as we have noted above. They are more likely to suffer greater exploitation, such as worse pay and/or working conditions than their local counterparts, just as their parents do. Where such vulnerable children work and their national counterparts do not, they are likely to receive discrimination in that country due to their lack of rights and skills compared to nationals, and have fewer chances as adults. If trafficked children are picked up by national authorities, they may be arrested, charged with illegal residency and criminal activities. Thus trafficked children are often criminalised while their recruiters, traffickers and middlemen and women are at liberty. Furthermore, many trafficked children will not be dealt with as minors in the criminal justice system. Other children whose work is deemed illegal may also be penalised and criminalized, increasing their vulnerability. This may also expose them to justice systems all too often ill-equipped to deal with minors and the particular issues faced by working children.

AGE

Age discrimination also affects child labourers - employers choose to employ children precisely because their young age makes them more vulnerable, more obedient and less aware of their rights. Some employers also use the argument that children's small size makes them more suitable for certain work than adults - whether it's their so-called 'nimble fingers' or their height. One employer in the cotton industry in Egypt told a researcher that he employed children since they were cheaper, more obedient and the appropriate height for inspecting cotton plants. Children's young age also means that they are often denied the right to participate in decisions affecting their lives. Often adults do not value children's insights into their problems and potential solutions. This includes child labourers, whose opinions may not be adequately sought or taken into consideration regarding how to improve and/ or resolve their situation.

Child Soldiers

Child soldiers merit a particular mention with regard to discrimination as a result of their work. Children who have killed or maimed others are likely to face discrimination on return to their communities, and many do not wish to return precisely because of this. Apart from the horror their activities may have caused in others, they may be linked with a particular side of a conflict - some have even had their skin branded - rendering it difficult for others to see them as neutral children or young people.

Discrimination amongst Child Labourers

Discrimination is also present amongst child labourers themselves. Older children may discriminate against younger children, foreign or minority children or children from a different caste. For example, in a household with more than one child domestic worker, there may well be a pecking order according to age, sex and region.

THE ROLE OF EDUCATION AND SCHOOL

The above sections on gender and race and ethnicity have touched on the links between education and discrimination. We have already stated that the discrimination in society is reflected in school. This may mean that teachers themselves and/or the education system as a whole discriminate against ex-child labourers, or those combining work and school, or just those who are poor/indigenous/migrants/disabled. Research shows that teachers often treat such different types of children as inferior, or may make them feel uncomfortable. Many ex-child labourers are older than their classmates, and teachers may feel that this makes teaching more difficult, discriminating against them as a result. In some cases, teachers have been known to refuse to accept certain children into their school or classroom.

Children also discriminate amongst themselves at school. For example domestic workers may be teased about their status, and children who have missed out on schooling may be made to feel stupid. All of this discrimination may mean that a working child or ex-working child does not want to attend school if what they will receive there is ill-treatment rather than education. For children combining work and school, school can help to reduce the hours a child works. Given that boys are more likely to be attending school than girls, these means that girls' exclusion from education also increases their working hours.

We hope that this chapter helps to illustrate the huge impact discrimination has on the phenomenon of child labour and on the daily lives of working children. We feel it demonstrates the need for two particular results:

- Much more research focussed on the issue, both by civil society, UN agencies and other institutions, and the need to include the element of discrimination while engaging in all research on child labour.
- The inclusion of how children as well as adults are affected by such discrimination in the ILO's Global Report

on Discrimination in Respect of Employment and Occupation 2003.

CHILD LABOUR IN INDIA

Millions of children in today's world undergo the worst forms of child labour which includes Child Slavery, Child Prostitution, Child Trafficking, Child Soldiers. In modern era of material and technological advancement, children in almost every country are being callously exploited. The official figure of child laborers world wide is 13 million. But the actual number is much higher. Of the estimated 250 million children between the ages of 5 and 14 who are economically active, some 50 million to 60 million between the ages of 5 and 11 are engaged in intolerable forms of labour. Among the 10 to 14 year-old children the working rate is 41.3 percent in Kenya, 31.4 percent in Senegal, 30.1 percent in Bangladesh, 25.8 percent in Nigeria, 24 percent in Turkey, 17.7 percent in Pakistan, 16.1 percent in Brazil, 14.4 percent in India, 11.6 percent in China.

ILO estimated that 250 million children between 5 and 14 work for a living, and over 50 million children under age twelve work in hazardous circumstances. United Nations estimate that there were 20 million bonded child laborers worldwide. Based on reliable estimates, at least 700,000 persons to 2 million, especially girls and children, are trafficked each year across international borders. Research suggests that the age of the children involved is decreasing. Most are poor children between the ages of 13 and 18, although there is evidence that very young children even babies, are also caught up in this horrific trade. They come from all parts of the world. Some one million children enter the sex trade, exploited by people or circumstances. At any one time, more than 300,000 children under 18 - girls and boys - are fighting as soldiers with government armed forces and armed opposition groups in more than 30 countries worldwide. ILO estimates that domestic work is the largest employment category of girls under age 16 in the world.

India has the dubious distinction of being the nation with the largest number of child laborers in the world. The child labors endure miserable and difficult lives. They earn little and struggle to make enough to feed themselves and their families. They do not go to school; more than half of them are unable to learn the barest skills of literacy. Poverty is one of the main reasons behind this phenomenon. The unrelenting poverty forces the parents to push their young children in all forms of hazardous occupations. Child labour is a source of income for poor families. They provide help in household enterprises or of household chores in order to free adult household members for economic activity elsewhere.

In some cases, the study found that a child's income accounted for between 34 and 37 percent of the total household income. In India the emergence of child labour is also because of unsustainable systems of landholding in agricultural areas and caste system in the rural areas. Bonded labour refers to the phenomenon of children working in conditions of servitude in order to pay their debts. The debt that binds them to their employer is incurred not by the children themselves but by their parent. The creditors cum employers offer these loans to destitute parents in an effort to secure the labour of these children. The arrangements between the parents and contracting agents are usually informal and unwritten. The number of years required to pay off such a loan is indeterminate.

The lower castes such as *dalits* and tribal make them vulnerable groups for exploitation. The environmental degradation and lack of employment avenues in the rural areas also cause people to migrate to big cities. On arrival in overcrowded cities the disintegration of family units takes place through alcoholism, unemployment or disillusionment of better life etc. This in turn leads to emergence of street children and child workers who are forced by their circumstances to work from the early age. The girls are forced to work as sex -workers or beggars. A large number of girls end up working as domestic workers on low wages and unhealthy living conditions. Some times children are abandoned by their parents or sold to factory owners. The last two decades have seen tremendous growth of export based industries and mass production factories utilizing low technologies. They try to maintain competitive positions through low wages and low labour standards.

The child laborers exactly suit their requirements. They use all means to lure the parents into giving their children on pretext of providing education and good life. In India majority of children work in industries, such as cracker making, diamond polishing, glass, brass-ware, carpet weaving, bangle making, lock making and mica cutting to name a few. 15% of the 100,000 children work in the carpet industry of Uttar Pradesh. 70-80% of the 8,000 to 50,000 children work in the glass industry in Ferozabad. In the unorganized sector child labour is paid by piece-by-piece rates that result in even longer hours for very low pay.

Inadequate schools, a lack of schools, or even the expense of schooling leaves some children with little else to do but work. The attitudes of parents also contribute to child labour; some parents feel that children should work in order to develop skills useful in the job market, instead of taking advantage of a formal education. From the time of its independence, India has committed itself to be against child labour. Article 24 of the Indian constitution clearly states that "No child below the age of fourteen years shall be employed to work in any factory or mine or employed in any hazardous employment". The Bonded Labour System Act of 1976 fulfills the Indian Constitution's directive of ending forced labour. A Plethora of additional protective legislation has been put in place. There are distinct laws governing child labour in factories in commercial establishments, on plantations and in apprenticeships. There are laws governing the use of migrant labour and contract labour.

A Recent Law

The Child Labour (Prohibition and Regulation law) of 1986 designates a child as a person who has not completed their

14th year of age. It purports to regulate the hours and the conditions of child workers and to prohibit child workers in certain enumerated hazardous industries. However there is neither blanket prohibition on the use of child labour, nor any universal minimum age set for child workers. All of the policies that the Indian government has in place are in accordance with the Constitution of India, and all support the eradication of Child Labour. The problem of child labour still remains even though all of these policies are existent. Enforcement is the key aspect that is lacking in the government's efforts.

Child labour is a global problem. If child labour is to be eradicated, the governments and agencies and those responsible for enforcement need to start doing their jobs. The most important thing is to increase awareness and keep discussing ways and means to check this problem. We have to decide whether we are going to take up the problem head-on and fight it any way we can or leave it to the adults who might not be there when things go out of hand.

THE IMPLICATIONS OF IMMIGRATION ENFORCEMENT

Madam Chairwoman, subcommittee members, and members of the Congressional Hispanic Caucus, thank you for this opportunity to testify before you today about the impact of immigration enforcement on America's children. The National Council of La Raza (NCLR) - the largest national Hispanic civil rights and advocacy organization in the United States - is a private, nonprofit, nonpartisan, tax-exempt organization established in 1968 to reduce poverty and discrimination and improve opportunities for Hispanic Americans. NCLR has a long history in the immigration debate; our work on this issue is focused on ensuring that we have an immigration system that functions in the best interest of the nation. Immigration to the United States should be orderly and legal, promote economic growth, sustain our families, and be implemented in a way consistent with our best values in the United States.

As you know, the country is far from achieving that goal. My organization, our Affiliates, and our many coalition partners are dedicated to an effort to reform U.S. immigration laws in a way that promotes order, fairness, and above all legality. Until a major immigration reform is enacted, the country will continue to cope with challenges resulting from the presence of roughly 12 million undocumented immigrants in our workforce and in our communities. There is substantial, growing evidence that the use of workplace raids as an immigration enforcement strategy is causing great harm to children, schools, child care centers, and communities well beyond the immigrant population. As with any set of laws, the nation should enforce them wisely and well. This requires an examination of the costs and benefits of particular enforcement strategies to ensure that the priorities and tactics we choose do not undercut other important laws, values, and goals.

Consequences of Immigration Enforcement for Children

There has been a significant increase in interior immigration enforcement operations by the Department of Homeland Security in the last year and a half. In 2007, according to U.S. Immigration and Customs Enforcement (ICE), more than 4,900 arrests were made in connection with worksite enforcement investigations, representing a 45-fold increase in criminal worksite arrests compared to fiscal year 2001. This year, ICE has stepped up its enforcement actions by raiding individual homes as well as worksites; in April ICE conducted a five-state sweep of Pilgrim's Pride poultry plants last month, and just last week it raided Agriprocessors, Inc., a kosher meatpacking plant in Postville, Iowa, a raid which ICE has called the largest in history.

The impact of immigrant enforcement raids on children is often disregarded and poorly understood. For these reasons, NCLR commissioned the Urban Institute to conduct a study of three communities where large-scale worksite raids occurred in 2007.

We had a strong interest in moving beyond the anecdotal

accounts reported by the media to documenting the challenges that children face as a result of immigration enforcement actions. NCLR believes that the impact on children and communities must be considered when making decisions about immigration enforcement - or any law enforcement - strategy. We believe strongly that such a debate should be based on facts and empirical evidence as much as possible, which is why we invested in a thorough report. NCLR released this report, *Paying the Price: The Impact of Immigration Raids on America's Children*, in October 2007. The findings confirmed the inevitability of hardship to children resulting from an immigration raid. There are approximately five million children in the U.S. with an undocumented immigrant parent, the vast majority of whom are U.S. citizens and under the age of ten. The Urban Institute researchers found that, for every two immigrants detained as a result of worksite raids, approximately one child is left behind. Further, the study shed light on the fact that many children slipped through the cracks as a direct result of ICE's enforcement protocols.

For example, ICE did not provide detained immigrants with access to telephones. This meant that parents were unable to notify family members and coordinate alternative child care arrangements, forcing some children to stay with landlords or babysitters indefinitely or, worse still, home alone. ICE also failed to consider hardship to children when making custody determinations. Some children experienced the loss of both parents who had been placed in detention locally or in detention facilities out of state, which made it virtually impossible for these children to visit them. There were also accounts of ICE detaining nursing mothers, resulting in infants being forcibly weaned from breast milk. In a 2006 raid in New Bedford, Massachusetts, an eight-month-old infant was taken to the emergency room to be treated for dehydration after her mother was detained.

The infant's pediatrician appealed to ICE officials to release the child's mother, citing medical reasons for which the child needed to continue breastfeeding. NCLR and our sister organizations in the Latino community wrote to the

Department of Homeland Security after this incident to raise concerns; we received a response stating that the incident never occurred, despite extensive evidence, including video footage of the child and interviews with the emergency room physician who treated her. In addition, the report found evidence of increased economic hardship, social stigma, fear, isolation, family separation, disruptions in schooling, and negative emotional and mental health consequences for children. Across the three communities examined in the report, teachers, caregivers, and mental health professionals consistently described children with symptoms of depression and other psychological disturbances such as sleep disturbance, loss of appetite, fearfulness, mood swings, and feelings of abandonment by their parent(s).

Beyond the negative consequences to children's well-being resulting from worksite raids, the report provides evidence that our nation's social institutions - such as school and child welfare agencies - that are tasked with protecting and nurturing children are playing the role of first responders in the aftermath of a raid. For example, school officials interviewed for our report discussed steps they undertook on the day of the raid to ensure the well-being of children, such as instructing bus drivers to release children only at homes where there was an adult present, asking teachers to stay late to help care for children, and coordinating mental health services. In the days following the raid, school personnel visited homes and attended community gatherings reminding parents that schools were a safe place for children and urging their return to school. A school leader in Grand Island, Nebraska made a poignant statement regarding how the raid served as a diversion from the school's primary mission of ensuring that no child is left behind.

Today, nearly every time there is a significant immigration enforcement operation, NCLR receives reports from the community similar to those noted above. There is a similar pattern with each raid: school systems and child care centers must scramble to find relatives or caregivers for children whose parents have abruptly disappeared. These institutions, along with community organizations, must grapple for days or weeks with an emergency situation in which families struggle to find the location of detainees, who are often unable to access legal services. Even since the implementation of ICE guidelines in response to these many problems, there are always cases of children left behind and nearly always cases of nursing mothers separated from their infants for long periods. Moreover, school systems and child care centers report enormous long-term challenges in meeting the needs of children whose families have been forcibly and suddenly separated in this way.

Continuing Impact

There is also growing alarm in our community about ICE's engagement in intimidation and enforcement tactics near our public schools and Head Start programs. For example, NCLR has several Affiliates who operate Head Start programs that serve the children of migrant farm workers. Last spring, many of these programs began reporting the following incidents:

- ICE agents parking near migrant Head Start centers during drop-off and pickup times.
- ICE agents and local law enforcement following school buses carrying children under the age of five, beginning as early as 4:00 a.m.; in some instances, ICE followed school buses for the entire route, as long as two hours.
- ICE agents and local law enforcement following migrant Head Start staff to and from the center during lunch breaks.

These actions on the part of ICE are having a chilling effect on the participation of migrant children in Head Start. Quite simply, the presence of ICE around Head Start centers is causing fearful parents to keep their children away from the program. In fact, the low rates of attendance registered by these programs has even garnered the attention of U.S. Department of Health and Human Services, Office of Head Start, which monitors Head Start enrollment and sanctions programs for failing to meet their enrollment targets. During the reauthorization of the Head Start Act, NCLR worked closely with this committee to ensure that migrant children benefit from greater access to Head Start. We were proud of this committee's bipartisan work to prioritize the expansion of migrant Head Start and its commitment to ensuring that migrant children exit the fields and enter classrooms where they can learn and grow.

It is deplorable that the laudable goals of this committee have been virtually undone by the current immigration enforcement strategy of this Administration. We are also aware of instances in which ICE has actually entered private homes and school buildings to remove children. For example, in October 2007, a Honduran immigrant mother, who was in her Ohio home breastfeeding her nine-month-old infant when ICE agents entered her home, was taken into custody while ICE agents went to her children's school to remove her children. In another account, an NCLR Affiliate, HELP-New Mexico, Inc., contacted NCLR in September 2007 to report that ICE agents and local police entered their preschool program, located inside the Sunrise Elementary School in Chaparral, New Mexico, to remove children whose parents had been detained in a local sweep of Hispanic businesses and homes. One child, Virginia Ana Rodriguez, was released to her father, who was in the custody of four fully armed Otero County police officers at the time.

The officers initially brought the father into the main office of Sunrise Elementary until the principal asked them to accompany her into the conference room so as not to alarm other students and staff. These same agents also entered the local middle and high schools to remove children of detained immigrants. In the immediate weeks following this incident, school officials at the Gadsden School District documented that approximately 200 students were absent and a small number returned to school during the remainder of the school year. The HELP-New Mexico preschool program also registered lower rates of enrollment in the ensuing weeks, and has yet to fully reach enrollment targets consistent with previous school years. A preschool teacher reports the challenges they now face in enrolling children in the program because parents remain afraid of the possibility that ICE agents will return to the center. Clearly, our current approach to immigration enforcement is instilling fear among our children and families and undermining our important social policy goals for children, and the programs designed to meet these goals.

Limitations of ICE Policies for the Protection of Children

Many of the problems that are documented in the NCLR/ Urban Institute report have also been the subject of media attention, litigation, and congressional inquiries. As a result of this pressure, during 2007, ICE developed and released three policy memoranda that consider children in the conduct of immigration enforcement actions. While these memoranda represent an improvement in ICE sensitivity to these important considerations, experience with immigration raids since the development of these policies suggests that they have significant limitations. The scope and the limitations of these guidelines are discussed as follows:

a. Guidelines for Identifying Humanitarian Concerns Among Administrative Arrestees for Worksite Enfor-cement Actions, November 16, 2007. Following the New Bedford, Massachusetts raid in March 2007, Senators Edward Kennedy and John Kerry and Congressman William Delahunt worked with ICE to develop guidelines for quickly identifying persons arrested who are sole caregivers or who should be released from custody for other humanitarian reasons. The guidelines apply to larger worksite raids that result in the arrest and/or detention of more than 150 immigrants. The guidelines stipulate that ICE will:
   - Develop a comprehensive plan for quickly identifying humanitarian issues among detainees.
   - Coordinate with federal health and/or state and local social services, including allowing these entities to serve as intermediaries to help screen and assess humanitarian issues among detainees.
   - Facilitate communication among detainees and their

family members by providing access to telephones; ICE is also expected to coordinate with nongovernmental agencies (NGOs) and make information on detainees and ICE personnel available to these entities in real time, so that they can help to screen for humanitarian concerns.

b. Memorandum Outlining Prosecutorial Discretion for Nursing Mothers, November 7, 2007. In response to mounting accounts of infants forcibly weaned from breast milk as a result of enforcement actions, ICE released guidelines highlighting the importance of discretion when making arrests and custody determinations of nursing mothers. These guidelines call for the following:
   - Nursing mothers should be released on an Order of Recognizance or Order of Supervision, and the Alternative to Detention programs should be considered as an additional enforcement tool.
   - In situations where ICE determines that nursing mothers should remain in custody, field personnel should consider placement in Berks or Hutto Family detention facilities.

c. Memorandum Regarding Juveniles Encountered During Fugitive Operations, August 24, 2007. In March 2006, ICE agents raided a home in San Rafael, California and apprehended Kebin Reyes, a six-year-old U.S. citizen. ICE agents kept Kebin in detention for ten hours alongside his father, who repeatedly pleaded for access to a telephone to make alternative care arrangements for Kebin. The ACLU filed a lawsuit that led to the development of a memorandum concerning the treatment of minor children encountered during enforcement actions. The memo stipulates the following:
   - ICE should not take into custody a legal permanent resident or U.S. citizen minor child.
   - ICE should coordinate the transfer of a minor child to the nearest child welfare authority or local law enforcement agency. If these options are not feasible,

ICE should document the parent's request for the transfer of the child to a third party.

- To the greatest extent possible, ICE should coordinate with child welfare authorities prior to an enforcement operation.

In general, ICE appears to have made attempts to adjust its enforcement policies to consider humanitarian issues, including hardship to children. There is even some evidence to suggest that ICE has adhered to its stated objective of promptly releasing nursing mothers. For example, recent large raids in Van Nuys, California and Postville, Iowa demonstrate that ICE has released nursing mothers with electronic monitoring devices. However, there is also anecdotal evidence that the release of these mothers can be significantly delayed and the conditions of their detention inappropriate. NCLR has learned that one nursing mother detained last week in Postville was not provided sufficient access to food over a nearly 24-hour period before she was released to care for her infant. However, the positive impact of ICE's guidance memoranda is severely limited with respect to providing any real assurances that children will be comprehensively and systematically protected in immigration enforcement activities. For example:

- The policy guidelines noted above are nonbinding, as they are not regulations and are not codified.
- There is no mechanism for holding ICE accountable for compliance with its own stated policies.
- The humanitarian guidelines for worksite raids only apply to larger raids of more than 150 people. Thus, it is unclear whether or not ICE will attempt to apply these guidelines in raids yielding less than 150 detainees.
- The guidelines noted above fail to address the undue burden placed on schools, early childhood centers, child welfare agencies, churches, and community-based organizations that are left to play the role of first responder in the aftermath of a raid.
- The guidelines fall short of accounting for all of the

situations and scenarios in which children could potentially be harmed in an enforcement action. Simply put, the guidelines do not stipulate that all children, regardless of any type of enforcement action of any size, will have their best interests taken into account.

Unfortunately, there is substantial evidence that ICE does not consistently follow its own guidelines. For example, Immigration and Naturalization Services (ICE's predecessor) policy guidance dating back to 1993 strongly discourages immigration enforcement actions near schools. The policy states that agents are to "attempt to avoid apprehension of and to tightly control investigative operations on the premises of schools, places of workshop, funerals, or other religious ceremonies."

In 2004, the Bureau of Customs and Border Protection of the Department of Homeland Security reaffirmed the 1993 guidance. However, as noted above, there are mounting stories of ICE presence near schools and Head Start centers, providing clear evidence that ICE does not uphold the guidelines and is actively conducting enforcement operations in violation of them. Even if ICE were to execute all of its existing policy guidance perfectly and expand its scope to include all children who are affected by immigration raids, there would still be a profound dissonance between the goal of enforcing our nation's immigration laws and the equally important goal of protecting America's children and supporting the institutions that are charged with meeting their needs. Even if the federal government were to use great care and attention when removing parents from their workplaces, homes, families, and communities – which is far from the case now – our current enforcement strategy relies heavily on raids which undeniably and inevitably has an impact on American children and creates difficult challenges for schools, child care centers, and the child welfare system in meeting their needs.

Impact of Raid in Postville, Iowa

Raid in Postville, Iowa provides the best evidence that, despite ICE's efforts to ameliorate some of the impact of enforcement actions on children, the negative effects of workplace raids on American children, school systems, and social service infrastructure can be catastrophic. A first major concern is that the raid itself appears to have undercut an investigation into the use of child labour at the Agriprocessors plant in Postville. There is substantial reason to believe that the employer in this case was highly problematic and was likely violating a number of laws in the treatment of his employees, including employing children - allegedly recruiting some of them from the local middle school. There is mounting evidence that state and possibly federal authorities were aware of labour law violations, including laws prohibiting child labour, in advance of the raid.

State authorities have confirmed that they were conducting an investigation, and the United Food and Commercial Workers Union wrote to ICE to request that an immigration enforcement action not take place, citing fears that it would undercut the enforcement of labour laws intended to protect all of the workers at the plant. ICE appears to have disregarded this evidence; indeed, as many as a dozen child workers - one as young as 13 -who were evidently poised to provide information that would assist in an investigation of labour law violations, were instead detained for several days by ICE authorities. As a result, the investigation into labour law violations has ground to a halt. The employer in this case, who is widely reported to have been abusive and was almost certainly illegally employing children, was able to reopen operations the next day, while the workers whose stories could lead to prosecution have faced detention and likely removal from the country.

Federal authorities missed an opportunity to prosecute abuse of workers - including children - which could have a profound impact on protecting workers in the state and in the meat processing industry well beyond the immigrant community. It is not only unjust that all of the penalties associated with this enforcement action have been borne by immigrant workers, rather than by the employer, it is also a clear example of how the actions of one federal agency enforcing one set of laws can undercut the enforcement of another important set of laws designed to protect all workers, including and especially children. There are also significant concerns about ICE officials failing to fully implement the ICE guidelines regarding nursing mothers. NCLR has learned that some nursing mothers were released for humanitarian reasons, however, in at least a couple of cases, there were substantial delays and inadequate nutrition provided to a mother in detention.

In addition, two major provisions of ICE humanitarian guidelines specifically intended to protect children appear not to have been followed in Postville:

- *Access to intermediaries:* ICE has said that it will allow for third-party intermediary entities - either federal health officials, or state and local social services, or other contracted third-party groups - to screen detainees for humanitarian reasons. This is important because many immigrants are reluctant to reveal to ICE that they are parents for fear that their children will also be detained. NCLR's contacts in Iowa have been unable to substantiate that any intermediary party assisted in screening of detainees.
- *Communication:* ICE has said that it will facilitate access to free telephones. According to NCLR's contacts in Iowa, very few families have been able to communicate with a detained family member. This complicates the ability of parents in detention to make alternative arrangements for their children and considerably increases the stress on nondetained family members, including children. Similarly, it adds a layer of uncertainty for school systems, child care centers, and social service agencies that are dealing with issues of finding appropriate adult supervision for children whose parents have been detained.

Finally, and perhaps most significantly, it is important for the committee to have a clear picture of what happens in a community like Postville when a worksite raid takes place. We have seen the same dynamics in nearly every major raid, both before and since ICE has changed its guidelines in the interest of protecting children. Specifically, as federal agents in trucks and helicopters descended on the plant in Postville, an uproar occurred in local schools, from which the helicopters were clearly visible, and students with immigrant parents were immediately affected, as were teachers and administrators. The situation for children in school was documented eloquently in the *Des Moines Register* by a teacher; I have attached it to this testimony.

Almost immediately, as the raid was taking place, the local Catholic Parish - St. Bridget's - became a focal point for community activity. NCLR spoke with individuals at the church who described the scene as being chaotic. About 150 children (most of whom are U.S. citizens) spent the night there, and the church provided food to more than 400 children throughout the first 24 hours following the raid. More than 24 hours after the raid there were at least 150 people still at the church, where they attempted to match up every child with a relative. The burden of ensuring that children are matched up with relatives and other caregivers has fallen squarely on the shoulders of the church, school, and community. As this testimony was being prepared, there were still families seeking sanctuary in the church.

Families have been afraid to go to their homes because of the continued ICE presence in Postville. The church was still feeding hundreds of children and families nearly five days after the raid. Children are being escorted on buses from the church to school and back. Church and school officials report that access to counselors and mental health professionals for children has emerged as one of many pressing unmet needs. In short, the disruption to the larger community in Postville, to its school system, churches, and community service infrastructure, has only just begun. As NCLR and the Urban Institute documented in the *Paying the Price* report, the impact of a major raid like this one is deep, long-lasting, and destructive.

We recognize that the nation can and should control its borders, and that it is reasonable to conduct interior enforcement activities. But it is also true that every enforcement agency must establish priorities and parameters for its work, and it is reasonable - indeed, essential - for these parameters to include consideration of other important policy and law enforcement goals. It is vitally important to the well-being of America's children and all communities that the federal government engages in a conversation that results in good judgments about how to enforce our immigration laws without undercutting other important goals, such as child protection, education, and worker protection.

In the Postville raid, immigration enforcement clearly trumped an important labour law investigation in a way that may have lasting implications for the workers - including children - in the meatpacking industry. To place children in detention while their exploitative employer regroups and reopens within a day is a clear indication that our enforcement priorities need examination. In Postville, as in other raids which preceded it, school systems, child care centers, and the social service infrastructure have been left with a huge challenge of meeting the needs of children whose parents literally disappeared from one day to the next. The *New York Times* has estimated that some 13,000 American children have had at least one parent removed from the country; surely this merits a conversation about whether workplace raids are causing more harm than good. NCLR believes that this committee has an important role to play in such a conversation.

While NCLR is glad to see that ICE has responded to these concerns, there is clear evidence that the workplace raids conducted over the last two years, as well as the ICE presence near Head Start centers and schools, are undercutting a variety of important priorities under the jurisdiction of this committee. It is also very clear that even ICE's carefully constructed guidance to avoid these problems will be insufficient to address this larger challenge. This problem is really a collision between very important policy goals. The longer that our immigration system remains broken and unaddressed by Congress, the longer that these and related problems - and the tensions surrounding immigration itself - will continue.

Literally every day, NCLR uncovers new evidence supporting the misguided notion that any immigration enforcement is considered good enforcement, even if it does grave damage to our American citizens and our nation's most cherished values, and we have tolerated this environment for too long. Last week alone provided three examples of the ways in which ill-considered policy and enforcement judgments do great, if unintended, harm. Every week the evidence mounts - evidence that we need to exercise judgment in the application of our laws affecting immigrants to avoid doing harm that we will later regret.

6

The Problems of Child Labour and the Need for International Labour Standards

The problem of exploitative child labour has received much attention in recent years. According to the International Labour Organization (ILO) there are approximately 250 million working children aged between five and fourteen, of which at least 120 million are involved in full-time work that is both hazardous and exploitative. Such labour is spread throughout the developing world. Measured in absolute terms, Asia has the highest incidence of child labour (152.5 million), followed by Africa (80 million) and Latin America (17.5 million) measured in proportional terms approximately 40 percent of African children work, while 20 percent of children work in Asia and Latin America respectively. Driven by public outrage in developed countries, the issue of exploitative child labour has received increasing attention. Yet solutions remain elusive, and they are made more complicated by the fact that the extent of child labour reflects a country's level of economic development. This means that developed country calls for prohibition can seem hollow in the eyes of developing countries, which maintain that the developed countries themselves relied extensively on child labour when they were at a similar stage of economic development.

Given this contentious environment there has been a tendency to promote policies of unofficial voluntarism whereby private-producers adopt codes of practice that bar the use of child labour. These voluntaristic practices are exemplified by private labeling schemes, such as rug mark in the carpet industry, which certify to consumers that a product has been produced without child labour. Such labeling policies focus exclusively on child labour and implicitly treat it as a stand-alone problem that can be addressed by independent stand-alone policies. This chapter argues for a profound reformulation of the child labour problem whereby it is viewed as a labour market and economic development problem. Child labour is intimately connected to the operation of labour markets, and solving the former therefore depends on solving problems that afflict developing country labour markets. Child labour is also connected to economic development, and addressing the child labour problem therefore also requires policies that foster development. Labour market dysfunction and under-development are the root causes of exploitative child labour.

Viewed in this light, the ILO's core labour standards become a critical instrument for solving the child labour problem because they tackle both of these root causes. Finally, there remains a place for voluntaristic codes of conduct, but it must also be recognized that such codes cannot address the underlying roots of the problem. More sunshine is always better than less, and voluntaristic codes can serve an extremely valuable function in galvanizing public opinion to move against child labour and labour market exploitation. However, it is important that codes not be presented as a substitute for official core labour standards. If this happens, voluntaristic codes will make a negative contribution by fracturing understandings and diverting support away from core labour standards.

LABOUR STANDARDS AND THE LINK TO INSTITUTIONAL ECONOMICS

Before turning to specific analysis of the problem of child labour and its relation to labour standards, it is worth noting how today's debate over labour standards has clear links with the early twentieth century Progressive Era-thinking of American institutional economists. One notable link is with John Commons' (1909) theoretical concept of "competitive menace." Commons developed the notion of competitive menace in his history of American shoemaking, describing it as operating through the marginal producer who is used to bid down standards and wages throughout an industry. Defining the "marginal producer" as the one with the lowest standards of living and cost and quality of work, he is the producer whose competition tends to drag down the level of others toward his own. It is not necessary that he be able to actually supply the entire market or even the greater part of it. His effect on others depends on the extent to which he can be used as a club to intimidate others against standing out for their side of the bargain. He is a menace rather than an actual competitor.

Now the extension of the market for the sale of goods is accompanied by an extension of the field for production of goods. This extension brings into competitive area new competitors who are essentially a series of lower marginal producers. Thus the extension of the field of production increases the variety and discovers the lower levels of marginal producers, and the merchant-capitalist emerges as the generalissimo, menacing in turn every part of the field from his strategic center. Glen Atkinson (1997) has emphasized the relevance of Commons' competitive menace framework for understanding today's process of globalization, and the parallels are clear. Globalization has extended the field for production of goods, which has resulted in entry at the margin of new low-standard producers. Though these marginal producers are unable to supply the entire market, the threat of production shifting is sufficiently credible that their entry can be leveraged to lower standards everywhere.

And at the center of the process remains the merchant-capitalist generalissimo, who in today's global economy is the multinational corporation which sub-contracts globally and then retails this production in developed country consumer markets. The "race to the bottom," which is discussed later in the chapter in terms of the prisoner's dilemma, partakes of a game-theoretic dynamic that is strikingly similar to Commons' competitive menace. And competitive menace is also germane to the problem of child labour, which is increasingly entwined with the globalization of production. Seen in this light, solving the problem of competitive menace, as it operates in the global economy, requires new institutions that promote a different path of development. Atkinson (1997) termed these institutions "rules governing bargaining transactions," and labour standards are just this. By blocking off the low road development path associated with the race to the bottom, labour standards compel business to shift to an alternative high development path that is more inclusive and deeper owing to its reliance on growth of domestic markets.

This rules approach echoes the Progressive Era approach to market economies outlined by Leo Wolman of the New School:

> Rules of the game prevail in business and industry as they do in sport; and in both the rules serve much the same purpose. They prevent confusion by supplying the players with an orderly procedure; or they assure the participants in the game that fair and equal treatment; or they provide standards of performance that establish the levels on which the games are played. Long experience with the lighter as well as the more serious activities of life has taught us that players can not always be trusted to make their own rules or, when they make them, to enforce them. (1924, 226)

A second link is with Progressive Era economists' discussion of the minimum wage. Robert Prasch (1998, 1999) provided a thoughtful survey of the arguments raised by these economists, and many have clear parallels with today's arguments for global labour standards and the points to the lasting vitality and relevance of institutionalism as a frame for understanding the economy. In making the case for a national minimum wage, Progressive Era economists emphasized the issue of bargaining power, and this, too, figures prominently in the case for labour standards. Interestingly, the bargaining power argument was raised by both institutionalists and neoclassicists. Thus, John Bates Clark, the originator of marginal product theory of income distribution, wrote:

> Hunger-discipline disqualifies the worker for making a successful bargain, and if the employer were everywhere at liberty to take men for what, under such pressure, they might individually offer to work for, he might get them for very little.

Another Progressive Era argument for a minimum wage was that of parasitic industries, whereby sweated industries paid less than that needed for subsistence, thereby forcing the cost of social reproduction on to others. This imposes an external cost on others. The real injury becomes diffused, not revealing its harmful effects except indirectly and after the lapse of time. This injury is none the less real. The industry is parasitic. Society is not entitled to the products of an industry that is not self-supporting on the basis of the human "live and let live" principle. Not until an industry has developed the ingenuity, the inventive and organizing ability, to make it self-sustaining in all of its returns, ought society to have that industry.

This parasitic industry argument has similarities with "race to the bottom" arguments for labour standards. The difference is that the parasitic industry argument is constructed in terms of a static externality, whereas "race to the bottom" arguments rest on a dynamic externality with standards compelling a high road development path in place of a low road one. Yet, even here Progressive Era economists anticipated elements of the contemporary debate. Thus, Florence Kelley of the National Consumer's League of New York wrote:

> The universally observed tendency is, however, that every improved standard of hours, wages, or conditions forced upon an industry for the good of the employees tends not to increase the retail price of the product, but to enhance

the efficiency of management. Improved apparatus already upon the market, but not installed for the reason of cost of installation, tends to be promptly installed when working-hours are shortened, or the age of the working child raised by statute, or the wage scale of home-workers fixed by an outside body.

M. Altman (2001) made some similar arguments in connection with child labour, maintaining that banning child labour need have no negative impact on costs if it results in the substitution of efficient adult labour in place of less efficient child labour. Whereas it is possible to find close similarities between a core labour standards-development approach to child labour and the minimum wage arguments of Progressive Era institutional economists, the same cannot be said for the modern neoclassical approach to child labour. Thus, K. Basu and P. H. Van (1998) portrayed the problem of child labour as one of multiple equilibriums. In their model the presence of child labour represents a case in which the bad equilibrium prevails. From their perspective all that is needed is to enforce a ban on child labour, thereby making the good equilibrium without child labour the only sustainable equilibrium. C. Grootaert and R. Kanbur (1995) adopted a more mixed stance.

On one hand they recognized that child labour is a problem of under-development. However, instead of identifying the problem as one of institutional malfunctioning of labour markets that can only be remedied by enforcement of core labour standards, they suggested neoclassical-styled incentive policies aimed at twisting relative returns to families in a fashion that makes school more attractive than child labour. Such adjustments can undoubtedly help at the margin, but they are unlikely to be sufficient if the root cause of child labour is lack of jobs paying an adequate wage.

ILO CORE LABOUR STANDARDS

The ILO's core labour standards consist of five articles. Three are prohibitive in character, banning forced labour, exploitative child labour, and discrimination. Two are affirmative in character, affirming workers the right of freedom of association and the right to engage in collective bargaining. These five core labour standards are elaborated in the ILO's Declaration of Fundamental Principles and Rights at Work, which was adopted in 1998. The five core labour standards, with reference to the fundamental ILO Conventions that give them content, are described below:

1. Freedom of Association-The ILO Freedom of Association and Protection of the Right to Organize Convention (No. 87) establishes the right of workers to form and join organizations, including unions, of their own choosing. Governments may not dictate the form, affiliations, or internal operations of such organizations and may not deny authorization to nor suspend such organizations.
2. Effective Recognition of the Right to Collective Bargaining-The Right to Organize and Collective Bargaining Convention (No. 98) protects unions from outside interference. Employers may not discriminate against workers who join organizations of their own choosing, nor may they pay for and establish their own workers' organizations. The state must establish legal mechanisms to prevent this interference. The government must also promote voluntary collective bargaining between workers' organizations and their employers.
3. The Elimination of All Forms of Forced or Compulsory Labour-The Forced Labour Convention (No. 29) and the Abolition of Forced Labour Convention (No. 105) require governments to suppress all forms of forced and compulsory labour in their territories. Forced labour is any form of labour which a worker performs under threat of penalty rather than voluntarily. Though there are very limited exceptions for the military and national emergencies, government prohibitions on forced labour must be comprehensive.
4. The Effective Abolition of Child Labour-The Minimum Age Convention (No. 138) sets a baseline minimum working age of fifteen. If a country is insufficiently developed, or if only light work is involved, the

minimum age can be lower; conversely, for hazardous occupations the minimum age is eighteen. States must adopt and pursue national policies that effectively end child labour and allow children to fully develop both physi-cally and mentally.

5. The Elimination of Discrimination in Respect of Employment and Occupation. The Discrimination Convention (No. 111) requires governments to establish national policies that eliminate discrimination on the basis of race, color, sex, religion, political opinion, and national or social origin. Discrimination includes unequal access to employment and training as well as disparate working conditions and the national policy must address both unequal opportunities and treatment. The Equal Remuneration Convention (No. 100) completes this standard by establishing the right of men and women to equal pay for work of equal value.

A particularly important feature is that they are "qualitative" in nature and not "quantitative." Unfortunately, all too often they are misrepresented as quantitative measures that set minimum wage levels or maximum hours of work, both of which are labour market interventions that are clearly contingent on the stage of development. This qualitative character of core labour standards reflects a recognition that some standards are universal and apply regardless of a country's stage of development.

THE CASE FOR LABOUR STANDARDS

The case for labour standards can be argued in a number of ways. This section briefly visits the "human rights" and "parity" cases for labour standards and then turns to examine the "economic" case in detail. This attention to the economic case for labour standards reflects the fact that economic arguments are increasingly decisive in the making of policy today. The first justification for labour standards rests on a human rights argument. Such an argument might be constructed on the grounds that work is a central activity of life, and as such plays a key role in the creation of self-identity, in personal development, and the achievement of personal fulfillment. Consequently, human beings should have some core rights at work to ensure that work contributes positively to these aspects of human growth.

A second justification that has much popular appeal is the parity argument. Here, the reasoning is that over the last several years various international trade agreements have conferred many global rights on investors and their intellectual property (IP), and consequently working people should also be given equivalent global rights and legal protections. Though having much popular political traction there are reasons for caution here. In particular, there are strong grounds for believing that existing investor and IP rights are wrong and unjustified. Lawyers love to talk of "intellectual property" because this makes any change in the law appear to be a form of "confiscation." However, the reality is that IP is a metaphor for a set of socially constructed constantly changing rules, and ranged against IP rights are a set of equally important values such as the right of people to imitate others, to work, talk, and write freely, and to nurture common cultures. Given this, there is a danger that the parity argument may link labour standards with unjustifiable IP rights that need to be repealed.

In contrast to the parity argument, the economic argument for labour standards makes an affirmative self-standing case for labour standards. This economic argument recognizes the labour market and economic development roots of the child labour problem. Addressing these roots leads to a focus on core labour standards, especially those concerned with the rights of freedom of association and collective bargaining. This is because these rights are key to success regarding child labour, discrimination, and forced labour. Given this, core labour standards should be made a central element of the system of global governance that is now being constructed, and all countries should be pushed to conform to these standards. Unfortunately, labour standards are frequently accused of being a form of "hidden protection" that gives unfair protection to industrialized country workers by taking away comparative advantage of workers in developing countries. As is argued below, this claim is fundamentally wrong. Labour standards are good for both developing and developed countries, and exemplify how good economic policy can promote win-win outcomes.

LESSONS FROM THE PAST

Before turning to abstract economic arguments it is worth briefly reflecting on the development history of the United States, which provides a concrete example of why there is a need for the type of rights embodied in core labour standards. In the nineteenth and early twentieth century the USA was marked by formation of an integrated national economy. This process was driven by the steamboat, the railroad, and the automobile, which integrated the component regional economies and it, was marked by many of same problems that are seen today in the global economy. Workplaces were unsafe, wages were low, and workers were subject to exploitation. All of these features were captured in books such as Upton Sinclair's The Jungle (1905). There was widening income and wealth inequality, and the national economy was prone to periodic booms and slumps, the most extreme example of which was the Great Depression.

Within the United States the response was to create rules and institutions that addressed these problems. Financial markets were tamed by the creation of the Federal Reserve System and the Securities Exchange Commission, while goods markets were stabilized by antitrust laws and the adoption of countercyclical monetary and fiscal policies. In labour markets the solution was the implementation of national labour standards. The Wagner Act (1935) and National Labour Relations Act (1938) granted workers the right of freedom of association to form trade unions and bargain collectively. The Fair Labour Standards Act (1940) established a national minimum wage and set the standard workweek at forty hours, and required overtime pay for work above this. Moreover, such legislation was developed on a federal basis explicitly to stop a race to the bottom among the states.

The result of this legislation was to improve workplace

standards, encourage firms to enhance productivity by innovation rather than exploitation, and give working people the income to buy what they produce, thereby solving the problem of demand shortages that previously contributed to gluts and depressions. These measures also made for "deep" development based on robust mass consumption markets, for ultimately a mass production economy requires mass consumption markets. Improved wages also helped reduce wealth and income inequality, which in turn reduced political conflict. Finally, the growth of trade unions contributed to the development of a healthy democratic politics in which the existence of balanced countervailing forces was able to check monopolistic tendencies.

The bottom line is that no country has experienced successful democratic market development without giving workers the rights embodied in core labour standards, and this historical experience should inform today's debate about the place of labour standards in developing countries. National economic integration was the problem of yester-year: global economic integration is the problem of today. Yet the two processes share a common underlying econo-mic logic, and it is for this reason that the policy responses that worked to create prosperity earlier remain an instructive guide for today.

Arguments for Today

Analogies with the past can help illuminate labour market and development problems of today, but they must be accompanied by arguments rooted in the analytic specifics of today. In many regards the core labour standards prohibition of "exploitative" child labour is the most complicated of the five standards. This is because the child labour problem clearly has a stage-of-development dimension that makes discussion more complicated. It is a paradox that the child labour question has greatest public traction, and yet it is also the most complicated owing to its stage-of-development dimension. That said, it is also clear that over any medium-term horizon the accumulation of human capital is key to economic development. This means that having children in school rather than earning a meager family income supplement is good development policy. Having rules that prompt developing countries to enhance education is therefore a good thing. However, for such rules to be successful three things are required.

First, there is a need to invest in education to provide school buildings and train and pay school-teachers. This involves government spending. If children are to be taken out of the workplace in the name of educating them, needed educational resources have to be funded? Second, work must pay wages that allow a family to subsist. Child labour exists because children earn vitally needed income for families. If society is going to stop children from working, then adult workers must be able to support their families. This is why core labour standards, as they pertain to freedom of association and collective bargaining, are so critical to solving the child labour problem. Third, if child labour is eliminated then there must be adequate numbers of jobs for adults so that they can earn the wages needed to replace child incomes. Once again, this is where labour standards have a role to play since they contribute to the building of a development dynamic that leads to deep economic development. In sum, these arguments illustrate how child labour is a problem that links with wider problems concerning labour markets and economic development, and solving the child labour problem therefore calls for policies that tackle these broader problems.

Prohibition of all forms of discrimination is another core labour standard, and here too there are implications for child labour. Discrimination is morally repugnant and it is also economically inefficient in that society fails to fully realize the economic potential of all it members. Ending discrimination should therefore be a goal of all. However, it also has child labour implications. First, to the extent that female adult workers are underpaid, it may make it harder for families to earn an adequate income and thereby may drive more children into the labour market. Second, some of the most exploitative forms of child labour-trafficking and sexual slavery-are concentrated among female children, and these practices are in turn connected to gender attitudes. Ending discrimination stands to empower women, and in doing so it can help reduce these especially abusive forms of child labour.

Eliminating discrimination, forced labour, and exploitative child labour are all ends. The rights to freedom of association and collective bargaining are both means and ends. Absent these rights, it is unlikely that prohibitions on discrimination and forced labour can be made effective in practice, nor will it be possible to create the labour market and economic development conditions necessary for the elimination of child labour. For these reasons, the rights to freedom of association and collective bargaining assume special importance. Yet, despite this, it is these rights that are frequently viewed with the greatest hostility by developing countries and labeled as "hidden protectionism." Granting workers the legal rights of freedom of association and collective bargaining is good development policy. By promoting improved distribution of income such measures can foster development of robust domestic markets.

This in turn allows wages to grow, giving rise to a virtuous circle in which rising wages support market development and market development supports rising wages. D. Rodrik (1999) provided evidence that democracies pay higher wages. Thomas Palley (1999) provided evidence that improved rights of free association correlate with faster growth in the five-year period after the improvements are made. Palley (2000) also provided evidence that income distribution is more equal in countries with better rights of freedom of association, as well as evidence that wages are higher in such countries. This finding potentially qualifies Rodrik's argument. Democracy still matters, but it matters because it creates the political conditions that allow for freedom of association, and freedom of association then becomes the actual instrument driving higher wages in labour markets.

Such arguments run completely counter to those advanced by the mainstream of the economics profession. According to the latter, unions are a "bad" in that they are not a market distortion, nor does income distribution matter for economic development. However, a labour standards perspective rejects the view that unions are a market distortion. Instead, it argues that they are a private sector corrective to market failure-namely a huge imbalance of power between individual workers and business. Unions serve to create a level bargaining field. This in turn is good for development as it improves income distribution, thereby fostering domestic development rooted in the growth of domestic markets. Such growth contrasts with the "enclave" model of development as exemplified by export processing zones, which are the modern form of plantation development. A second contribution of labour standards is that they promote good governance. There is now widespread recognition that good governance promotes successful development, and labour standards fit with this new view.

Good governance, characterized by transparency and accountability, is necessary to prevent corruption and the misallocation of capital. Freedom of association and unions contribute to good governance by creating the countervailing power that can check such practices. Contrary to mainstream thinking, competitive markets alone cannot do this. Simply opening and liberalizing markets will not compete away the problem of corruption as market participants just get captured by corruption. Each firm must make a decision to "bribe" or "not bribe." In equilibrium where neither firm bribes are socially optimal as neither firm wastes resources on bribing, and contracts are allocated on the basis of which firm is the most efficient. However, if one firm chooses not to bribe, then the other has a private incentive to bribe and secure the business. Consequently, both end up bribing, and the market left to itself is characterized by bribery.

The only way to sustain the optimal "no bribery" equilibrium is to have political institutions that prevent bribery. Bribery and corruption are political problems, and their elimination requires political reform. Labour standards, through the right of freedom of association, can foster political conditions that promote such reforms. Palley (2000) reported evidence that countries with better rights of freedom of association have lower corruption, have greater economic security, and are more democratic. Not only do labour standards promote conditions of good governance that facilitate domestic economic development, but there are also grounds for believing that labour standards can help resolve some of the contradictions that currently afflict the international economy. This accounts for the international win-win dimension of labour standards. In particular, the international economy is afflicted by the contradiction of export-led growth. The export-led growth paradigm embodies a "fallacy of composition" in that it leads all countries to aim for export surpluses. However, one country's exports are another's imports, and this means that not all can run surpluses. What works for one cannot work for all. If all try to run surpluses and grow on the backs of their neighbors' markets, the result is a shortage of demand and global deflation.

For developing countries, a particular manifestation of the export-led problematic is ever-declining terms of trade. This is an old finding, first identified by Hans Singer and Raoul Prebisch in the 1950s in connection with commodity prices. Now, owing to the persistent spread of export-led industrialization, developing countries may have entered a new era marked by secularly declining terms of trade for low end manufactured goods as well as commodities. In effect, developing countries may face the prospect of having to run to stay where they are. Moreover, this situation promises to increase financial instability since these countries must export ever more to pay their foreign debts, which then drives down prices further. The only long run solution is to have developing countries consume a greater portion of what they produce, thereby slowing the growth supply on international markets and driving up prices. However, for this to happen these countries need to fix their hugely unequal income distributions, and this is why labour standards are so crucial.

Another failing of the export-led growth model is that it

is marked by an incentive structure that produces a race to the bottom. This is because each country has an incentive to try to gain international competitive advantage by exploiting every possible margin. Good competition focuses on productivity and quality; bad competition eats away at workplace safety, the environment, and income distribution. Labour standards can help by ruling out bad competition, and once again this can be understood in terms of the logic of the prisoner's dilemma. Each country has a choice whether to maintain or lower standards. The socially optimal equilibrium has both maintaining standards, but left to itself the market produces a socially sub-optimal outcome in which both lower standards. The logic is as follows. If one country maintains standards, the other has an incentive to lower standards and gain a competitive advantage. Consequently, both end up lowering standards. The only way to sustain the socially optimal equilibrium is to have global labour standards that bar countries from taking the low road.

Interestingly, this race to the bottom dynamic has usually been conceived in terms of competition between north (industrialized countries) and south (developing countries). However, there appears to be a growing recog-nition that it may operate principally between southern countries. Thus, G. Berik (2001) found in her study of the Pakistan soccer ball industry that moves to restrict the use of child labour contributed to production moving out of Pakistan to India. In this instance Pakistan tried to maintain standards, and it was then undercut competitively by India.

Making Part of the System of Global Governance

Labour standards are good development policy and should therefore become a core piece of the global governance structure now being constructed. The ILO will retain a critical role regarding the monitoring of country adherence to standards, and it also has special capabilities to advise governments as to how to develop systems for enforcing labour standards. However, beyond this, the international financial institutions (IFIs)-as represented by the International

Monetary Fund, the World Bank, and the regional development banks-must all officially promote core labour standards as part of their mission. The articles of agreement of the IFIs require them to adopt policies that are "economically justified," and labour standards pass this critical (and appropriate) test. The IMF, the World Bank, and the multi-lateral regional development banks are all in the "business of development," and this is why labour standards should be part of their standard operating procedures.

With regard to the IMF, annual Article IV country reviews conducted by the IMF should explicitly report on countries' adherence to labour standards. This can help spotlight behaviour as well as contribute to the emergence of a global labour market policy norm. Countries should also be obliged to meet labour standards conditions to receive enhanced structural adjustment fund loans (ESAFs) from the IMF. These conditions need not require that countries immediately meet labour standards, but they must at a minimum require an effective plan that will ensure compliance by a reasonable date certain. Finally, to receive IMF special drawing rights (SDRs) countries are obliged to follow IMF policy, and this policy should now be amended to require countries to commit to labour standards. Just as the IMF now requires countries to pursue policies that promote good governance, so too the IMF should require that countries commit to ILO labour standards.

With regard to the World Bank and the regional development banks, country assistance strategies (CAS) which guide all bank lending should incorporate an explicit focus on labour standards. All loans are currently screened with regard to their environmental impact, and loans should now also be subject to a "core labour standards" assessment. Once again, countries that do not currently meet core labour standards could satisfy this assessment by putting forward a satisfactory plan that details how they will achieve compliance by a reasonable date certain. Finally, there is also a place for core labour standards in the world trading system as administered by the World Trade Organization (WTO). The

WTO should have the right to penalize countries that violate labour standards. Trade-related labour standards disputes should be administered through a dispute resolution process similar to that governing the administration of intellectual property rights, and this dispute resolution process should also have access to the same set of remedies.

Child labour is now widely recognized as an unacceptable scourge. Less widely understood are the policy implications that follow from recognizing that it is a problem that is rooted in labour market dysfunction and economic under-development while voluntary corporate codes of conduct and "free of child labour" product-labeling programs have an important role to play in highlighting the problem of exploitative child labour, they fail to tackle the root causes of the problem. Elimination of exploitative child labour requires the global adoption and enforcement of the entire body of ILO core labour standards. These standards address the root causes of child labour-namely inefficient functioning of labour markets and lack of economic development. Unfortunately, core labour standards are all too often misrepresented as a form of "imperial bullying" and "hidden protection for industrialized countries" when the reality is that they constitute good economic policy.

Labour standards are good for developing countries because they help remedy the problem of labour market exploitation. They also contribute to deep economic development by positively impacting the distribution of income in a way that fosters robust domestic markets and by promoting institutional developments conducive to good governance. Finally, they are good for the international economy because they tilt country development away from reliance on export-led growth, which is a strategy that is inconsistent when considered at a global level. The scourge of exploitative child labour can only be eliminated by building labour markets that function for the benefit of working people and by fostering economic development. Core labour standards contribute to realizing both of these goals and for this reason are at the heart of the solution to the child labour problem.

CONCEPTS AND METHODOLOGY

This study focuses on cross-border trafficking of children into prostitution other extreme or intolerable forms of child labour. Attention is, however, paid to use of child labour and child trafficking which take place within the country but connect with cross-border or international trafficking. Definitions of child labour and child trafficking, conceptual framework and research methodology are discussed in this chapter. There are three important points in relation to concepts and methodology of this study that need to be stressed here first. Firstly, the emphasis of the study on cross-border trafficking in children does not confine its samples to interview the trafficked children only, as it is wiser to also cover the interviews with persons whose current age are 18 or over but were recently trafficked when they were aged below 18.

Findings from previous studies have consistently shown, however, that in most, circumstances, the actual procedures through which people are recruited seem to follow the same pattern for childen and adult. Where relevant, practices related young women trafficking are also explored. The study also designs to obtain information from key informants in sending and receiving communities and other key informants, such as children's parents, children's employers, GO and NGO staff dealing with child trafficking problem. By doing so, it is anticipated that meaningful insight of child trafficking problem and its impacts will be gained. Second, the definition of child trafficking that will be discussed in the next section is specifically framed to meet to aims of this study. It is not aimed to set a definition to be used as an international standard or an agreement between countries or among countries in this sub-region for coordination or mutual assistance. This working definition is only the proposition from the research team. Lastly, the study also intends to investigate exploitation of child labour in each country in the sub-region whenever the patterns or situations would link to cross-border or international trafficking in children.

Cultural values in this sub-region accept and sometimes

encourage child employment. Children assisting their parents in farmwork or family business and household chores are widely practiced. A large number of children, however, work in exchange for money, in jobs such as factory workers, service workers, and domestic workers. To parents in this sub region, having their children working in order to obtain supplement family income is very common and is not greatly recognized as a problem even if their children are engaged in destructive and exploitative working conditions. But it is generally agreed for the states in this sub region that use of child labour in extreme exploitative forms, such as a form of bonded labour and slavery, cannot be tolerated and must be eliminated. Therefore, it is appropriate to start with defining what is child labour and what are the extreme or intolerable forms of child labour that are the emphasis of this study. In this study, a child refers to a person aged below 18 which is a definition universally used by states, the United Nations, and international organizations.

- A child labourer refers to a native child or a foreign child who engages in any types of work in exchange of income or in kind at the time of the interview or at anytime of one's life when that person was aged below 18 years. A child labourer may receive any type of payment regularly or irregularly. A foreign child must migrate crossing a border from one country to another in the Mekong Sub region.
- The extreme forms of child labour are: the use of children in prostitution, pornography, the drugs trade, and other forms of forced or compulsory labour, debt bondage and serfdom, and their employment in any types of work that is dangerous, harmful or hazardous.

These exploitative forms are prioritized as a core problem of child labour that is currently being combated by the states and international organizations world-wide. The International Programme on the Elimination of Child Labour, ILO, for instance, has identified four types of child employment which need to be eliminated without further delay: (1) children in slave-like and bonded labour; (2) children in dangerous and hazardous working conditions; and (3) vulnerable children such as the very young aged below 12 and girls (ILO 1997). Various definitions are currently used to describe trafficking in women and children. There is some common dimension of the definitions of children trafficking used by various international organisations. But none of them are clear and cover all forms of trafficking in children and women as documented by the UN Special Rapporteur on Violence Against Women. Thus, there have consistently been calls for reformulating international standards and straightforward definitions of children and women trafficking.

Major differences in the definitions of trafficking in children and women are found to be differences in terms of approaches, gender, age, sexual exploitation, and legal or illegal moves crossing national borders. In an effort to obtain the inclusive definition, it is recommended that the definition should not discriminatory and exclude any trafficked person due to their age, gender, type of work, location and means by which they were trafficked. It is widely accepted that trafficking for sexual exploitation is the major form of trafficking in children and women. But as a matter of fact, any persons at any age regardless of their sex can be trafficked within a country or crossing border for different purposes which may or may not involve sexual exploitation. And girls are more prone to be trafficked and abused for sexual purposes.

Although, emphasis of this study is on children trafficking associated with use of child labour in any extreme forms, some forms of children trafficking across national borders which are not labour in nature, such as false marriage and adoption, are included if the trafficked children are put into coercive and exploitative conditions associated with use of child labour. For instance, in most circumstances, Vietnamese girls who are sold to be wives in Chinese families are forced to be unpaid servants or to help in family agriculture or business under slavery-like conditions.

- A profitable act undertaken by person(s) other than the

children themselves.

- Transportation of a child within one national border and/ or across national borders.
- Frontier-crossing movement is usually but not always an illegal move with or without a child's consent.
- Using false or deceptive information.
- Trading a child for the purpose of work or services by means of violence and abuse, or other forms of coercion.
- Destructive and exploitative work conditions.

Conceptual Framework

The vulnerable groups of children to trafficking: There are specific groups of children that are customarily vulnerable to trafficking and thus are the prime target group of traffickers. These include children of minorities, migrants, lower caste or indigenous people which are usually at high risk of exploitation for both cultural and economic reasons (ILO 1997). With special reference to migrant children, it is particularly true that children of undocumented migrant workers have to encounter at least two problems: no or limited opportunity for education, and to health care services existing in the destination country. As a result, many of young kids have to work at a very young age. Some start to help their parents as young as 4-5 years old. The older kids have to become a wage labourers working in places notorious for their poor health and safety conditions with very low pay. It is understandable that the foreign child workers do not have much choice. Consequently, children of illegal migrants largely end up, later in life, following the path of their parents and becoming illegal migrant labourers. They are easily coerced and trafficked to work in extreme forms of child labour since they often lack stability.

The migrant children are the target population in this study. Use of child labour is deliberately divided, according to actual situation of cross-frontier trafficking in children in this sub region, into three types of labour:

- First, children in commercial sex-industry are paid more

attention as compared to the other two types. This is primarily because the nature and extent of children trafficked into prostitution has been recognised the most intolerable form and is receiving the most attention practically and theoretically. There have been a large number of studies, government reports and international papers on this issue. It is also the topic that the core research team has been involved in for more than 2 years. Networks and trust building from previous work with key informants: children and women in sex work, owners of the establishments, NGOs and local authorities working on this issue, have eased confidentiality to disclose a variety of trafficking patterns. Accordingly, more cases of children in sex work than children in other forms of labour are interviewed arid presented in this report.

- Second, trafficking children into the begging and soliciting business is a new form of bonded labour in this sub region. It covers a few thousands of children and small scale of areas. However, it is included not because of its visibility but also because of its degree of seriousness as a violation of the fundamental rights of the human persons.
- Third, children engaged in other extreme forms of labour is compared to the above two types covered, the largest scale in terms of number and types of work. The work that children are engaged in can be either illegal or legal as well as voluntarily or forcibly. The actual situation of foreign children engaged in the extreme forms of child labour is more or less the same as life of poor children working for survival in reality.

RESEARCH METHODOLOGY

This research project puts importance on obtaining the most updated, valid and informative data in order to truly improve an understanding of child migrants trafficked into extreme forms of child labour in the sub region. Several data collection methods were employed; however, the primary methods were in-depth interview, and documentary analysis which can be categorized as qualitative research. The samples generally cover a small number of interviews (as compared to random samples of population used in quantitative research or 'survey research') and texts/documents. The analysis is usually aimed to elaborate what and how the situations happen in concrete reality like telling stories. In most circumstances, the research teams made filed trips to collect data in the worksites or in the sending and receiving communities and interviewed the target populations. During the filed visits and along the interviews the researchers also observed behaviour of people and situations related to the topic under study. This method is generally called 'substantive field research' which intends to elucidate a sense of 'action' taking place in particular setting.

The data collection methods varied from team to team. The core research team, for example, combined many data collection techniques ranging from qualitative and quantitative methods, conducting estimations, gathering information from discussions and exchange of ideas at conferences on the issue of trafficking in women and children which research investigators attended, to taking a role as a committee member for the government's sub-committee on sex work and unskilled labour contrast. Cambodia report mainly relied on documentary study.

Major methods of data collection

a. In-depth Interview (IDI): The Thai, Vietnam and Yunnan teams used the semi-structured questionnaire or interview guideline as a major tool of data collection. However, the Thai team and Yunnan also used informal and unstructured interviewing in the field settings where the research teams are familiar to or with the respondents in their trust in the researchers have been built from the previous study. Theoretically speaking, the unstructured interview which places the control over the interviewing process lies in hands of the interviewees is more appropriate when the researchers are in the field for a longer period of time and/or are able to interview the same individual on many separate occasions. The semi-structured questionnaire on the other hand, which follow an interview guide, allows for similar degree of flexibly as unstructured interviews, but place more of the control in the hands of the researcher. The interview guideline consisted of a written list of questions and topics specifying an order for how the inquiry should occur. In practice, not all questions were asked due to many reasons: time and place of the interview, willingness of the interviewees to answer some questions, and the presence of interference.

Both techniques discussed above refer as IDI were selected not only because of limited time of data collection which all research teams encountered, but because of the need for flexibility. The sampling methods mainly were; (1) nominations—the respondents were chosen by local NGOs, local leaders or the authorities.; and (2) snowball sampling— once each key informant or a child or parents of child labourers was selected and interviewed, they were asked for names of others to be interviewed. These are major and recommend sampling techniques in qualitative research. However, some government officials were purposively chosen according to their positions and responsibilities with regard to the problem.

Interviews were conducted with key informants including: trafficked children parents of child workers, migrant children in employment in various business sectors, government officials and NGOs locally working on issues of women and children. For most of the interviews, the researchers asked the respondents' permission to take notes during the interviews. When and wherever possible, the interviews were taped with the respondents' consent and were mostly transcribed immediately after the interviews. Group discussions with the community members and with government officials were also carried out. Altogether, almost 200 respondents were interviewed by the IDI technique with somewhat over 100 cases conducted by the Thai team, 41 cases by the Yunnan team and 38 cases including group interviews by the Vietnam team.

It should be noted here that language barriers for interviews migrant children and their families conducted by the Thai team were very minimal. For Burmese migrants, interviewers were native speakers of the Burmese language. For Laotian migrants, all of them could communicate in Thai because of similarities of languages used in the two countries. For Cambodian migrants, most of them have lived in Thailand for sometime, mostly over one year, they can speak and understand Thai language used in daily life quite well.

b. Assessing secondary data: Each research team made their best effort to try to gain access to related secondary data or documents from governmental agencies working on child labour and trafficking of women and children in order to obtain a macro figure or history of child trafficking in the country. Three main sources of documentary data were obtained: GOs, NGOs and related research papers. In addition, news and features published in daily newspapers and magazines also provided updated information about child trafficking problems. This method was used by all research teams.

c. Co-operation of the GOs and NGOs: It is not surprising if this technique is not considered as a data collection method but rather a facilitating process for easing the data collection. Due to the hidden nature of trafficking problem, it is usually difficult to begin any interview with the trafficked victims either in the sending or receiving settings. This is why all research teams stated that cooperation from various organizations was extremely important in conducting their field research. In general, these organizations assisted in nominating or locating potential key informants. Then the researcher tried to approach them in their worksites or their own local communities and ask permission to interview.

In some circumstances, they introduced the research team to the respondents as well as helped in explaining the purposes of the interview. Moreover, with this assistance, it proved to be the most important tool to obtain not only reliable information but to gain access to inaccessible sources of data. For example, this method helped the Thai team to access and interviews the women migrant prisoners who were trafficked from Myanmar to Taiwan passing through Thailand, Malaysia and the Philippines as well as to data base files of aliens detained at the Immigration Detention Center (IDC) in Bangkok. In Yunnan study, selection of the interviewees relied very heavily on the local governmental agencies, such as women's federations, public security, and other organization. They helped in disclosing the files of those being trafficked and repatriated or returned to their communities.

RESEARCH SITES

Apart from conducting filed research in the 16 selected provinces in Thailand, the Thai team made visits to 2 provinces in Myanmar (1 capital city and a border province), Vientiane, the capital city of Lao PDR, and Koh Kong, a border province of Cambodia. The Vietnam team carried out their survey in 2 Northern border provinces and 3 Southwestern border provinces. The Yunnan team conducted the interviews in 8 counties and cities from 4 prefectures which altogether have a total borderline of over 1,200 kilometers with Myanmar. The Cambodia team made observations during on-site visit to crisis centers run by NGOs in Phnom Penh.

CONCEPTUAL REMARKS AND POLICY RECOMMENDATIONS

This study has tried to examine and analyze current situations of child trafficking in the Mekong Sub-region. The findings indicate in general that the phenomenon of child trafficking is complicated and encompasses numerous factors both in sending and receiving communities. This chapter will summarize an overview of the child trafficking situation and discuss the study's conceptual findings. Recommendations for further development of programmes and strategies to prevent child trafficking and to reintegrate trafficked victims into their home communities will also be explored.

The study results indicate that cross-frontier child trafficking in the six countries of the Maekong sub-region has increasingly been a problem throughout the sub-region. The number of victims has increased. Types of business which children are trafficked into have been various and unexpected of. Areas of procurement have expanded and reached small remote communities. Many well-defined trafficking routes have been established. Sending communities are more likely clustered in the bordering areas of the sending countries adjacent to the receiving countries. The routes and the extent of the problem differ by types of business children are trafficked into. The type of child trafficking most commonly found is abduction of girls into prostitution. Others are trafficking of children into begging gangs and other types of manual labour.

Exact number of child trafficked victims is not available. This is mainly because child trafficking involves illegal and clandestine activities and access to information in order to understand its reality and extent is not conveniently available. As a result, no systematic quantitative study is carried out, whether it be a micro and macro study and whether it be conducted in sending or receiving countries. It is also partly because the problem has not been fully recognized and addressed at an official level in many countries in the sub-region. For example, although main factor determining the migration of ethnic minorities from Myanmar is clearly rooted to the country's political unrest and economic hardship, the government of Myanmar still seems reluctant to perceive the problem and recognize that the majority of trafficked children are ethnic minorities whose home communities are in the Myanmar war-zone areas. Vietnam, Yunnan and Laos are in the early stages of studying the child trafficking problem. For Cambodia, a number of studies on child trafficking have been conducted and they indicate that many thousands of Vietnamese child prostitutes in Cambodia.

1. The Context of Trafficking

Poverty has been one of the most important factors that drive children out of their homes and into the workforce with promises for money and better lives. Children are naturally vulnerable and often become repeatedly victimized by child trafficking. The following figure reflects the conceptual findings which the author conclusively analyzed from research projects on combating child trafficking in the Maekong basin countries as well as from various studies on transnational migration she has earlier conducted.

a. Victims forced and/or kidnapped, and trafficked.
b. Victims are given false information, and trafficked into types of business other than promised. (Often found with victims from Laos, Cambodia, and Vietnam.)
c. Victims realize the nature of the work, but not the work conditions. (Common among sex workers.)
d. Victims realize the nature of work and work conditions, but are not aware and/or are able to foresee the difficult situations they may encounter. (Victims are inexperienced and are given partial information.)
e. Labourers (could possibly be formerly trafficked) realize the nature of work and work conditions, but are not given alternative worksites.
f. Labourers (could possibly be formerly trafficked) realize the nature of work, work conditions, and are able to select their worksite.

The Trafficking Continuum shows that there are different degrees of being trafficked. The most abusive trafficking method is to force victims out of their normal lives or kidnap them and force them into the workforce (A). The least abusive method is at the opposite end of the line (F) where the people are mostly former child trafficked victims, but no longer regarded as victims or as children. A trafficked victim usually starts being trafficked at young age from point A and moves to points further right on the line as their trafficking experiences are accumulated. The movement is usually from the most abusive form of trafficking to the least abusive form (from left to right or from point A to point F). The movement is also apparently made step by step, for example from point C to point D rather than from point C to E or F.

Although the people at points further right on the line are no longer children nor regarded as victims, they hold experiences from being at least once trafficked as a child. Furthermore, although these people are considered experienced in the trafficking world and have learned to survive in difficult circumstances, they could be trafficked all over again and their skills and experiences may not protect them. The reverse movement from right to left on the line as indicated is apparently made step by step as well. For example, a woman could voluntarily enter sex industry but was consequently left with no choices, and finally trafficked into types of work she did not anticipate (from point F to E or from point E to D). The fact found identical for any trafficked victim at any point of their life along the continuum line is that, every trafficked victim carries loads of debt which they owe to the trafficking agents. According to recent studies, more trafficked victims are engaged in workforce voluntarily. It is often found that trafficked victims from the Maekong basin countries actually realize to some extent that they are brought out of their communities in search for employment in a foreign land. They usually have some idea of what they are brought into. Recently, victims are less likely to be forced or kidnapped. One trafficked victim could therefore appear at any point on the line and move left or right on the Trafficking Continuum line.

Studying trafficked victims' biographies will provide interested people a whole picture and all-sided views of trafficking. A trafficking study that focuses only on trafficked children under the actual definition of children (persons under the age of 18 years old) may fail to completely allow one to understand trafficking and its impacts. For example, a professionally satisfied 25 year-old sex worker could have been forcefully trafficked into prostitution as a child and managed to finally end up as a voluntary sex worker. As discussed earlier, trafficked victims might have been trafficked as a child, grew up, have been repeatedly trafficked but to lesser degrees, and finally voluntarily enter the workforce on their own. Other important factors which expose children to being easily trafficked and victimized are the children's legal status and education. The populations most trafficked are evidently disadvantaged groups of people such as marginalized people and people who have little or no access to education. The marginalized populations include stateless people who hold none or limited legal status such as hill tribe people, ethnic minorities from Myanmar and Laos, and low-income people including their children from Cambodia.

2. The Root Causes of Trafficking

Trafficking in children has developed rapidly from a simple high profit underground human trade to a more complicated and more acceptable network business. Trafficking players have changed from conventional ones such as strangers, non-community-based procurers to recently groups like trafficked victims' parents, community leaders, and authorities such as police and other law enforcement officers. It is frequently claimed that lack of cheap labour, and children being obedient, quick learners, not being able to refuse all forms of abuses and violence are the reasons why children are being trafficked. It was also reported that child trafficking is the most profitable business that receives the least attention from generally all governments in the Maekong sub-region, as compared to other 'underground' businesses such as drug and weapon smuggling, and logging business. Has an in-depth analytical questions regarding trafficking in children been asked, the answers to which why child trafficking, how it is well maintained, and how it is progressively developing, would be as follow.

a. *Gender Sensitivity*: Although vary in degrees, most countries in the Maekong sub-region share the male dominated culture. Thailand is one leading male dominated country in the sub-region. Sex worker patronage is commonly practiced among men in Thailand. It has become common in some areas geographically close to Thailand and in some cultures where their people have exposed to the Thai men culture. It was reported that such cultures have recently included some ethnic and hill tribe groups in Myanmar and Laos, and some populations in Cambodia, Vietnam and China. The male dominated cultures usually express their beliefs by providing different treatment for boys and girls. For example, in most countries in the sub-region, boys and girls are given unequal education opportunities. Especially regarding sex, boys and girls are given different sets of sex education and sex norms by parents and schools.

The gender insensitivity leads girls and women to being vulnerable subjects of trafficking. Schooling opportunity is necessary for adequate physical, emotional, and social development of a child. It is also important for the children's future job placements and their space in a society. Equal schooling opportunity between boys and girls are therefore needed in order to provide all children with equal opportunities in their lives. It will lead boys and girls to equal employment placements, relatively equal social status and respect from a society. As previously mentioned, Thailand is the largest receiving country of girl children trafficked into sex business. Some cultures such as in border towns of Vietnam, Cambodia and Myanmar, and in inner cities such as Kengtung in Shan State of Myanmar, and among ethnic groups such as Mon from Myanmar, have taken such male's sex worker patronage culture and procured girls from their communities for prostitution. The tradition has been widely practiced and well received among men, and some women across the Maekong sub-region. The trafficking in girl children has therefore grown in the recent years and more girls are procured and used for sexual purposes. The gender insensitivity remains while girls are being more complicatedly exploited.

b. ***Cultural Factors***: An attitude in which children have to pay gratitude to their parents is a common practice among countries in the Maekong Sub-region. Girl children in particular, are expected to support their family from a very young age. A girl has to learn to take care of younger siblings and perform household chores, and continue to do so in whatever possible ways throughout her life. Especially if a girl is an older sister, she is expected to even generate income to support family as well as sending brothers to school. Being raised to be obedient, girls are usually cornered into protecting and supporting their families, come what may. Many girls as young as 12 or 13 years old have been reported to enter the sex industry to generate income for their family.

Girls are often subjected to being trafficked more than boys, and they are usually trafficked into sex business more than other types of business. Paying gratitude to parents is a social value and culturally practical. It should not be, however, expected of daughters only. New perspectives where both boys and girls pay gratitude to their parents should be created and initiated. Several programs have been developed and implemented in the Maekong Sub-region communities to eliminate trafficking in girl children. Some countries in the sub region like Thailand and Vietnam have also amended their regulations and set a heavy penalty against parents who directly and indirectly engage their children into prostitution.

c. ***Materialism*:** It is evident that materialism has influenced the lives of people in the Maekong sub-region. From China and Vietnam, across Lao PDR and Cambodia, and onto Thailand and Myanmar, the general populations in the sub-region are affected by the rapid economic growth in Asia. Private sectors have put tremendous effort in advertising and marketing their products. Products are mass-produced. Advertisement to release the products takes place. Customers are usually persuaded and manipulated to purchase and consume. Signs of success have been newly constructed concrete furnished houses, electric appliances, automobiles, and fashionable clothing. Most communities in the Maekong Sub-region favor easy money and convenient life, become less self-sustained, and depend rather heavily on external factors. The attitude among the general populations has been changed towards materialism. The people are nurtured by such attitude throughout most countries in the Maekong Sub-region. Especially among the disadvantaged groups people, they struggle to keep up with such rapid change. As girls are not equipped with education but are obliged to support families, girls have become easier subjects of trafficking.

7

Related Issues of Child Labour

"India is a developing nation". It may be true in certain areas or issues. But, when it comes to literacy, per capita income, social justice, child labour, infrastructure facilities, social awareness, India cannot project itself as a developing country, but has to call itself as an underdeveloped country. Among the above mentioned problems, child labour is continued to be a more serious problem which hampers the health and growth of the child (i.e.) the growth of future India. Moreover, the mind set of the Indian's who worry only about themselves and not about the society in which they live in is a major cause for the social evils like child labour to prevail continuously. Child labour implies that who are in the age group below 14 yrs and who work for themselves or for their family for an income and who contribute a significant share to the labour force of India.

May be the GDP of India has grown significantly during the recent years, but it cannot be proudly stated that the entire contribution is by the adult labour force. This is a serious problem which has to be curtailed through social engineering and transformation of ideas among the people in the society. Among the total child labour force, a significant portion of them work in organized sector which is governed by all social security legislations and government appointed inspectors like Inspector of Factories PF Inspector, ESI Inspector, and their higher ups. If this is the fate in the organized sector, it is not necessary for us to think about the children working in their own families or in an unorganized sector.

REASONS FOR CHILD LABOUR AND THE STRATEGIES TO OVERCOME

The following are the major reasons for child labour in India and strategies to overcome it.

Inhumane attitude of the Employers

The managements of the corporate/organized sector have an inhumane attitude towards children, as their only intention is to make profits at the costs of children's health and growth without a moral or social responsibility. Children come to work or parents send them to work due to poverty and this is exploited by the organized sectors. These corporate do not even think that the health and growth of a child is being pampered as they employ them, but think only about the percentage of profits they can make out of this cheap labour. The official/governmental machinery which is to prevent child labour are just puppets in the hands of the job providers and are onlookers of this social injustices after getting their individual needs fulfilled by them.

Strategies to be Adopted

The following strategies may be adopted to curtail this injustice made to children.

- People from the organized sector should not entertain child labour at the first instance and make it as their policy, so that generations together may not follow it.
- If they are forced to employ children, due to competition, or any other business situation, they should take care of the children by offering them jobs which may not be health hazardous, and easy to be performed so that their health does not get affected.
- They may reduce the working hours of the children and offer them free education and free food, so that they grow parallel along with their job, both physically and mentally.

- There are professional business houses and corporate which expand, diversify they make their growth overseas without employing child labour. The organized sector should learn business lessons to make their profits, from them, by adopting their strategy or formulate tailor made strategies with the help of them. The professional business houses should also help the organized sector to formulate their strategies as a corporate social responsibility towards prevention of child labour.
- "To make profits is business, to do profiteering is not business. It is exploitation". It is nothing wrong in expanding or diversifying or utilizing new business opportunities but the job providers should not think of creating assets for generations together as this may force them to indulge in all unethical practices including child labour.
- When employers pay their employees, they should have at least a minimum consideration on The Payment of Wages Act, The Minimum Wages Act, The Equal Remuneration Act, because if they are paid with a minimum salary they may not be in a position to send their children for work, by which, they may play a vital role in the eradication of child labour.

Lack of Awareness among the Parents

Parents of the children who send them to work may be illiterates who are not much awareness of the consequences of child labour to the child, to their family and in total to the society. Poverty may also be one of the reasons but the parent should take up a moral responsibility of not shouldering their financial burden on the shoulders of the children. Unplanned family may also be one of the reasons for the parents to send their children for work and there are instances where parents give birth to more children as all the children together can contribute for a larger income for the family.

Strategies to be adopted:

- Large corporate houses along with the NGO's and the

government must help in creating awareness among the parents about the evils of child labour.

- Awareness about the legislations against child labour should be created among the parents.
- The children should be made aware of this rights and privileges and when forced to work, the avenues to get rid of it.
- Individual campaigning, group campaigning, family campaigning may be resorted to educate parents, children and the promoters of business houses.

Inefficient Government Machinery and its Legislations

Legislations are enacted to protect the evils in the society along with loop holes to bypass it. They must be enacted in such a way that, not a single citizen of India should think of neglecting the provisions in the legislations. The governmental personnel who are responsible in administering the provisions of the legislations have a neglecting attitude as they are not given adequate protection when they discharge their duties. Political pressure from the politicians of the ruling government and opposition parties contribute in a significant way by preventing the government, the official machinery and by helping the managements to continue with the evils of child labour without eradicating it.

Strategies to be Followed

Severe provisions may be made in the enactments like closing down of the organization, attaching the assets of the promoters of the organization to the government to rehabilitate the students who were working in that organization. Government staffs may be given due power and they should be dismissed from their jobs with a fine and imprisonment if they are found guilty of neglecting their duties within their jurisdiction. Legislations like Goondas Act or as a non bailable offence should be enacted and administrated against the erring business promoters, parents, government officials and labour contractors, if any.

Ways to Adopt Strategies

Following ways may be adopted to implement the strategies suggested.

Corporate/business houses and organised sectors:

- Performance based incentives and increments may be adopted as a HR policy, so that the efficiency increases and the organizations may not seek to adopt child labour to increase their profits.
- If the employers are forced to use child labour, due to various situations, they may allocate a portion of their available surplus of profits to spend in maintaining the growth and health of the children whom they employ.
- The employers can apportion a certain percentage of their profits, and help the government in eradicating child labour and the government may in turn give a tax rebate to the organization who do not use children as labour.

Government:

- The government should provide safety to the staff who implements the legislations against child labour by taking care of their family and dependents, if anything untoward happens to him/her.
- Inspector of factories should be given more powers of closing down the place of working, if they find that the establishment works against the provisions of the child labour legislations.
- Punishments against erring organization should be made severe so that they may not be repeated in future. For example companies in Tirupur which were guilty of utilizing child labour have been asked to pay RS 10,000 as a fine. This amount when compared to the profits they earn through child labour is very meager and therefore this may not prevent them from using child labour.

Awareness creation:

- All Medias like televisions, radios, hoardings, slide shows, documentary films should be utilized to create awareness among the general public and the parents about the evils of child labour.

- Movies, which are a tool of mass media communication, should be utilized efficiently; this can be done by compulsorily screening the documentary films before the screening of main movie.
- The government and the NGO's should take the responsibility of appointing/utilizing professionally trained social workers to create awareness/ through social casework and social group work.

Any number of awareness programs or strategies cannot by itself solve this problem, unless there is an initiative, understanding and acceptance by the parents, employers and the general public that child labour is an evil to the society. When we are finding it difficult to eliminate the practice of child labour from the organized sector, it is very difficult to think about the same in the unorganized sector and in the agriculture sector. Improvement in the literacy rate, improved awareness among the parents, humanitarian gestures from the employers, efficient legislations and machineries to combat it are the general and open avenues which are available to eradicate child labour from our society.

A COMPREHENSIVE APPROACH TO LABOUR POLICY

Labour standards have been imposed on economies since the 14th century. While such laws initially served the interests of the elite, standards began to address the rights of low-skilled workers during the industrial revolution of the 19th century. Today, the International Labour Organization (ILO) and several international agreements exist to coordinate global labour standards. Domestic laws and international institutions have focused particularly on the issue of child labour. Virtually every country in the world attempts to regulate and limit child employment. International conventions, such as the ILO's Convention on Child Labour, call for a minimum employment age of 15 throughout the world. However, national and international attempts to regulate and/or eliminate child labour have had limited success. Policymakers must better understand the role of child labour in the modern economy in order to create more effective labour regulation. This chapter will examine the economic implications of child labour and labour regulation, revealing that economic development is the ultimate path to the elimination of child labour. Literature Review Analysis of child labour often focuses on the moral imperative to prevent exploitative labour practices.

While humanitarian concerns are relevant to some studies of labour regulation, this chapter uses economic theory to model and explain child labour participation and regulation. Krueger's work (1996), which demonstrates a strong correlation between child labour and poverty, has been particularly significant in the literature. Dehejia and Gatti (2003) add, "Income is the single most important household-level predictor of child labour". Brown (2001) extends this claim, asserting that child participation in the labour force is negatively correlated with per capita GDP. Considerable literature also explores the relationship between child labour and variables that correlate with income, such as development, family size, and education. Scholars have developed many theories to explain connections between these variables. Evidence suggests, however, that the relationship between income and child labour dominates all others. Edmonds and Pavcnik (2004) claim that 75% of cross-country variation in child labour can be explained by income variation.

The relationship between income and child labour illustrates that child "nonwork" is a luxury good that households "consume" when they can afford to do so. Basu and Van (1998) substantiate this commonly held theory with evidence that children of the non-poor seldom work, regardless of national economic or political factors. Krueger (1996), furthermore, observes that people with high socioeconomic status tend to support government regulation of child labour. Economists use several models to explain the continued existence of child labour in a world that strongly prefers that children not participate in the workforce. Dehejia and Gatti (2003) determine key explanatory variables for child labour by analyzing the type of bargaining that leads households to a particular outcome. The intra-household bargaining framework describes child labour as an outcome of bargaining between members of a household. In this framework, variables associated with family dynamics affect decisions about child labour. Such variables include wealth, family size, family member age, and gender of children. The extra-household bargaining framework, alternately, considers each household a single unit. This framework asserts that family units bargain with employers to determine the necessity of child labour.

Access to credit and other household wealth variables significantly affect the outcome of the extra-household bargaining process. Scholarly work that identifies market failure as the cause of child labour expands on the importance of household-level decision-making and bargaining. Most economists agree that child participation in the workforce results from a household preference for immediate benefits of income rather than possible long term-benefits from human capital accumulation. Specifically, the literature suggests that families support child labour because they perceive that the benefits of work outweigh the benefits of school. Beegle et al. (2004), however, note that school and labour are not perfect substitutes. Children may attend school and engage in work during the same time period. Conversely, children may choose not to work or attend school. None-theless, most evidence suggests that children participate in either school or labour. Moreover, those who work at a young age are unlikely to return to school in the future. Assuming that child labour and education are largely substitutable, households engage in a cost-benefit analysis to choose between human capital investment (education) and maintenance of a stable income (child labour).

Grootaert and Kanbur (1995) explain that child labour is inefficiently high when private returns to education are lower than social returns. Child labour is also more likely when parents have not attained high levels of education. This evidence suggests that parents may place less value on education due to personal experience, an inadequate school system, or a perception that education does not provide benefits on an individual level. Evidence confirms that the returns to education are not distributed evenly across societies. Beegle et al. (2004) note that, education is a better investment than child labour because the returns to education increase with age whereas the returns to work experience decline monotonically. Rural communities, however, may not experience the same benefits from education as urban areas. While primary education raises productivity for all sectors of an economy, secondary education does not increase returns for agricultural activity. A household's choice to support a child's education or to promote child labour also depends on the family's ability to manage living expenses. Households in poverty choose to engage in child labour as a means of survival. Market mechanisms can help households survive in the short-term, providing families the means to engage in long-term human capital investment.

For example, Dehejia and Gatti (2003) illustrate that credit access allows households to "trade resources intertemporally" in order to reach an optimal tradeoff between current income and future returns. They find a strong link between incidence of child labour and access to credit, even after controlling for a range of confounding variables. Dehejia and Gatti (2003) also discuss the importance of negative bequests, which allow parents to borrow against the future and tend to be linked with lower levels of child labour. Transitory income shocks, such as accidental crop loss, significantly increase levels of child labour by decreasing household income stability. Income volatility, stemming from unstable markets or income shocks, correlates with higher incidence of child labour. Households suffering from sudden income loss and lacking stable financial institutions or credit access resort to child labour as a means of survival. Beegle et al. (2006) find that households with assets can offset shocks without resorting to child labour because they use assets as collateral for borrowing.

The Benefits and Necessity of Intervention Child labour

policy cannot effectively be analyzed using the extensive literature without first determining that child labour limitations are beneficial and that intervention is necessary. The International Labour Organization states that the global benefits of eliminating child labour exceed the costs by a ratio of 6.7 to 1. All regions of the world would experience large net gains if child labour was eliminated, although some regions would benefit more than others. Reducing child labour also benefits the economy because child labour is inefficient. Children are imperfect substitutes for adult workers. By definition, children have less experience and are less capable of work than adults. Furthermore, the availability of child labour encourages economic inefficiency by increasing the supply of low-skill workers. Eliminating child labour would encourage development by forcing firms to increase efficiency in order to increase profits. Some claim that international labour standards are a form of protectionism and impede the LDC low-wage advantage. Evidence shows, however, that US legislation supporting international standards for child labour does not stem from protectionist interests. Krueger (1996) finds that legislators who voted for the Child Labour Bill were less likely to come from districts whose jobs were threatened by foreign low-skilled labour.

Legislative support for broad trade agreements, such as NAFTA and the GATT, does correlate with economic interests of constituents, but policymakers and voters seem to place child labour in a category separate from other labour standards. While the concern that labour regulations might reduce the Low-wage advantage of LDCs is compelling, comprehensive child labour policy that addresses the root causes of the issue will limit the negative effects of regulation. Policy can provide net gains on a national and global level by addressing economic development in combination with regulation. Although limiting child labour provides overwhelming long-term economic benefits, child labour will continue unless regulatory policy is imposed because regulation requires short-term sacrifice. For example, although the returns to education eventually dominate the gains from child labour, the payoff is realized at least 10 years after a household would have received earnings from child labour.

The global benefits discussed by the ILO also do not apply in the short term and are only relevant a decade after policies have been implemented. Competitive markets make it difficult for employers to accept short-term losses imposed by child labour standards, even when they understand the long-term benefits. The nature of the problem necessitates intervention as a means of ensuring that individuals cooperate to withstand loss and achieve long-term mutual gains. Basu and Van (1998) explain the mechanism by which labour regulation may achieve long-term economic benefits. According to the economists, child labour policies may achieve Pareto efficient change because labour markets often have multiple equilibriums. For example, a market may have one equilibrium in which wages are low and children work, and a second equilibrium in which wages are high and children do not work. Effective child labour policy "jolts" the economy into the Pareto efficient equilibrium. Comprehensive external intervention is necessary in order to achieve this change. Thus, limiting child labour through regulation is ultimately possible, necessary, and beneficial. Policies Used to Limit Child Labour.

CHILD LABOUR BANS

Basu and Van predict that child labour bans might effectively "jolt" an economy into Pareto efficiency. They describe a simple mechanism by which a ban might change the nature of child participation in the workforce of an economy. According to the academics, a ban on child labour creates a shortage of labour because adult and child labours are substitutes. Adult wages increase in response to excess demand for labour. Increased wages reduce the demand for child labour, ultimately eliminating the need for the ban. Several flaws exist in Basu and Van's reasoning regarding the efficacy of a simple child labour ban. The economists fail to consider that child labour and adult labour are not perfect substitutes. Basu and Van also do not address the difficulty of enforcing regulations, particularly in underdeveloped nations lacking strong political infrastructure, where child labour is most prevalent. Moreover, bans on child labour are more difficult to effectively implement than other regulations. The literature explains that people around the world already prefer that children not engage in work.

Effective policy must do more than encourage an existing preference. Effective policy must help people gain the capacity to engage in this preference. The equilibrium shift described by Basu and Van can therefore occurs only through policy that changes the economic opportunities of individuals and societies. Partial bans (created through policy or lack of enforcement) ultimately harm children by shifting labour such that adults work for higher wages in better conditions and children work for lower wages in poorer conditions.

Education

Policies that improve the education system—directly or indirectly—may limit child labour by increasing its opportunity cost. Households decide to engage in child labour based partially on the perceived costs and benefits of attending school. People are less likely to choose child labour if education is a more attractive option. However, education policy alone cannot eliminate child labour. Other factors, such as income and credit access, will affect the household choice between work and school, regardless of the appeal of education. Evidence confirms that educations laws alone do not prevent child labour. Less developed nations with compulsory education laws, such as Brazil, continue to experience significant rates of child labour.

Financial Programs—Credit Access, Monetary Transfers

The most effective child labour policies address financial and capital markets. Evidence shows that improvements in financial development are strongly associated with decreased levels of child labour. The relationship between financial market development and child labour is particularly large and robust in poor countries with less developed markets and greater levels of child labour. Specifically, financial markets can be improved through mechanisms such as increased access to credit, insurance programs, and monetary transfers. Access to credit allows households to borrow against the future, providing families in poverty an increased ability to send their children to school instead of work. Access to credit and strong financial markets also minimize the effects of income variability and instability on child labour. Without access to credit, households are forced to rely on child labour during income shocks. Credit access and insurance programs reduce child labour by providing families with income stability in times of crisis.

Many nations use conditional cash transfers to stabilize income and enforce human development. These social assistance programs reduce child labour, even when they do not explicitly address labour standards. Conditional cash transfers promote social services, such as compulsory education, in two ways. The programs increase demand for services by lowering the opportunity cost of participation and providing information about the services. Cash transfers might also increase the supply and quality of social services. The problems with conditional cash transfers stem primarily from an implementation perspective. Many nations that need such programs lack the resources to sustain them. Furthermore, programs based on transfer of funds may lead to a populace of dependents.

Trade, Development, and Economic Growth

A recent World Bank study claims that "increases in per capita incomes explain nearly all of the reductions in worldwide child labour since 1950". The overwhelming income-child labour correlation suggests that policy that affects income and GDP will have the most significant effect on child labour. Development and trade correspond with child labour and labour regulation primarily because integration into the modern economy correlates strongly with other factors that link to child labour. For example, development and trade are significantly linked to income. Furthermore, the dynamic effects of trade and development—such as capital accumulation and improved political infrastructure—also discourage child labour and encourage regulation. In a cross-country analysis, Edmonds and Pavcnik find that incidence of child labour is lower in countries that engage in international trade (2004). The relationship between trade and child labour is particularly strong for LDCs that trade with developed countries. Increased integration into the world market affects child labour through a variety of mechanisms. Trade primarily affects labour by raising income.

Improving the endowments of unskilled labour and reducing credit constraints decreases the incidence of child labour. Expansion of trade also increases wages via the Stolper-Samuelson theorem and thus reduces supply of child labour as predicted by the Basu and Van model. However, trade might also induce child labour by increasing demand for products that are low-skill intensive. The effect that dominates increased trade depends on variables in the market—such as the slope of the labour demand curve, the impact of trade on labour demand, and the elasticity of substitution between child and adult labour -and variables associated with national institutions.

Sanction

Multilateral and bilateral trade agreements often link trade and child labour regulation through specific standards. While some international conventions do not have compliance mechanisms, nations often accept global norms in order to participate in the global economy. Sanctions are sometimes used to enforce compliance with international treaties, but they are not effective in limiting child labour. Evidence shows that sanctions are more likely to harm workers more than improve working conditions. Sanctions are generally ineffective because governments lack resources to enact changes in national policy. Households also may not have the ability to change behaviour based on international standards. For example, Rogers and Swinnerton (1999) estimate that if GDP per worker falls below $5020, families cannot afford to keep children out of the workforce regardless of the policy.

Thus, sanctions cannot effectively change behaviour in the case of child labour.

Analyzing the economic roots of child labour and the effects of existing regulation policy illustrates the need for an innovative solution. Effective policy must have the ultimate goal of eliminating child labour—a goal that will benefit individuals, nations, and the international community at large. An examination of the economic implications of child labour illustrates that elimination can be accomplished only through the eradication of extreme poverty and income instability. Effective child labour policy must address the economic roots of child labour by developing credit access, financial markets, and general economic growth. International treaties, bans or sanctions that impose labour standards without addressing economic realities only exacerbate the problem of child labour. The world has a clear interest in eliminating child labour. The international community must therefore encourage economic growth and the development of strong financial markets around the world.

IMPLICATIONS FOR POLICY AND PROGRAM DESIGN

Around the globe, millions of children are working under conditions that are detrimental to their education, health, and moral development. According to the International Labour Organization, there are approximately 246 million children ages five to seventeen years who are working around the world. An estimated 171 million of them work in hazardous conditions that threaten their health and safety. When the number of children in the unconditional worst forms of child labour (such as forced labour and sexual exploitation) is counted, the magnitude of child labour is even greater. Not only does child labour violate the fundamental human rights of children, it perpetuates poverty and hinders economic growth and development. Exploitive work often deprives children of education or training that could lead to a productive adult job. Without an appropriate education, the chances of a child remaining in low-paying, unskilled work, or even out of work altogether, are much greater. Furthermore, the low levels of human capital and high health costs that are associated with child labour often result in decreased labour productivity and stagnant or low levels of economic growth.

Some forms of child labour lead to reductions in adult wage rates and increases in adult unemployment rates. While the life-chances for working children may seem bleak, many national and international governmental and non-governmental organizations have made a strong commitment to the elimination of child labour. In 1989, the members of the United Nations (U.N.) approved the Convention on the Rights of the Child (CRC) and, in 1999; the member states of the International Labour Organization (ILO) unanimously adopted Convention No. 182 on the Worst Forms of Child Labour. This Convention has been ratified more quickly by more member states than any previous ILO Convention. In addition, the U.N.'s May 25, 2000 adoption of Optional Protocols to the CRC (addressing the sale of children, child prostitution and child pornography, and child soldiers) demonstrated the growing international commitment to protect children from the worst forms of child labour. Despite growing national and international concern, for many years there was an absence of reliable data and research on child labour.

Recommendation 190, accompanying C. 182, recognizes the need for more and better data, stating, "detailed information and statistical data on the nature and extent of child labour should be compiled and kept up to date." To this end, the ILO, UNICEF, and the World Bank have partnered with national governments and research institutions to collect quantitative and qualitative data on child labour. Measuring child labour, especially its worst forms, is a difficult task. Measurement involves decisions of what and how to measure. Because numbers have important policy implications, this chapter focuses on the ability to convey and accurately report data on child labour. The first section of the current chapter discusses the commonly used definitions for studying children's work and child labour. The second section reviews the current state of the data and the strengths and limitations of the available data sources. The third and fourth sections demonstrate the use of data for policy development, program design, and project evaluation. These sections address the usefulness, interpretation, reliability, and comparability of the indicators across countries and over time.

Definitions Related To Children's Work

Generally, children of different ages perform "work" of different types, for different reasons, and under different conditions. It is extremely important to be aware of the differing perceptions, and accompanying definitions, of "child labour" when collecting, analyzing, and comparing data from various sources. Child Labour The ILO Convention No. 138 on the Minimum Age, provides the most comprehensive and authoritative international standards on minimum age for admission to employment or work. Prior to the adoption of C. 138, ILO conventions addressed minimum ages only for specific types of employment. Convention 138 requires countries to set a minimum age for employment or work, which ideally should not be less than the age for completing compulsory schooling and, in any event, should not be less than fifteen years of age. It obligates countries to pursue a national policy aimed at effectively eliminating child labour.

The convention was designed to allow flexibility among countries with differing social and economic structures, and "is aimed at encouraging the progressive improvement of standards and of promoting sustained action to attain the objective." As a result, different minimum ages have been established both between countries and within a single country, between different types of work or over time. They range from as low as twelve years for "light work" in developing countries to eighteen years for "hazardous work" in any country.

Worst Forms of Child Labour

The ILO unanimously adopted the Convention on the Worst

Forms of Child Labour (C. 182) in 1999. This convention and its accompanying Recommendation (R. 190) were designed to complement C. 138 by encouraging immediate and comprehensive action to abolish the worst forms of child labour. According to C. 182, the worst forms of child labour comprise: (a) All forms of slavery or practices similar to slavery, such as the sale and trafficking of children, debt bondage and serfdom, and forced or compulsory labour, including forced or compulsory recruitment of children used in armed conflict; (b) The use, procuring, or offering of a child for prostitution, for the production of pornography, or for pornographic performance; (c) The use, procuring, or offering of a child for illicit activities, in particular for the production and trafficking of drugs as defined in the relevant international treaties; and, (d) Work which by its nature or the circumstances in which it is carried out is likely to harm the health, safety, or morals of children. While the types of worst forms of child labour identified in parts (a)-(c) of C. 182 are quite clear and unambiguous, the hazardous forms of work identified in part (d) leave room for national decision-making and are therefore likely to differ between countries. How can a line be drawn between "acceptable" forms of work by children (even regarded as something positive) on the one hand, and child labour slated for abolition (because of negative consequences) on the other? Furthermore, within child labour, how can a line be drawn between "the worst forms," which require action as a matter of urgency, and the other forms of child labour?

Economically Active Children

Because children's economic activity has so often been used interchangeably with—or as a proxy for—child labour, it is important to describe the strengths and limitations of this concept. The widespread use of data on the economically active child population as a proxy for data on child labour primarily stems from the difficulty of translating ILO child labour standards into statistical terms. According to the ILO, the economically active population is defined as: all persons of either sex who furnish the supply of labour for the production of economic goods and services as defined by the United Nations systems of national accounts and balances during a specified time-reference period.

According to these systems the production of economic goods and services includes all production and processing of primary products whether for the market for barter or for own consumption, the production of all other goods and services for the market and, in the case of households which produce such goods and services for the market, the corresponding production for own consumption. The definition of economic activity includes not only those in paid employment (paid in cash or in kind) but also self-employed children, own account workers, apprentices who receive pay in cash or in kind, unpaid family workers who consume or produce economic goods or services for their own household consumption, and the unemployed.

CURRENT VS. USUAL ACTIVITY

Within the concept of economic activity, persons can be categorized as those who have "ever" been economically active (different from the adult concept of "usually" economically active) and those who are "currently" active. The population of children who have ever worked is comprised of individuals who were involved in a main activity (determined by the number of weeks or days) at any time during a long period, such as the last year. The concept of "ever worked" is particularly useful among children because it captures seasonal work and children who are at risk of working, as well as children's work during school holidays. However, because children are typically unable to accurately recall activities over a year, questions regarding hours of work, duration of work, and type of work can be fraught with measurement error. Previous research has also shown that children's work activities occur intermittently throughout a given year, and therefore may only be captured in a household survey through the measurement of "ever worked." The currently active population (or the labour force) is defined as individuals who satisfy the definition of economically active, as defined above, for a specified brief period such as the last seven days or one day. The measurement of current activity and its follow-up questions is less fraught with recall bias given the shorter reference period. However, depending on when the survey is conducted, measures of current economically active children often exclude children who primarily work seasonally or during school holidays. In some countries, the figures for current and "ever" economically active vary widely.

STRENGTHS AND LIMITATIONS

Some children's activities are either difficult to capture when measuring economic activity or are not considered economic activity. Among adult wage-earners and to determining whether a person is economically active or not is often unambiguous. However, because most children work in informal businesses, which are not usually included in surveys of economic activity, estimates of economic activity, are likely to underestimate the true number of working children. Informal sector employment can consist of unpaid family workers, work with unregistered businesses, or establishments with less than five or ten workers. Because informal enterprises are often excluded from surveys, the economic activity of unpaid family workers or those working for family consumption is not captured. This is particularly problematic among children, since the majority of children work as unpaid family workers or are involved in non-market production for own family consumption. In Kenya, for example, 79% of all working children (ages five to seventeen) worked as unpaid family workers.

Many children carry wood or water (economic activity), particularly in African countries. A group of experts convened by the U.N. to revise the Systems of National Accounts (SNA) agreed that carrying water should be included as an economic activity on the grounds that carrying water was similar to gathering fruits and vegetables and therefore should be treated as the production of a good. When agencies carry out surveys of economic activity within a particular country, they determine whether to consider carrying water or gathering wood as an economic activity, based on whether the water or wood is carried over long distances. The definition of "long distances" is left to national determination, but these activities can take up significant amounts of children's time. In South Africa, for example, 5.4 million children aged five to seventeen reported fetching wood and/or water for the household during the week. Of all children engaged in fetching wood and/or water for their households almost a quarter spent eight hours or more per week on this activity.

Other children's activities that are difficult to capture or are not at all captured in surveys of economic activity are illegal activities and begging. Children who beg for money or food are not considered to be involved in an economic activity, as there is no concept of production involved in begging activities. Moreover, the SNA does not address the legality of an "economic activity." In principle, therefore, activities such as prostitution or the production or transporting of illegal substances should be included when measuring economic activity. Whether or not these activities are actually captured in a survey is a methodological rather than a definitional issue. Furthermore, the economically active population by definition does not include those who carry out household chores within one's own home. This exclusion is particularly relevant to children since many children, especially girls, perform household chores.

The Choice of Criteria for Data Collection and Compilation

The above discussion provides an overview of definitions of child labour and the types of information needed to identify child labour-based on these definitions. If any data or indicators are to be used to monitor national compliance with ILO child labour standards, they must be assessed in terms of their ability to provide information-based on the ILO definitions. If data on economically active children must be used as a proxy for data on child labour, it should be borne in mind that some economically active children are working in forms of work that are "acceptable" in terms of ILO standards. Efforts should therefore be made to disaggregate the data on economically active children by age groups and types of work in order to separate out those who are in prohibited child labour, using the criteria set by ILO Conventions Nos. 138 and 182. Cross-country comparison is also difficult because the ILO's flexible child labour standards do not offer a single set of definitions applicable throughout the world. For example, if two neighboring countries had the same number of working children by age, and one established a higher minimum age for work, that country would, as a direct consequence, score worse in child labour figures compared with its neighbour.

SOURCES OF DATA

During the past ten years, researchers have gained experience in using quantitative and qualitative data collection methods to better understand the complex phenomenon of child labour. Quantitative data collection methodologies have taken the form of censuses, household surveys, establishment surveys, and school-based surveys. With quantitative data, researchers can make generalizations about the incidence, characteristics, and causes and consequences of child labour. Researchers and policy-makers can also use quantitative data to develop, carry out, and monitor policies and programs aimed at the abolition of child labour.

Researchers have made progress in learning about the hidden and illegal forms of child labour through qualitative methods. These methods help to shed light on children's activities that may not be captured by surveys of households or take place in a region where little prior information exists. In addition, qualitative methodologies help to provide a more thorough understanding of concepts and indicators of child labour that can be used to refine survey methodologies and instruments. Quantitative and qualitative data collection methodologies complement each other, providing a more complete picture of child labour to inform and improve policies and programs aimed at the elimination of child labour.

Household Survey Data

In the early 1990s, the ILO, through the International Program on the Elimination of Child Labour (IPEC) and the Bureau of Statistics, experimented with survey methodologies to identify the best way to probe into children's work. In Ghana, India, Indonesia, and Senegal, researchers tested a household survey, an employer survey, a survey of street children, and a time use survey. Based on their findings, ILO concluded that the household-based sample survey, supplemented by surveys of employers and street children, was the most appropriate methodology for inquiring about children's work and educational activities. While the house-hold survey method is the most commonly used approach to collecting information on child labour, it has limitations.

Children who are homeless are often missed when the unit of measurement is the household. Many children both live and work in the street, and excluding them may therefore lead to an underestimate. Furthermore, unless special efforts are made to capture children working in the unconditional worst forms of child labour, it is highly likely that household surveys will miss these children. Children's work is also often geographically clustered and if the design of the household survey sample does not take this into account, clusters of working children may be inadvertently omitted. Likewise, in urban areas, where children engage in very diverse economic activities, household surveys may not capture all of these activities, or may do so only with large sampling errors if the sampling methodology does not address this need.

The three international organizations that have led the way in collecting data on child labour using household surveys are the ILO, under the auspices of the Statistical Information and Monitoring Program on Child Labour (SIMPOC); the World Bank, through its survey instrument of the Living Standards Measurement Study (LSMS); and UNICEF, through the Multiple Indicator Cluster Surveys (MICS). Currently, the SIMPOC program is the only program with the sole aim of collecting data and information on child labour. The LSMS surveys are aimed at measuring poverty and the influence of governmental policies on living standards in developing countries. The MICS are designed to measure various countries' progress toward the goals laid out in the 1990 United Nations World Summit for Children. Each of these major survey programs (SIMPOC, LSMS, and MICS) is described and evaluated below, based on its appropriateness for measuring children's economic activity and child labour.

All of the household surveys discussed below suffer from the usual non-sampling biases, such as non-response, erroneous response, interviewer errors, data entry, and processing errors to some extent. Efforts to reduce these biases through interviewer training, pre-testing, and data quality controls are discussed below. The Statistical Information and Monitoring Program on Child Labour (SIMPOC) of the International Labour Organization SIMPOC was created in 1998 in response to the growing need for reliable, comparable, and gender-sensitive data and information on child labour. Since its inception, SIMPOC has led the way in child labour data collection, and has gained a vast amount of experience working with countries to conduct national household-level child labour surveys. Currently, SIMPOC is assisting over forty countries in conducting household surveys of child labour. When selecting countries for SIMPOC surveys, the ILO considers country requests, whether a government is committed to collecting and disseminating data on child labour, and whether a country has a great need for child labour information.

SIMPOC works with partner organizations, including national agencies, research institutions, non-governmental organizations (NGOs), employers and workers organizations, and international organizations. SIMPOC surveys are varied and often country specific. In all cases, the appropriate government agency—most often the National Statistical Office (NSO)—carries out the child labour surveys with technical assistance and, in most cases, funding from SIMPOC. In some countries, child labour survey modules are added to existing labour force surveys or any other continuous household-based survey, while in other cases, SIMPOC surveys are conducted on a stand-alone basis. In each country, the NSO oversees the SIMPOC survey, selecting, training, and managing the team of interviewers, based upon its particular methods, experiences, and needs. The SIMPOC survey in Zimbabwe, for example, was conducted by the Ministry of Public Service Labour and Social Welfare (MPSLSW) and the Central Statistical Office (CSO). These agencies selected 195 interviewers and trained them with theoretical instructions, mock interviews, and field practice using real respondents, as well as post-practice discussions and a test on the concepts and definitions in the training manual.

The interviewers were familiar with the culture and local languages of the respondents, and were thoroughly informed about the purpose of the survey in order to help elicit honest responses from the children and parents. The agencies also launched a publicity campaign to sensitize the public about the child labour survey and to ensure that respondents accepted it as a study and not a punishment for parents of working children or employers of children. According to the 1999 Zimbabwe SIMPOC Child Labour Report, "this made respondents contribute willingly and honestly without any suspicions." Most SIMPOC surveys ask numerous questions about children's work, such as the type of work, hours of work, working conditions, workplace characteristics (including its physical and mental safety), parent's perceptions of child work, and hours spent on household chores. In addition, the surveys collect data on the household's basic demographic, social, and economic characteristics. In some SIMPOC surveys, interviewers ask questions regarding children not currently residing in the household, in order to capture children who are living away from home. In addition, some surveys include inquiries about the household's awareness of child recruitment.

The SIMPOC methodology is designed to ensure that a large enough sample of working children is captured in the survey. In general, SIMPOC surveys consist of relatively large sample sizes (10,000 households or more). The sampling design methodology used in SIMPOC surveys requires an up-to-date master frame of households with information on the total number of children in the age group five to seventeen. In some cases, level of income, region or provincial residency, and urban/rural residency are used for stratification and the selection of the required number of households. In some cases, households in the lower income levels or slum areas are over-sampled. Most SIMPOC surveys over-sample urban areas in order to capture the different types of occupations, industries, and wage levels of working children. Segmenting by region, province, or other relevant geographic breakdowns ensures that reliable estimates can be computed at sub-national levels. It also ensures that certain types of child labour will be captured within the national surveys if it is known a priori that a large proportion of working children exist in the specific regions.

In terms of measuring economic activity, the basic questions on work are included in all of the SIMPOC surveys. Based on previous experience, the ILO has found that probing questions are the most successful method for collecting detailed information on work activities. For example, in methodological surveys conducted by the ILO in Costa Rica and Kerala, India (1983/1984), the use of additional probing questions resulted in a 4.2% increase in the reported number of persons engaged in economic activity in Costa Rica and a 5.4% increase in Kerala, India. As a result, the more recent SIMPOC survey includes more probing questions than other surveys. This has led in general to higher child work-population ratios when compared to other surveys. The questions used in SIMPOC surveys to measure economic activity differ by country, depending on the needs, experience, and expertise of the implementing agency. SIMPOC interviewers ask about work over the last seven days (currently economically active) and over the last twelve months (ever economically active). Because children's recall tends to be poor when referring to long periods of time, such as during the last year, detailed questions on the child's occupation, hours of work, etc. are posed only to children who reported working in the last seven days.

Many SIMPOC surveys include questions for measuring the extent of "child labour" and "hazardous child labour" as defined by ILO conventions and national laws. As a starting point, all SIMPOC surveys include questions about the industries and occupations that employ children. The surveys also yield information on hours of work, which can be used to aid in the measurement of "light work" and excessive work. Many of the newer surveys include a question on the time of day or night when children carry out their work. Questions aimed at measuring the extent to which children participate in household chores and the hours they spend on these activities are also addressed in many SIMPOC surveys. Finally, questions on whether a child is exposed to a hazardous work environment (i.e., work at heights or underground, work with tools or machinery, work in excessive noise or dust, work in extreme temperatures, etc.) or hazardous agents or chemicals (such oxygen, ammonia, pesticides, or glues) are included in the more recent SIMPOC questionnaires.

The World Bank Living Standards Measurement Study Surveys

The World Bank established the Living Standards Measurement Study (LSMS) in 1980. Its main objectives were "to develop new methods for monitoring progress in raising levels of living, to identify the consequences for households of current and proposed government policies, and to improve communications between survey statisticians, analysts, and policymakers." Since 1985, LSMS household surveys have been conducted in numerous developing countries. An LSMS survey includes questionnaires aimed at different groups in order to collect information on expenditures, income, household composition, and economic activity. Interviewers use household questionnaires to elicit general information from the head of household (or best-informed family member) and information about economic activity from each individual household member. The sampling methodology generally consists of two stages based on the designated enumeration areas and a random selection of households within these areas.

However, in considering whether a particular LSMS survey adequately captures child labour, it is important to keep in mind that LSMS survey methods, like SIMPOC methods, vary widely among surveys. Therefore, each survey should be evaluated on its own accord. As the main objective of the LSMS is to measure household living standards and the effects of various government policies, the sample sizes are relatively small. Most LSMS surveys sample between 1,500 and 5,000 households with a few rare exceptions of over 5,000. The smaller sample sizes reduce the costs of the survey and keep non-sampling errors to a minimum. In addition, these relatively small sample sizes are suited to understanding relationships or "why" a certain phenomenon is happening, and not necessarily to identify incidence. The relatively small samples may make it difficult to disaggregate detailed data on child labour in particular occupations and industries. The majority of the LSMS surveys collect information on the economic activity of young persons, asking about such activity in the last seven days and last year. However, the ages for which information on children's work is collected varies widely across countries.

Typically, the lower age limit for which economic activity data are collected corresponds to the age at which formal schooling begins. The LSMS surveys generally follow the ILO definition of economic activity. In the past, no special attention was given to working children and the diversity of their activities, but this has changed in more recent years. In general, estimates of the economically active population of children based on the LSMS surveys are lower than estimates based on SIMPOC data. This is likely due to the fact that the main objective of the SIMPOC surveys is to capture the work activities of children, and therefore the sampling methodology and questionnaires are designed around this aim.

These variations greatly reduce cross country comparability of the raw data and require the use of standardization techniques. In terms of measuring child labour, the LSMS surveys generally collect information on occupation and industry, hours of work, and school attendance. A few of the more recent surveys include information on household chores, hours spent on household chores, and injuries and illnesses (not necessarily work-related injuries or illnesses). However, with relatively small sample sizes, it is often difficult to obtain the detailed information necessary to determine whether the work a child is doing constitutes hazardous child labour. This may be the reason why most of the research to date that utilizes the LSMS survey data defines child labour in terms of economic activity.

Multiple Indicator Cluster Surveys of the United Nations Children's Fund

UNICEF developed the MICS as a response to the 1990 World Summit for Children where governments committed themselves to the Declaration and Plan of Action for Children; UNICEF has identified seventy-five indicators aimed at monitoring children's rights. The specific indicator for monitoring child labour is the "proportion of children in households aged 5-14 years who are currently working (paid or unpaid; inside or outside the home)." UNICEF recommends that this indicator be calculated separately for children working outside the home, and for paid and unpaid work. The MICS surveys, like the SIMPOC surveys, were designed to be carried out as stand-alone surveys or as modules attached to other existing household surveys. By 1996, over 100 surveys had been conducted in developing countries, and in 1997 independent experts conducted a detailed evaluation of these surveys. The evaluation concluded that the surveys provided a quick and economical way to collect quality data, and that the process of conducting the surveys enhanced the capacity and skills of both the country offices and the UNICEF staff.

Finally, the evaluation found that government involvement and expertise varied across countries, and that some MICS results were inconsistent when compared to results from other surveys. MICS sample sizes are relatively large, in keeping with UNICEF's recommendation of samples in the range of 2,500 to 14,000 households. The MICS typically consists of three questionnaires. The household questionnaire includes the household listing form and orphan hood questions, and modules on education, child labour, water and sanitation, and salt iodization. The questions in the child labour module are addressed to the caretaker, usually the mother, of each child aged five to fourteen who resides in the household. However, caretakers may tend to underestimate the activities of their children, particularly if the society views child labour negatively. Furthermore, caretakers may not accurately recall all of their children's activities. The recommended child labour survey module consists of seven questions designed to collect information on work in the last week and work in the last twelve months.

The questions are divided into work done for a member outside the household (both paid and unpaid) and family work. In addition, there are questions about hours of work and household chores. Like the LSMS surveys, MICS surveys are lacking in some key areas related to measurement of child labour. For example, MICS do not typically measure children's occupations or industries, making it impossible to determine whether children are working in hazardous occupations. The surveys also do not lack any detailed information about working conditions, such as with machines, chemicals, or other hazardous agents, nor is there information on children suffering from work-related injuries or illnesses. In addition, interviewers collect information only for children ages five through fourteen years. On the other hand, all MICS surveys consistently measure hours of work and housekeeping activities.

National Labour Force Surveys and Censuses

Most countries have conducted a labour force survey, and many do so at regular intervals. In addition, most countries conduct censuses with questions about the economic activity of the population; however, these data tend to be less frequent, less detailed, and insufficient for children in the lower age ranges. Unfortunately, labour force surveys also tend to be "notoriously weak at measuring labour force participation at the tails of the age distribution." According to Anker, the measurement problems associated with collecting data on women's work are even greater when collecting information on child labour, because the sampling plans of labour force surveys are generally designed to measure the situation of adults, thus it is likely that the coverage of the samples are deficient with respect to children.

Many labour force surveys do not collect data on persons under the age of fifteen, under the assumption that children are not in the labour force. The work of women is often difficult to measure because the respondents (including the working women themselves) and the interviewers may hold the preconception that women should not work or they may not consider the work of women as actual work activities. Instead they may consider the activities as part of their daily life. This is even more likely to be the case for children. There are inherent difficulties in measuring child labour since children are even more likely than females to work on a part-time basis, in seasonal work, or as unpaid family workers. Despite these limitations, labour force surveys and censuses can be useful sources of information when no other sources of data on working children exist in a country. In addition, labour force surveys and censuses, depending on their quality, can be used to evaluate and verify data from other sources such as the SIMPOC or LSMS programs.

ILO Database on the Economically Active Population

In 1996, the ILO released the fourth edition of its database on the economically active population for the years 1950 through 2010. This database contains estimates and projections of the economically active population. Data are presented for 178 countries with populations of 200,000 or more and world and regional aggregates. The estimates and projections of the economically active population are based on data provided voluntarily by countries and are based on countries' labour force surveys and censuses. The data reflect adjustments and extrapolations where necessary to conform to a standard concept of the economically active population, comparable age categories, reference periods, and date of surveys/ censuses.

The ILO database includes data on economic activity among children ages ten through fourteen for most countries. However, users should be cautious when interpreting the data because different countries gather data on work among children beginning at greatly different ages, ranging from age ten to age fifteen. In countries where economic activity data are collected for persons twelve and over, for example, the activity rates presented in the ILO database are not adjusted to account for younger working children, ages ten and eleven. Therefore, the economic activity rate for ten-to fourteen-year-olds is the ratio of active twelve- to fourteen-year-olds to the population of ten- to fourteen-year-olds, and is likely to be an underestimate.

Rapid Assessments

In response to the dearth of information on the worst forms of child labour, the ILO and UNICEF developed the Rapid Assessment (RA) methodology. RAs have been conducted on children in bondage, child domestic workers, children engaged in armed conflict, child trafficking, drug trafficking, hazardous work in commercial agriculture, fishing, garbage dumps, mining and the urban environment, sexual exploitation, and working street children. The RA methodology provides qualitative and descriptive information on the characteristics of working children, their families, and communities at the local or micro level. It can provide a detailed picture of the daily lives of working children and can also be used to identify appropriate interventions in the first stages of program planning, when often little information on child work is available. Findings from the RA can be used to complement the findings of national household-based surveys.

The RA methodology uses a participatory approach and is designed to be flexible, relatively quick, and inexpensive, often including both quantitative and qualitative survey tools. Generally, the research team begins by collecting background research and then identifies and interviews key informants, who may range from police officers to trade union officials or healthcare workers. The researchers observe both working and non-working children, and gather information from children, parents, and other adults through focus groups, household surveys, or casual interviews (with re-interviews to verify findings). The resulting findings may be "partly descriptive, partly analytic and partly statistical . . . [and] reasonably accurate and representative of the issue that was investigated. They can even be replicated, with a fair degree of reproducibility [although] they will never have the validity of scientific inquiry."

Obtaining quality information on all types of the worst forms of child labour is especially difficult for several reasons. First, many of the worst forms of child labour (e.g., use of children in drug production and trafficking, prostitution, and pornography) are illegal in most countries, and criminals generally hide these activities. Even if the children are located alone, they may refuse to talk to the interviewers for fear of being further harmed. If their employers or parents/guardians are present during the interviews, the children may be afraid to answer the questions truthfully. Furthermore, children may feel distrustful of the interviewers and may not want to lose money by taking time away from work to participate in the research. In the RA of child domestic workers in Nepal, for example, employers were present during most of the interviews and, in fourteen cases, participants were dropped from the study after their employers refused to continue with the interviews and in addition, according to the RA on child porters in Nepal, "adult porters were often present and influenced the responses" of the children being interviewed.

The sampling design and selection of respondents varies greatly from study to study. For the most part, the RA methodology uses non-probability sampling in the form of purposive "snowball" sampling. In some cases, the children are contacted through the rehabilitation programs they are involved in, or through the knowledge of other key informants. In other cases, the interviewers take to the streets and interview any child they find working in the form of child labour being studied, while in other studies, researchers select households for interviews. The numbers of respondents in the RAs conducted to date average a little over 100 children. It is important to note that the RA methodology is not designed to extrapolate figures or make generalizations outside the scope of the interviewed respondents.

Other Sources of Data and Methods of Collection

Countries wishing to effectively abolish child labour require national and sub-national data on the unconditional worst forms of child labour in order to understand the size and shape of the problem, including target areas that require immediate attention. Although data on the unconditional worst forms of child labour have been notoriously weak, the situation has improved considerably in recent years, as many organizations have attempted to quantify such data, while acknowledging the difficulties of the task and highlighting the methodological limitations. A recent study on child labour in the cocoa sector provides an example of the different sources and methods used to collect data on hidden forms of work.

The International Institute of Tropical Agriculture (IITA) conducted the study using a combination of quantitative and qualitative survey methods. IITA conducted three surveys: (1) the Baseline Producer Survey (BPS), (2) the Producer/ Worker Survey (PWS), and (3) the Community Survey (CS). The PWS and the CS were conducted in Côte d'Ivoire, and the BPS was conducted in the remaining countries of Cameroon, Ghana, and Nigeria. The PWS carried out in Côte d'Ivoire was the only source of national estimates and used the national census of cocoa and coffee farmers conducted in 1998 from which the sample was drawn.

The BPS surveys conducted in the other countries only yielded estimates specific to the interview regions. Thus, the study identified one of the main limitations to be the lack of up-to-date statistical frames. Other limitations that may have introduced bias in measurement included the sensitive nature of the child labour issue and the timing of the survey outside the peak harvest season. With a growing literature on and movement toward children's participation in making decisions and setting policies about child labour, children have begun to participate in the data collection process.

Save the Children UK has involved children in collecting and analyzing information on hazardous forms of child labour in Bangladesh, Burkina Faso, and Honduras. Study teams researched the current child labour laws and met with various stakeholders in each country. In Bangladesh and Burkina Faso, the teams organized interviews with children. In Bangladesh, based on filmed interviews with eighty working and non-working children, the team determined that a sectoral approach to defining hazardous work is not appropriate if it does not address children's working conditions. In Burkina Faso, children were trained and used to conduct interviews with other children working in gold mining. The team found that using children in data collection was particularly valuable because child interviewers were better able to draw out and capture the perspectives of the children being interviewed.

NGO and Government Reports

Governmental agencies and NGOs report data and information on child labour in general, and selected worst forms of child labour in particular. These include the Global March against Child Labour's *Status Report on the Worst Forms of Child Labour*, the United States Department of Labour's *Findings on the Worst Forms of Child Labour*, and the United States Department of State's *Human Rights Report* and *Trafficking in Persons Report*. A major contribution of these reports is that they provide information from many different primary sources of data in an easy to read, organized format.

NGO Reports

Information found in the Global March's *Status Report on the Worst Forms of Child Labour* is gathered from international organizations, national governments, NGO reports, academic research, journal and newsletter articles, and newspaper reports. Whenever possible, the original sources of the data are cited; however there is no evaluation of the reliability or accuracy of the data presented. Instead, the report is intended to be an all-inclusive repository for research and information on the worst forms of child labour. The report is very useful for understanding the child labour situation—particularly the worst forms—in numerous countries. Nevertheless, the data and estimates should be scrutinized carefully, compared to other figures when available, and the original sources should always be consulted for methodological explanations and accuracy.

For example, the report states that "Official statistics reveal that there are approximately 900 child prostitutes in Italy coming from Albania" while, based on another source, the report states that "There were 1,880 to 2,500 minors working as street prostitutes, of whom 1,500 to 2,300 were trafficked illegal immigrants, predominately Albanians, and some Nigerians." Even more disparate are the estimates of children in prostitution in Thailand, which range from about 20,000 to 800,000. Anker suggests that "advocacy statistics" released by NGOs may purposely dramatize the magnitude of child labour thus supporting the need for careful evaluation of these figures.

Government Reports

The U.S. Department of Labour prepares its *Findings on the Worst Forms of Child Labour* annually in response to the Trade and Development Act of 2000. That law requires the Secretary of Labour to report on government efforts to eliminate the worst forms of child labour among countries receiving benefits under the U.S. Generalized System of Preferences. It contains information on the incidence and nature of child labour—and on government policies and programs aimed at eliminating child labour—in 146 countries and territories. Each country report provides the sources of information, including the U.S. Department of State and other government agencies,

U.S. consulates and embassies abroad, and a wide variety of reports and materials from foreign countries, international organizations, and NGOs. The report also includes a data section that describes how statistics on child labour from various sources are prioritized and used in estimating the number of working children in each country.

The *Country Reports on Human Rights Practices* published by the U.S. Department of State compile information from U.S. embassies, other government departments, foreign governments, the U.N., and other international organizations, academic reports, and the media. Each country report includes a section on the status of child labour practices and working age laws, and a separate section focusing on children that often includes observations and analyses of the child labour situation in the country, such as the situation of street children in Angola and child trafficking in Thailand. The U.S. Department of State also publishes the annual *Trafficking in Persons (TIP)* report in response to the Trafficking Victims Protection Act of 2000.

The *TIP* report classifies countries with documented cases of trafficking in persons into three tiers indicating the extent of government action to address its trafficking problem. Country reports include a description of the magnitude of trafficking, the geographic regions that persons are trafficked to and from, and the experiences and fates of trafficked persons. Government efforts are also described. A limitation to U.S. Department of State's publications is that data cited in these reports are not often adequately sourced, so it is difficult to determine where the information is coming from; while government reports provide a wealth of information on child labour, the extent to which they are free from political influence is uncertain.

Empirical Research

To be effective, policies and programs aimed at eradicating child labour must be designed based on an intricate understanding of child labour, and the community of child labour researchers has contributed greatly to such understanding. Researchers have generated a tremendous amount of original research with explicit intent to inform policy. They generally use data on children, their families, and communities to test the validity of a given theory about the causes and to better understand the consequences of child labour. Characterizing the empirical literature on child labour is a challenge since its contributors hail from a broad set of disciplines, and include sociologists, demographers, educators, economists, psychologists, public health researchers, and legal scholars. In addition, studies of child welfare have contributed to the understanding of the causes, dynamics, and consequences of child labour. This chapter does not provide an in-depth review of the child labour literature, since this has been accomplished by other researchers including Brown et al., Basu, and the ILO. Instead, it provides information on research that has involved the collection of original data or matching techniques to better understand the child labour phenomenon.

Some investigators have overcome the scarcity of data on the worst forms of child labour by conducting their own studies. Richard Estes and Neil Weiner have developed and applied a methodology for measuring the commercial sexual exploitation of children. These two researchers have made a tremendous contribution to the extraordinarily difficult task of studying this illicit activity. As part of their study, Estes and Weiner, along with collaborating investigators, have interviewed current and former child prostitutes, traffickers, and adult customers of child prostitutes in Canada, Mexico, and the United States. In the course of their U.S. work, Estes and Weiner identified seventeen distinct groups of children at risk of sexual exploitation, underlining the complexity of the problem, since each group may have a different entryway into sexual exploitation and require a specialized response. They were also able to identify the major countries of origin of children trafficked to the United States and the international gateways used by traffickers.

The authors provide a range of estimates for the number of children in the United States at risk of falling victim to commercial sexual exploitation, including a conservative estimate of over 244,000 children. They conclude with recommendations to prevent exploitation and respond to current victims. It is worth noting that, in addition to his work with Neil Weiner, Richard Estes has put together an extensive six-part guide to the literature on the sexual exploitation of children. Original data collected by researchers contributes to the understanding of child labour by providing access to information about specific communities. In addition, this approach reduces the need to use proxy variables for participation in labour since the data collection instruments are often designed by the researchers themselves. However, the samples are typically small and geographic coverage is limited, so the results cannot be generalized to the larger population of child laborers.

Another strategy is to match data from several sources. Duncan and Strauss combine data from the 1974-1975 Brazilian household survey with data on 4,000 counties in Brazil from another survey to learn if child height is correlated with household and community characteristics, including access to child services. Case and Yogo use data from two national surveys of school quality and the 1996 South African Census to assess the impact of school quality on returns to education. Although not yet widely used in the empirical child labour literature, the approach of combining data sets is expected to increase as multiple sources of data relevant to child labour become available.

The Extent of Child Labour

Indicators are an important part of the policy process, providing information about problems and a systematic way to monitor programs. Two basic indicators that are useful in describing the extent of child labour in a given country are the number and proportion of economically active children (ages five to seventeen) and the number and proportion of children (ages five to seventeen) who are child laborers. These indicators should, at the very least, be presented by gender and age. Providing both numbers and proportions of economically active children and child laborers is important because the policy planning, resource mobilization, and advocacy implications may differ for countries with high numbers of child laborers, compared to countries with large proportions of child laborers.

The ILO, for example, found that while Asia and the Pacific region harbors the largest number of working children, Sub-Saharan Africa has the largest proportion of working children. As described above, measures of the economically active child population have their weaknesses. Nevertheless, these measures are important for three main reasons. First, any interventions aimed at reducing child labour in a given country will most likely have an effect on the ratio of economic activity. Second, because most data are based on the definition of economic activity, information will be available for more countries, making cross country comparisons more feasible than when using any other indicator.

Finally, according to the ILO global estimates of economic activity and child labour, approximately 88% of the economically active children (five to fourteen years of age) were also considered child laborers. This figure, however, was much smaller (42%) when considering the youth population (fifteen to seventeen years of age). The number and proportion of children who were child laborers while most relevant to monitoring ILO child labour standards, is difficult to define, and not likely to be comparable across countries. Each country may have its own definition of child labour—based on its own national legislation. Few countries participating in SIMPOC surveys have attempted to define and measure child labour according to national legislation. Instead, these countries report information on economically active children. Some researchers suggest that the ratio of children not enrolled in school is a complementary measure of the economically active children. However, children who are not enrolled in school are not necessarily economically active. For example, among children ages ten to fourteen in Colombia, 8.4% were neither attending school nor working, while 10.6% of children in El Salvador were neither attending school nor working.

In addition, some children who are not enrolled in school may be forced to stay at home to conduct household chores or other non-economic activities. If household chores or domestic activities are not taken into account, these children, particularly girls, are presumed to be "idle." Therefore, another helpful indicator of children's activity, particularly girls (as recommended by the Sixteenth International Conference of Labour Statisticians), is the proportion of children participating in household chores at home by ranges of hours of work. These data should be tabulated separately from indicators of economic activity and child labour since these activities are generally excluded from international standards on minimum age. Many children not attending school spend numerous hours on domestic chores in order to allow adult household members time to work. In addition, children who attend school may spend a significant amount of their non-schooling hours on household chores. Another useful indicator is the percentage of children working in the various industrial sectors such as agriculture, mining, construction, transport, manufacturing, etc. This indicator can be used to target programs and monitor progress in specific industries, including those industries that have been identified in national legislation as unfit for children below the determined minimum age.

Over time, this indicator is likely to show whether children have shifted from one particular sector of employment to another. However, the indicator may not reveal whether children move to more hazardous forms of child labour, such as prostitution, drug trafficking, or armed conflict, which are rarely measured in survey data. Another important indicator of the severity of work as outlined in the two main ILO Conventions on child labour is the percentage of children working by ranges of hours worked per week. This indicator aids in identifying the extent to which children work excessive hours, considered hazardous child labour. These data are collected in most SIMPOC and MICS surveys and in some LSMS surveys. Finally, there are numerous other variables that help to understand child labour within the national context and may have some influence on child labour and investments in children. These indicators have been discussed in great detail by Jensen and Anker. They include both micro- and macro-level indicators, for example, school attendance, health status, adult education and literacy, public school expenditures, school quality, poverty, income per capita, income inequality, adult employment and unemployment, and HIV/AIDS prevalence rates.

THE "EFFECTIVE ABOLITION OF CHILD LABOUR"

The most obvious measure of a country's progress toward the abolition of child labour would compare, over time, the quantitative indicators on economic activity and child labour discussed above. However, such indicators are usually available for only a single time period. In addition, comparisons over time should be based on a thorough understanding of the national context, including education policy and the definitions used. For example, national survey data from Turkey indicate that the percentage of economically active children decreased from 8.5% to 4.2%. However, compulsory education in Turkey was extended to eight years in 1997, which likely explains part of the decline in the economically active child population.

Further, although economic activity decreased, children engaged in domestic chores increased, largely among girls. In addition, comparing these indicators over time may show that child labour has decreased in certain sectors or nationally; this may be because children have moved into other sectors not captured in household surveys. For example, children may move from working in a factory (measured in national surveys) to being sexually exploited in prostitution (likely to be missed from structured surveys).

This problem highlights the need for sound, accurate, and reliable measures of the worst forms of child labour on a timely basis. In the absence of time-series data on child labour, a country's action toward the "effective abolition of child labour" can be used to measure progress. Countries can make elimination of child labour a national priority by developing policies, legislation, programs, and monitoring functions. For effective abolition, child labour programs should be integrated with related government programs, such as those aimed at poverty reduction, job creation, health, and education. Governments can publicize the problems associated with child labour and encourage workers' and employers' groups and NGOs to assist in making progress toward "effective abolition." In addition, countries can support the extensive research needed to determine the extent, distribution, and forms of child labour in the nation, as well as its causes and consequences. One important indicator of progress toward the elimination of child labour is a country's ratification of the two main ILO Conventions on child labour.

The ILO makes this simple indicator of progress readily available on its Web site on an updated basis. By mid-June 2002, of the 175 ILO member states, 125 countries have ratified C. 182, and 117 have ratified C. 138. Another indication of progress may be measured by the existence or development of basic legislation related to child labour. Although this measure does not include the evaluation of the effectiveness of the legislation, it can indicate that the country is taking steps (however small) toward addressing child labour. The ILO collects information on national laws from subscriptions to official gazettes, legislative databases, its field offices, and other publications, making it publicly available through the NATLEX on-line database. As discussed in the companion article by Constance Thomas, additional information on national legislation can be obtained through the ILO supervisory process on ratified conventions and the ILO follow-up to the 1998 Declaration. Although international supervision and follow-up do not provide a quantitative indicator of the country's progress in the elimination of child labour, they point to the existence of problems or obstacles that need to be removed. In addition, the information provides a broader context for understanding the situation of countries with regard to child labour.

Although researchers are still learning about collecting

data on child labour, great strides have already been made. Within the next three years, over forty countries will have conducted SIMPOC child labour surveys. In addition, because they view child labour as important, officials are adding child labour questionnaires to existing surveys and collecting employment data on younger children than previously. As the global movement against child labour grows, better, timely, and regular data have become a necessity. High quality, reliable data are needed to increase public understanding of child labour and its causes and consequences and to design and implement programs aimed at eradicating child labour. Such data require not only initial surveys, but also follow-up surveys on child labour. Continuing government interest and action are necessary to support the ongoing surveys needed to measure a country's progress toward effective abolition of child labour. Based on SIMPOC's experience, ongoing surveys also require additional donor support.

Moreover, quantitative methods for collecting accurate data on the worst forms of child labour must be developed in order to monitor progress toward abolishing these forms of child labour. As outlined above, there is no one source of data or one indicator that will accurately represent a country's situation with regard to child labour. Rather, researchers and policymakers should consult numerous data sources and indicators when trying to understand the overall picture. Definitions of "child labour," including age coverage, need to be clearly stated when presenting data. Likewise, comparing data based on national standards across countries should be avoided, as such comparisons could lead to misinterpretations and unwarranted conclusions. In addition, because of the diversity of the child labour surveys and data sources, each survey and its methods should be evaluated individually. Now, with new data sources available, additional research on the complex phenomenon of child labour is urgently needed.

Efforts are being made to harmonize the data on child labour collected by international organizations within the confines of the joint ILO, UNICEF, and World Bank project Understanding Children's Work; these efforts need to be not only continued, but expanded as well. This includes research on the effect of child labour on children's school performance. In addition, researchers should develop methods to measure hazardous child labour (such as working in sectors like agriculture) and its impacts on children's health and development. Research is also needed on the relationship between HIV/AIDS and child labour, and there is an especially urgent need to develop and test new methods to measure the worst forms of child labour at the national level.

BIBLIOGRAPHY

Adepoju, Aderanti (2005) "Review of Research and Data on Human Trafficking in Sub-Saharan Africa." International Migration 43:75-98.

Aghatise, Esohe (2004) "Trafficking for Prostitution in Italy: Possible Effects of Government Proposals for Legalization of Brothels." violence Against Women 10 1126-1155.

Allred, Keith J. (2006) "Peacekeepers and Prostitutes: How Deployed Forces Fuel the Demand for Trafficked Women and New Hope for Stopping It." Armed Forces and Society 33:5

Andrees, Beate and Mariska N. J. van der Linden (2005) "Designing Trafficking Research from a Labour Market Perspective: The ILO Experience." International Migration 43:55-73.

Andrews, Sara, K. Winter (2004) "U.S. Domestic Prosecution of the American International Sex Tourist: Efforts to Protect Children from Sexual Exploitation." Journal of Criminal Law & Criminology 94 (2):415-453.

Arnold, Christina and Andrea M. Bertone (2002) "Addressing the Sex Trade in Thailand: Some Lessons Learned from NGOs, Part I." Gender Issues 26-53.

Bastia, Tanja (2005) "Child Trafficking or Teenage Migration? Bolivian Migrants in Argentina." International Migration 43:54-87.

Belser, Patrick (2005) "Forced Labour and Human Trafficking: Estimating the Profits," Geneva: International Labour Office.

Bennett, John W. (1996) Applied and Action Anthropology. Ideological and Conceptual Aspects. Current Anthropology 36: S23-S53.

Bruckert, Christine and Collette Parent (2002) Trafficking in Human beings and Organized Crime: A Literature Review. Research and Evaluation Branch. Royal Canadian Mounted Police.

Bump, Micah N. and Julianne Duncan (2003) Conference on Identifying and Serving Child Victims of Trafficking. International Migration 41(5): pp. 201-218.

Bump, Micah N., Julianne Duncan, Elzbieta M. Gozdziak, and Margaret MacDonnell (2005) 2nd Conference on Identifying and Serving Child Victims of Trafficking. International Migration 43 (1/2): pp. 343-363.

Burke, Alicia., Stafania Ducci and Giuseppina Maddaluno (2005) Trafficking in Minors for Commercial Sexual Exploitation: Costa Rica. Torino. UNICRI.

Cadet, Jean-Robert (1998) Restavec: From Haitian Slave Child to Middle-Class American. Autin: University of Texas Press.

Caldwell, Bruce K. and Indrani, Pieris et al. (1999) Sexual Regimes and Sexual Networking: The Risk of an HIV/AIDS Epidemic in Bangladesh. Social Science and Medicine 48(8): 1103-16.

Caliber Associates (2003) Needs Assessment for Service providers and Trafficking Victims. Fairfax, VA: Caliber Associates.

Chapkis, Wendy (2003) "Trafficking, Migration, and the Law: Protecting Innocents, Punishing Immigrants." Gender and Society 17:923-937.

Chase, Elaine and June Statham (2005) "Commercial and Sexual Exploitation of Children and Young People in the UK - A Review." Child Abuse Review 14:4-25.

Chuang, Janie (1998) "Redirecting the Debate Over Trafficking in Women: Definitions, Paradigms, and Contexts." Harvard Human Rights Journal 65.

Claramunt, Maria Cecilia (2002) Commercial sexual Exploitation of Minors: Costa Rica. Geneva: ILO.

Cole, Jeffrey, Sally S. Booth (2007) Dirty Work: Immigrants in Domestic Service, Agriculture, and Prostitution in Sicily: Lexington Books.

Constable, Nicole (1996) "Jealousy, Chastity, and Abuse: Chinese Maids and Foreign Helpers in Hong Kong." Modern China 22:448-479.

Coonan, Terry and Thompson Robin (2005) "Ancient Evil, Modern Face: The Fight Against Human Trafficking." Georgetown Journal of International Affairs 6:43.

Curtol, F.; Decarli, S.; Di Nicola, A.; Savona, E. U. (2004) "Victims of Human Trafficking in Italy: A Judicial Perspective." International Review of Victimology 11:111-141.

Finger, Carla (2003) "Brazil pledges to eliminate sexual exploitation of children." Lancet 361:1196.

Government Accountability Office (GAO) 2006 Human Trafficking: Better Data, Strategy and Reporting Needed to Enhance U.S. Antitrafficking Efforts Abroad.

Goode, Erich (1997) Deviant behavior. Upper Saddle River, NJ: Prentice Hall.

Hennink, Monique; Simkhada, Padam 2004 "Sex Trafficking in Nepal: Context and Process." Asian and Pacific Migration Journal 13:305-338.

James, Allison (2007) Giving Voice to Children's Voices: Practices and Problem, Pitfalls and Potentials. American Anthropologist 109(2): 261-272.

Journeys of Jeopardy: A Review of Research on Trafficking in Women and Children in Europe. (2003) International Organization for Migration. (Migration Series, No. 11). 2002. 69p.

Kempandoo, Kamala with Jyoti Sanghera and Bandana Pattanaik (2005) Trafficking and prostitution reconsidered: new perspectives on migration, sex work and human rights. Boulder, CO: Paradigm Publishers.

Petros, M. (2005) "The costs of human smuggling and trafficking." Global Migration Perspectives, 31.

Pochagina, Olga (2007) Trafficking in Women and Children in Present-Day China. Far Eastern Affairs 35(1): 82.

Scheper-Hughes, Nancy (1995) The primacy of the ethical: propositions for a militant anthropology. Current Anthropology 36(3): 409-440.

Sheldon, Zhang X, Ko-Lin Chin, Jody Miller (2007) Women's participation in Chinese transnational human smuggling. A gendered market perspective. Criminology 54(3): 699.

Shigekane, Rachel. (2007) "Rehabilitation and Community Integration of Trafficking Survivors in the United States." Human Rights Quarterly 29:112.

Tyldum, Guri. and Anette Brunovskis (2005) Describing the Unobserved: Methodological Challenges in Empirical Studies on Human Trafficking. International Migration 43(1/2): 17-34.

Weitzer, Ronald (2005) Flawed theory and method in studies of prostitution. Violence against Women 11(7): 934-949.

Williams, Suzanne and Rachel Masika (2002) Editorial. In Rachel Masika (Ed.), Gender, Trafficking and Slavery. Oxfam Focus on Gender. Pp. 2-9.

INDEX